D1563925

THE GOLFER'S LIBRARY

A READER'S GUIDE TO THREE CENTURIES OF GOLF LITERATURE

Daniel Wexler

SPORTS MEDIA GROUP

All inquiries should be addressed to:
Sports Media Group
An imprint of Ann Arbor Media Group LLC
2500 S. State Street
Ann Arbor, MI 48104

Printed and bound at Edwards Brothers, Inc., Ann Arbor, Michigan, USA

08   07   06   05   04   1   2   3   4   5

Library of Congress Cataloging-in-Publication Data
Wexler, Daniel.
  The golfer's library : a reader's guide to three centuries of golf literature
    / Daniel Wexler.
    p. cm.
  Includes bibliographical references and index.
  ISBN 1-58726-107-3 (alk. paper)
  1. Golf--Bibliography. I. Title.
Z7514.G6W39 2004
[GV965]
016.796352--dc22
2004007289

*For Bernard Darwin, Henry Longhurst, and
Herbert Warren Wind, whose monumental prose has
elevated both the game and our eternal appreciation of it.*

CONTENTS

INTRODUCTION

A book about golf books.

Not even a new idea, really, for Mr. Cecil Hopkinson of England gave life to it back in 1938 and others—most notably the late Joseph Murdoch—have, from time to time, pushed the legacy substantially forward. But while these volumes have generally been both interesting and thorough, they are not, alas, even remotely available to the average interested reader. Indeed, copies of such books as Hopkinson's *Collecting Golf Books* or Murdoch's *The Library of Golf,* when findable at all, generally run into the many hundreds of dollars—and are significantly outdated relative to thousands of subsequently published titles as well.

But aside from providing an accessible and affordable contemporary update, my goal in writing *The Golfer's Library* is to furnish something of a buyer's guide to readers and collectors; an easy-to-use catalog offering salient details about content, importance, availability, and price of 400 of the game's finest volumes. In this era of Internet shopping, where so many used book purchases are made sight-unseen, the practical value of such a work seems self-evident. But if, in the process, it succeeds in relating even a fraction of the style, flavor, and diversity of golf's great body of literature, so much the better.

Naturally the reader will wonder what criteria were used in selecting the chosen volumes, and here we must be clear: In no way should this be construed as "The 400 Best Golf Books Ever Written," for any such judgment would be entirely subjective and likely raise as many arguments as it purports to settle. Rather, this collection is intended to highlight a broad and representative sampling of excellence in 10 areas central to golf's timeless appeal: Ancient Volumes, History, Tournaments and Tours, Anthologies, Instruction, Biographies, Architecture, Courses and Travel, Reference/Miscellaneous, and Club Histories. It does not dabble in equipment, agronomy, cartoons, all manner of metaphysical fiction, or several other areas that, quite frankly, I find either highly specialized, less important to the bigger picture, or both.

Regarding the individual books listed, several things should be noted. First, all editions profiled are hardcover unless marked with a PBK (paperback) designation. Also, I have generally presented the names of authors as they appear on a book's title page, though for the sake of consistency, the occasional book-to-book discrepancies have been resolved by consulting *the* bibliographic source, Murdoch and Donovan's *The Game of Golf and the Printed Word*.

I have included for each selection the title, author, publisher, number of pages, year(s) of publication, and reprints/alternate editions. It should be explicitly understood that while the vast majority of this bibliographic material is 100 percent accurate, it is not being deemed complete, particularly in the case of limited-edition reprints (often produced by private tournaments), which can occasionally slip by undetected.

Some further bibliographic points:

- I have chosen not to waste valuable space listing multiple printings of single editions, as the first and 21st printings of a particular edition generally will be identical. Second or third *editions*, however, may well contain substantial changes and are thus listed to the fullest extent possible.
- For internationally printed volumes I have generally noted only the editions published in the United States and the United Kingdom. This again lies mostly in the interest of brevity and the reader should not be surprised to discover the occasional Canadian or Australian printing not accounted for here.
- I have refrained from including such additional information as dimensions, jacket descriptions, binding construction and the like, again in the interest of clarity and space, though such specs can be easily obtained on the Internet (see chapter two).
- The contemporary prices listed do not represent any sort of official appraisal, but rather are educated estimates based upon recent availability and sales. More details regarding pricing appear on page xxxiii.

Beyond its book listings, *The Golfer's Library* includes two additional chapters. The first, "A Brief History of Golf Literature," is just that, recapping the genre's development with particular attention paid to landmark volumes and writers. The second, "Some Advice on Building a Golfer's Library," is equally self-explanatory and hopefully of some relevance in today's worldwide, Internet-dominated book collecting market. A short appendix also follows the text, listing every title published by 15 of the game's landmark writers and 25 of its greatest players. As these lists include more than 340 volumes, only 119 of which are profiled herein, they manage to comprise a rather substantial reference source in their own right.

Finally, a word about reprints and facsimiles. For the past 20 or so years, publishers such as Classics of Golf/Flagstick Books, Clock Tower Press (née Sleeping Bear), and, most recently, the Ann Arbor Media Group have taken to reproducing numerous rare golf books, making them accessible to entire generations of new readers. First-edition collectors may turn a condescending cheek toward these inexpensive replicas but the average reader should consider the following: With such reprints, roughly a dozen of golf's legendary, time-honored books can be purchased, in flawless condition, for about the same amount one might pay to acquire a single tattered original—with an up-to-date foreword (frequently by Herbert Warren Wind) and other extras often included in the bargain.

Assembling this book required only a limited degree of outside help, but I do wish to impress the reader with three very important acknowledgments. The first is to the aforementioned Joseph Murdoch, likely the first man ever to attempt the complete codification of golf's thousands of published volumes. In addition to his rare and thorough *The Library of Golf,* Murdoch partnered with book dealer Richard Donovan to research and write *The Game of Golf and the Printed Word,* by far the most detailed bibliography of the field ever assembled. It is a book in which, even after several years of research, one seldom finds even minor omissions, and it has been an invaluable source in compiling much of the bibliographic information presented here.

Second, I wish to salute the Amateur Athletic Foundation of Los Angeles, a nonprofit organization founded with proceeds from the 1984 Summer Olympics. The AAF maintains one of the world's finest repositories of sports information and, in 2002, absorbed the entirety of the Ralph W. Miller Golf Library (formerly housed in the City of Industry), allowing continued public access to this utterly remarkable collection.

The third acknowledgment goes to Mr. Ralph W. Miller himself, a man about whom I feel I should know more, and to whom countless golfers and historians should be eternally grateful. It is truly difficult to imagine the time and resources Mr. Miller must have dedicated to assembling his private golf library, but I can categorically state that this volume and many, many others have benefited immeasurably from the fruits of his labor.

I think that when considering the 400 volumes that follow, most learned readers would agree on at least 300, leaving something less than one-quarter open to debate. In this context then, *The Golfer's Library* certainly isn't guaranteed to include every fine book ever written on golf. It does, however, represent a varied and rich collection, one that would afford anyone fortunate enough to own all 400 volumes the knowledge that very little grass—either fairway or rough—has grown beneath their book-collecting feet.

—Daniel Wexler

A Brief History of
Golf Literature

One of the pleasures in assembling a volume such as this is the degree to which it has reinforced, at least in my own mind, the oft-stated notion that golf enjoys a body of literature superior to that of any other sport. This idea has long been observed by literary types—both golfer and nongolfer alike—but I suspect that a more compelling piece of evidence is the utter lack of similar claims made by supporters of other sports. Football? Tennis? Basketball? The comparisons seem almost silly. Baseball? Well, there at least we have a worthy contender. But with all due respect to the American national pastime, I shall leave it to George Plimpton, a prominent and neutral observer who has written of both, to conclude that baseball "has produced some interesting books, but golf is by far the best."

The reasons for this superiority may be many but several obvious ones stand out. First, golf enjoys a much greater variety of subjects about which to write, as history, biography, instruction, architecture, and championship play are vastly differing topics, yet all important components of the game. Second, golf has historically appealed to an educated (and frequently affluent) clientele—the type of audience that can recognize, appreciate, and afford quality writing. Third, golf has been blessed with some splendidly talented reporters—men like Darwin, Longhurst, and Wind, all of whom were not so much great golf writers as great writers who happened to write primarily about golf. And finally, with ample time between shots and a challenge that is really more mental than physical, golf is likely the most ruminative of all sporting pursuits. Further, as the ruminations of Tiger Woods do not always differ so much from those of the 18 handicapper, golfers can view much of their game's literature on relatively equal footing. Far more so, at any rate, than the average baseball fan can see their game through the eyes of Roger Clemens.

Naturally, golf's remarkable longevity is also a factor in the advanced nature of its literature. And though the game's earliest roots shall forever remain lost to antiquity, we can at least cite the first known written reference to it, the famous 1457 Acts of Parliament, in which Scots were banned from golfing for fear it might diminish the practice of archery—a much-needed skill in those days of a not-so-United Kingdom. Other early references were similarly incidental, with fleeting mentions of the game popping up in books, diaries, and other nonsporting texts, including several prominent profiles of the village of St. Andrews. Occasional records also exist of equipment being shipped to faraway English colonies, the earliest thus far discovered dating to 1743.

The first identified writings with golf as their sole subject appear primarily to have been poems or songs, the poorly recorded nature of which makes present-day assessment difficult. The earliest work thus far recorded is *Glotta,* a verse penned by Scotsman James Arbuckle in 1721. Considerably more famous, however, is Thomas Mathison's *The Goff,* an "Heroi-comical Poem in Three Cantos" first published in 1743, with subsequent editions appearing in 1763, 1793, and, as the first entry in the USGA's rare book series, 1980. A similar poetic work, George F. Carnegie's *Golfiana,* debuted in 1833.

The last noteworthy effort among these early texts is James Cundell's 1824 *The Rules of the Thistle Club,* a 50-page document that features a good deal more historical information than the title might suggest. Also a future USGA reprint (1983), it, like *The Goff, Golfiana,* and several other early works, is omitted from *The Golfer's Library* for the simple reason that it cannot truly be considered a book, at least in our modern sense of the word.

An Era of Firsts (Pre-1911)

The era of golfing books really began with 1857's *The Golfer's Manual,* a 96-page effort authored by "A Keen Hand" (actually one H.B. Farnie). Essentially an introductory mix of history and instruction, Farnie's groundbreaking volume was followed shortly by similar "get acquainted" books like *A Few Rambling Remarks on Golf* (Robert Chambers, 1862), *Historical Gossip about Golf and Golfers* (George Robb, 1863), and *The Golfer's Handbook* (Robert Forgan, 1881), all milestone works to be sure, though hardly grand in their scope.

The first book to break this topical mold—and undoubtedly golf literature's first true classic—was *Golf: A Royal and Ancient Game*, a collection of the game's important writings assembled by Edinburgh's Robert Clark in 1875. Including all manner of club records, royal proclamations, and early excerpts (plus a full reproduction of *The Goff*), it stands even today as both a uniquely splendid record and a warehouse of information for historians.

In broader terms, however, one must look to the 1890s as the true dawn of golf literature, for it was this decade that spawned an unprecedented run of important firsts. In 1891, for example, Horace Hutchinson's *Famous Golf Links* was the first volume built around the profiling of great courses, while Willie Park Jr.'s *The Game of Golf* (1896) was the first work to be authored by a professional. On the west side of the Atlantic, the game debuted in book form with James Lee's *Golf in America* (1895) and, though historically outshone by later works, H.J. Whigham's *How to Play Golf* (1897) was America's initial instructional book. Finally, at the very tip of the new century, John L. Low's *F.G. Tait: A Record* (1900) was the game's first true biography.

It was also during this turn-of-the-century period that Hutchinson, a two-time British Amateur champion, managed to establish himself as the first true giant of golf literature. Though perhaps not the equal of the soon-to-arrive Bernard Darwin, Hutchinson was a fine and prolific writer, authoring/editing not less than 13 books covering every aspect of the game. His first was the diminutive *Hints on the Game of Golf* (1886), a primarily instructive foray whose timelessness eventually led to a 1987 Classics of Golf reprint. *Golf Greens and Green-Keeping* (1906) was perhaps the earliest book to substantially address agronomical issues, while 1897's stunning *British Golf Links* was decades ahead of its time in the coffee table genre. Yet the best remembered of Hutchinson's portfolio is almost certainly 1890's *The Badminton Library: Golf*, an omnibus volume designed to acquaint Britons with this suddenly burgeoning sport. It remains today, more than a century later, one of the game's more important and readable works.

Two more period writers of note were Garden Smith and Henry Leach, both editors of Britain's venerable magazine *Golf Illustrated*. Between 1897 and 1912, Smith would be responsible for four prominent volumes, the most memorable of which, *The Royal and Ancient Game of Golf* (1912), was assembled with seven-time Major champion Harold Hilton. Leach, for his part, authored three original works and compiled another, *Great Golfers in the Making* (1907), a really splendid book that began as a series of *Golf Illustrated* articles.

Shortly after 1900 came the first of what we might call encyclopedic instruction books; that is, tutorial volumes created by great players which manage also to cover history, courses, architecture, the author's life, and other areas of interest. J.H. Taylor's *Taylor on Golf* (1902) was likely the pioneer of this attractive subgenre, while Harry Vardon's *The Complete Golfer* (1905) was surely the most popular.

The first instruction books written specifically for women appear to have been May Hezlet's *Ladies' Golf* and Genevieve Hecker's *Golf for Women,* both of which appeared (in Britain and the United States, respectively) in 1904. The use of illustrations for instructive purposes began with Sir Walter G. Simpson's classic *The Art of Golf* (1887), though the first book designed strictly around the photographic study of great swings was George W. Beldam's impressive *Great Golfers: Their Methods at a Glance* (1904).

Several additional works from this pioneering period also command a mention including W.W. Tulloch's 1908 *The Life of Tom Morris* (the author being a contemporary of Old Tom's!), H.S.C. Everard's *A History of the Royal and Ancient Golf Club, St. Andrews* (1907) and John L. Low's *Concerning Golf* (1903), the game's first traditionalist manifesto.

Finally, this era of firsts also witnessed the debut of those early mainstays among yearly volumes, *The Golfing Annual* (1887–1910) and the still-running *Golfer's Handbook*, which has missed only five World War II–era editions since 1899.

A Golden Age (1911–1939)

American golf's Golden Age can loosely be defined as lasting from the opening of Charles Blair Macdonald's National Golf Links of America (in 1911) to the late-1930s onset of World War II. During this period, golf's popularity literally exploded from coast to coast, with the number of courses jumping roughly eightfold, Bobby Jones and Walter Hagen taking over the championship stage, and the game becoming a recreational darling of the nation's affluent sporting elite.

Naturally, the number of golf books published in the States expanded substantially during this period, though not necessarily in proportion to the game's overall growth. With so many new players, instructional books were an obvious cornerstone, though in hindsight the efforts of even the biggest American stars were comparatively modest. For example, Jones, Hagen, and Gene Sarazen—clearly the nation's three biggest prewar names—were involved with the writing of not less than 15 booklets of instruction among them, but these were generally shorter, pamphlet-like efforts, only three of which exceeded 100 pages. Of course, the lone full-sized work to emerge from the three, Jones's 1927 *Down the Fairway*, became one of golf's enduring classics, but the paucity is interesting just the same.

Meanwhile in the United Kingdom, where the game remained better established, all sorts of interesting things were happening. The Old School voices of the Triumvirate, Sandy Herd, Andrew Kirkaldy, and others remained especially active, boosting both the instructional and autobiographical genres throughout the 1920s and '30s. The relative lack of playing success enjoyed by the Triumvirate's heirs (George Duncan, Abe Mitchell, and Archie Compston) resulted in only a modest literary place for the younger men, but a decidedly older one, elder statesman Horace Hutchinson, managed to produce one final classic with 1919's retrospective *Fifty Years of Golf*.

A fabulous new arrival of the era was humorist P.G. Wodehouse, whose highly entertaining books *The Clicking of Cuthbert* and *The Heart of a Goof* were published in 1922 and 1926, respectively. Another expanding realm was the field of anthologies, where Peter Lawless's wonderful *The Golfer's Companion* (1937) set an admirable prewar standard.

But in the golfing world, the word anthology can only be synonymous with the legendary Bernard Darwin, and it was during this era that roughly the first third of the great man's collections were published (see appendix). This run of seven books—their contents nearly all drawn from articles in the *Times* or *Country Life*—began with 1911's *Tee Shots and Others* and concluded with 1936's *Rubs of the Green*. During these same years, however, Darwin also produced his first autobiographical work, *Green Memories* (1928), and his epic *The Golf Courses of the British Isles* (1910), establishing him as an unparalleled icon both at home and abroad, and by far the dominant golf writer of the age.

Another area experiencing rapid growth was that of the annual yearbook. Pioneered some three decades earlier by *The Golfing Annual* and *Golfer's Handbook*, such almanac-type volumes, with their thorough listings of clubs, rules, and champions, now proliferated on both sides of the Atlantic. In America the leading entries were the *Golfer's Year Book* and the longer-running *American Annual Golf Guide,* while in Britain the all-encompassing *Golf Clubs of the Empire* quickly came to the fore. France's *Continental Golf Yearbook* was similarly impressive, and is also significant as the only prominent annual (save for the uniquely resilient *Golfer's Handbook*) to survive past 1933.

An additional genre that blossomed during the Golden Age was that of golf course design. For during this period, prominent architectural volumes appeared on either side of the ocean, many of which still enjoy profitable reprints today. Among the legendary names contributing full-length books were H.S. Colt and C.H. Alison, Dr. Alister MacKenzie, George Thomas, and the father of American golf design, Charles Blair Macdonald. Additionally, both Dr. MacKenzie and Donald Ross completed (and lost) period manuscripts that were not published until the 1990s, while three volumes compiling A.W. Tillinghast's entertaining prewar articles did not begin appearing until 1995.

Finally, we must mention an often-overlooked American classic, H.B. Martin's 1936 retrospective *Fifty Years of American Golf,* by far the most comprehensive history of the stateside game then attempted, and a genuine milestone work.

The War and Its Aftermath (1940–1969)

While there can be little doubt that the life-altering upheavals of World War II derailed much of golf's Golden Age momentum, it did not altogether sidetrack its literature, particularly in Britain. For during those bleakest of years, a relocated Bernard Darwin penned three major retrospective works, the semi-golfing *Life Is Sweet Brother* (1940), the nearly golf-less *Pack Clouds Away* (1941), and the golf-saturated *Golf Between Two Wars* (1944). Shortly after the cessation of hostilities, some small sense of normalcy was perhaps reestablished with the publication of Darwin's first anthology in a decade, 1946's *Golfing By-Paths.* Now well into his 70s, the Dean then closed out his book-writing career with the 1952 biography

James Braid, 1954's *Golf* (part of the Pleasures of Life Series), and one last autobiographical work, *The World That Fred Made* (1955). He would pass away, at age 85, in 1961.

Replacing the likes of a Bernard Darwin was well nigh impossible, but during this period British golfers were fortunate indeed to discover a wonderful alternative, the incomparable Henry Longhurst. Longhurst's ode to the prewar years, the immensely pleasing *It Was Good While It Lasted*, first appeared in 1941, and was followed, postwar, by numerous anthologies and golfing travelogues. Of these, *Only on Sundays* (1964) and *Never on Weekdays* (1968), both of which compiled decades worth of *Sunday Times* columns, have surely had the most lasting impact.

Several other prominent British columnists crossed over into books during and after the war including *The Scotsman's* Frank Moran and the inexhaustible Louis Stanley, golf correspondent for *The Field* and author of nearly 20 related volumes. For sheer output, however, one doubts if anyone will ever top the longtime editor of *Golfing* magazine, Robert Browning, who during this period was responsible for a dizzying 350 club handbooks or regional guides. Guaranteeing himself acclaim for something beyond simple productivity, however, Browning also published *A History of Golf* (1955), one of the game's definitive historical volumes.

From the professional ranks, it would be impossible to ignore the writing of the great mid-century British star Henry Cotton. Strictly speaking, Cotton did publish two relatively minor volumes well before the war, but his eight major works (including *This Game of Golf* and *My Golfing Album*) ran between 1948 and 1980. Also prominent during the 1960s were *Guardian* and *Country Life* columnist Pat Ward-Thomas and an extremely talented amateur, Sir Peter Allen, whose fine guidebooks *Famous Fairways* and *Play the Best Courses* crossed over into the modern period.

Golf writing on the west side of the Atlantic, largely on hiatus during the war years, picked up again soon thereafter, and again relied upon the game's top players to attract an audience. Byron Nelson, Ben Hogan, and Sam Snead all obliged with high-profile instructional works, and were soon joined by Lloyd Mangrum, Cary Middlecoff, Ken Venturi, Tony Lema, Julius Boros, and others. The dominant work of the period, however, was surely Hogan's epic *Five Lessons: The Modern Fundamentals of Golf,* a truly seminal work written with Herbert Warren Wind in 1957.

Interestingly, some of the most successful titles of the era came from the stars of yesteryear. For example, 1956's autobiographical *The Walter Hagen Story* finally recounted the Haig's legendary career, while Bobby Jones scored with two relatively late entries, *Golf Is My Game* (1960) and *Bobby Jones on Golf* (1966). But coming from furthest off the pace was the Silver Scot, Tommy Armour, whose last Major championship had come way back in 1931. Some two decades later, Armour hit it big with 1953's blockbuster *How to Play Your Best Golf All the Time*, then managed something of an encore with the popular *A Round of Golf with Tommy Armour* (1959).

This proliferation of nostalgic entries notwithstanding, however, postwar American golf writing did experience the arrival of two major new contributors. The first was Herbert Warren Wind, simply this country's greatest-ever chronicler of the game, who would eventually ply his trade for many memorable years at the *New Yorker*. Wind's comprehensive 1948 epic *The Story of American Golf* remains, fully a half-century later, as *the* domestic golf history, having been revised and/or reprinted thrice. Similarly, his partnerships with Gene Sarazen (1950's *Thirty Years of Championship Golf*) and Jack Nicklaus (1969's *The Greatest Game of All*) produced two of the finest golfing biographies of all time.

Somewhat lost in Wind's wake was the fine scribe Charles Price, whose opus *The World of Golf* (1962) is another first-class historical survey. Price's 1964 compilation, *The American Golfer*, an anthology of articles culled from that excellent Golden Age magazine, was another important work that enjoyed reprinting during the late 1980s.

Finally, we close out this era with an instructional volume that has turned heads for 35 years, Homer Kelley's thoroughly unique *The Golfing Machine* (1969). It's probably just as well that this cultish legend was produced so far ahead of its time, however, for despite such a head start, I doubt that even those who started reading it in 1969 have fully digested it yet.

The Modern Era (1970–the Present)

The early years of the modern era represented, by any measure, a slow awakening from golf's literary doldrums of the 1950s and '60s. To be sure, several established writers from the past remained at the peak of their game, carrying forward the great tradition of eyewitness tournament coverage and knowledgeable, pertinent columns. Chief among these was Herbert Warren Wind, whose twin anthologies *Herbert Warren Wind's Golf Book* (1971) and *Following Through* (1985) are perhaps the finest general works of the period. Also remaining highly relevant were Pat Ward-Thomas and Charles Price, who were joined in the modern pantheon by Englishman Peter Dobereiner and Texan Dan Jenkins, both popular writers with entries on their résumés prior to 1970.

But beyond this traditional, faintly nostalgic approach, things were changing. With jet engines making the world a much smaller place, books profiling the world's famous courses became commonplace. Many were fairly limited volumes, designed more for the coffee table than any serious examination of great golf design. One grand exception, however, is the superb *World Atlas of Golf,* a colorful volume authored jointly by Ward-Thomas, Wind, Price, and the great Australian champion Peter Thomson. In its fifth edition at the time of this writing, it has remained the industry standard since debuting in 1976.

Additional stars among "golf course" authors include the aforementioned Sir Peter Allen, American James Finegan, and architect/writer Tom Doak, whose uniquely entertaining *The Confidential Guide* (1996) stands as one of the more forthright golf books ever published.

The mention of Doak reminds us that for the first time since the Golden Age, course architecture has recently returned to the literary limelight. Doak's thorough *The Anatomy of a Golf Course* (1992) stands tall in this realm as do a pair of books by historian/architect Geoff Shackelford, *The Golden Age of Golf Design* (1999) and *Grounds for Golf* (2003). As a combination historical volume and reference source, however, nothing can approach the encyclopedic *The Architects of Golf,* an epic 1993 effort produced by Geoffrey Cornish and Ron Whitten. Avid readers can also locate attractive biographical works on a number of Golden Age designers, a trend that continues strong at the time of this writing.

Though the modern game seems powerfully intent upon losing touch with its past, some very thorough research has, in recent years, produced several important historical volumes. Perhaps the most interesting (and elusive) among these is Alastair Johnston's privately produced *The Chronicles of Golf, 1457–1857* (1993), while David

Stirk's *Golf: History & Tradition* (1998) and David Hamilton's more narrowly focused *Golf: Scotland's Game* (1998) stand out among those commercially available.

As it ever was, instruction continues to remain the game's most popular literary genre, with the post-1970 era producing the usual mix of excellence and silliness. Jack Nicklaus's *Golf My Way* (1974) and Byron Nelson's *Shape Your Swing the Modern Way* (1976) were perhaps the era's first standards, though a series of highly popular works by Texan Harvey Penick (beginning with 1992's *Little Red Book*) contain material that the author began gathering many years earlier. Among more recent entries, former NASA physicist Dave Pelz's *Short Game Bible* (1999) and *Putting Bible* (2000) have been highly successful, as have several volumes produced by the chief of modern swing gurus, David Leadbetter. Among contemporary player-authored books, Ernie Els' *How to Build a Classic Golf Swing* (1996), Nick Faldo's *Faldo: A Swing for Life* (1995), Tom Watson's *Getting Up and Down* (1983), and Raymond Floyd's *The Elements of Scoring* (1998) might be selected to head a wide and ever-growing field.

An additional area of golf literature largely new to the modern era is the club history book. The quality and scope of these volumes generally run the gamut, from simple staple-bound pamphlets to colorful hardcovers on par with the product of major publishing houses. For *The Golfer's Library* I have selected 25 of the very best, though it's a good bet that these will be challenged by many attractive competitors in the years ahead.

Finally, the library of golf seems over the years to have suffered only from a lack of high-quality reference books. However, the modern era has provided a pair which I believe any avid reader will find essential: Donald Steel and Peter Ryde's marvelous *The Shell International Encyclopedia of Golf* (1975) and Joseph Murdoch and Richard Donovan's bibliographic bible *The Game of Golf and the Printed Word 1566–1985* (1988). Though not entirely current, they remain, at the time of this writing, indispensable.

Such, then, is the briefest recounting of golf literature's evolution, one that provides only a loose framework with which to tackle this book. We may find it worth noting, however, that as the ethos of the corporate mentality seeps into the publishing industry and increasingly more books are produced away from the major houses, certain enduring aspects of golf's written charm still hold fast. To wit: The Spring of 2003 saw the publication of *Bernard Darwin on*

Golf, the 14th collection of Darwin's work to be assembled, six of them in the modern era. Very soon now the great Bernardo will have more anthologies published posthumously than when he was alive—and if that sort of longevity doesn't suggest some hope for the game's future, I surely don't know what does.

Some Advice on Building a Golfer's Library

While the Internet has affected international and domestic commerce in all manner of positive ways, I doubt that any field has been so profoundly influenced as the buying and selling of used books. For with the arrival of this groundbreaking technology, anyone with a personal computer can now access and do business with literally thousands of bookshops all around the world, securely closing transactions from the comfort of their desk chair. True, the overall process may have lost some luster for the old-fashioned "thrill of the chase" types, but to my mind this must certainly be compensated for many times over by the ability to locate even the rarest volumes, worldwide, with the click of a mouse.

For those unfamiliar with the process, the mechanism itself is a simple one. Web sites such as abebooks.com (the current industry standard and thus our working example) essentially operate as clearinghouses for thousands of book dealers who pay a fee and/or a small percentage of each sale to post their offerings on the sites. Buyers utilize search engines to shop, choosing from whatever copies of a particular volume are available from any of the chosen site's vendors at a given moment. Payment is then arranged either through a secure server or directly between buyer and seller with the book being shipped—generally at the speed of the buyer's choice—shortly thereafter.

All in all a simple exercise, and one that I daresay a great percentage of this volume's readers are already quite familiar with. For these truly experienced buyers, much of what appears below may be superfluous. However for newcomers and the less-practiced, most of what follows can help to save valuable money and time—not to mention assuring that the volume received is, in fact, the very one desired.

We begin then with some thoughts on the search, a process that can always be conducted using a book's title and/or author. The problem with so superficial an approach is that it can often lead to an overwhelming number of results, the sorting of which can be both time-consuming and frustrating. If one doubts this assertion, run a search by simply typing "Bernard Darwin" in the author box as I have just done at ABE. A stout 737 hits was the result.

Thankfully, additional search options are offered to help narrow one's choices. At ABE, we can specify hard- or softcover, first editions, ISBN number, signed copies, date of publication, and/or price ranges of our choosing. We can also refine the search by opting to see only the copies available in a particular country and, in America, those being offered in a single state. Finally, we can choose how we'd like our search results to be arranged, with "Lowest Price," I'd imagine, being the runaway favorite. Thus the above Bernard Darwin search, when refined to include, say, only hardcover first editions currently available in the state of Florida, now yields exactly four books.

A final important point regarding our search—and one which runs consistent to all areas of Internet usage—is the reminder that as a computerized process, there is no flexibility whatsoever so far as spelling is concerned. As proof of this, I will only point out that a search of books written by "Bernard Darrwin" yields exactly zero responses, worldwide.

Having located one or more prospects with our search, we must then set about determining what we can of their various physical conditions. While this generally isn't too difficult, we must remember that each individual volume's Internet entry is written directly by its dealer, thus a good deal of stylistic variance may be encountered. Many vendors, for example, will describe a book's flaws in great detail (e.g., "Slight foxing to final 30 pages, rear endpapers lightly stained"), so that one might visualize the volume as clearly as if it sat in his or her hand. Others provide only skeletal information, leaving potential buyers largely to wonder. Thankfully, however varied their presentations, nearly all subscribe to a common six-grade standard for rating the fundamental condition of both book and dust jacket, a scale reading: Poor, Fair, Good, Very Good, Fine, Mint/New. The meanings of these terms are relatively self-evident, and I am happy to report that they tend to be applied quite consistently. Still, given the obvious subjectivity of such phrases, developing a familiarity with certain dealers will naturally provide a greater sense of confidence. For while Mints and Fines tend seldom to disappoint, the delineation between Good and Very Good might, on occasion, be an issue.

Beyond general physical condition, several additional factors may affect our final decision and here again, a grasp of terminology can come in handy. Specifically, we may first wish to verify that a book is in fact either a hardcover or paperback, depending upon our preference. Often this is as simple as spotting the word "hardcover" or "paperback" in its description, but synonyms for these designations abound and are not always entirely obvious. Paperbacks, for example, might be abbreviated as logically as PB or PBK, but they may also be referred to as wraps, cards, or proofs. Similarly, hardback volumes are frequently listed as cloth, leather, embossed, boards, buckram, and so on. Though searches theoretically do limit the field to one type or the other, verification by double checking the book's description is highly recommended.

One simple way to recognize a hardcover edition is the mention of a dust jacket, the external covering that not only protects the book from wear and tear but often adds a good deal of ambience in its own right. The words "dust jacket" are frequently abbreviated as DJ or DW ("dust wrapper") and a jacket's condition usually follows the same six-grade scale as the book itself. Thus entries will generally appear something like F/VG (a Fine volume with a Very Good dust jacket) or VG/Poor (a very good volume with a poor jacket). As an F/F book often will be considerably more expensive that an F/Poor one, those less interested in dust jackets can often enjoy substantial savings if willing to purchase the latter and either ignore or discard the old wrapper. On the other hand, many frayed or damaged jackets have already been encased in Mylar (the clear plastic we often find on library books), protecting them from further decay and making them, from a handling perspective, rather like new. As many used bookstores are willing to wrap an old jacket for a minor fee, the saving of a tattered but attractive jacket does remain a viable and inexpensive option.

Assuming that one has, based on price, condition, or divine intervention, narrowed down the field to a particular volume, it is time to actually make the purchase. This is a fast and easy process made even easier by leaving a credit card number on file, the advantages of which are twofold. First, an on-file card represents the fastest method of payment, one which requires no further contact with vendor or Web site and generally results in the shipping of the book within 48 hours. Second—and of no small consequence—it places one's credit card information into the fewest hands possible, while also removing the need to send such sensitive material via e-mail. Excepting either vendors with whom one has an ongoing relationship or cases where specific questions must be answered regarding the book, I cannot imagine ever needing to contact a dealer directly when such a secure and direct method is so readily available.

All of which brings us to shipping. Generally, the buyer has two options, which usually equate to ground or air mail. As ground shipping can be excruciatingly slow, I tend always to choose the faster air option. On American domestic shipments, the difference in cost frequently is no more than $2 and thus easily worth it. For overseas packages the difference can often be as much as $10—but should the less expensive option be chosen, be prepared to wait at least a month to receive your books. Though not presented as an automated option, overnight shipping can usually be arranged, at a proportionally steeper cost, by contacting the book's dealer directly.

It is also worth noting that one can save a great deal on shipping by purchasing multiple volumes from a single vendor. Though I believe them to be unique in this regard, ABE allows the searching or browsing of a particular vendor's entire on-line inventory, providing the opportunity to hunt for second or third titles once one discovers an initial desired item. Though this is sometimes impractical when the inventory is presented *en masse*, vendors who focus heavily on the Royal & Ancient game will often have their golf books cataloged separately, making for an interesting (and often fruitful) browse.

And finally a few additional thoughts.

First, for the benefit of the novice, let me state confidently that buyers really can shop on-line with few misgivings, even when large sums of money are involved. Obviously the use of secured servers minimizes theft concerns, but I suspect that for many the bigger fear is of ordering a volume from halfway around the world, only to have it arrive in a condition different than advertised. The concern, I'll admit, seems a reasonable one, yet in reality a couple of things render it moot. First, Internet-based book purchases inevitably carry a money-back guarantee should the buyer find that his or her new acquisition fails to live up to expectations. Perhaps more importantly, I am quite certain that no one has ever pursued a career in used books with the chief goal of getting rich. Indeed, the independent book business must surely be among the most honest-going, filled with avid and dedicated people. In short, orders seldom—if ever—show up less than advertised.

A second thought speaks to the quality of a volume's condition. Specifically, comparatively few of us purchase books either for prestige or potential financial gain; we simply wish to add certain volumes to our collections for pleasurable reading or research purposes. In this light, the need to acquire Mint or even Fine copies is generally minimal, while a willingness to purchase volumes categorized as Very Good (or the frequently seen "Very Good +") can provide both a wider selection and ample savings. Reprints, of course, offer a similar dynamic; if you're simply looking for a good-quality copy that will last a while, a Mint or Fine facsimile provides like-new conditioning at a relatively cheap price.

A third point comes in the form of a basic recommendation: Do *not* shy away from overseas dealers simply because they may be located 10,000 miles away. The temptations to do so may be several (including concerns over currency conversion, shipping costs, and delivery time) but often the advantages gained far outweigh the negatives.

To begin with, an American's books of choice are often surprisingly inexpensive overseas; cheap enough, in fact, to more than cover any difference in shipping costs. So far as I can tell, this price differential stems from two things. First, many foreign countries are simply less money-oriented than we here in the States, making their pricing much closer to fair than usurious. And second, one will occasionally encounter volumes stocked overseas that are simply less desirable to foreign readers than to Americans, pushing down their prices accordingly. To wit: A quick check of ABE reveals the autobiography of the great American amateur Francis Ouimet, *A Game of Golf,* to range in price from $150 to $2,012.50 (the latter, of course, being signed). Yet two years ago, I managed to secure a copy in England—where Ouimet's 1913 defeat of Harry Vardon and Ted Ray did *not* play quite so well—for about $90, including shipping. Favorable monetary exchange rates, especially in places like Australia and New Zealand, also represent a foreign advantage, as volumes intended to be priced at a "normal" level end up, for American buyers at least, considerably less.

Lastly, when in doubt, be patient!

More than once I have seen a coveted title offered only in the $150 range, a price that, for whatever reason, I chose not to pay. But by exercising patience and checking back regularly, I eventually discovered a very good copy at roughly half that price. It is true, of course, that most books (particularly old, out-of-print editions) will appreciate over time. However in the world of Internet sales, golf volumes are frequently offered by dealers for whom the subject is not a specialty. Consequently, bargains *do* exist—if one has the time and patience to hunt and wait for them.

Because of the Internet, contemporary readers and collectors are living in a time of unparalleled opportunity, a point powerfully brought home when considering the international letter-writing and phone-calling lengths to which the late Joseph Murdoch had to go in assembling his 3,000-volume library. Murdoch's task, of course, would be infinitely easier today, and though this convenience surely minimizes the much-romanticized thrill of the chase, it is a palpably good thing for buyers and sellers everywhere. What's more, its popularity is such—even at this relatively early stage—that ABE reports the sale of up to 15,000 books per day on their site, worldwide.

Now that's something to think about.

Top Internet Used Book Sites

abebooks.com—The world's largest on-line used book dealer, the British Columbia–based ABE claims to list over 40 million books from over 10,000 vendors at any given time. Offers affiliated sites catering to buyers in North America, the United Kingdom, Germany, and France.

*a*libris.com—Claiming a regular inventory of over 30 million used volumes, this Emeryville, CA company represents the most viable alternative to ABE. *a*libris also offers customizing options for hardcore collectors and libraries.

Bibliofind—Formerly an independent competitor of ABE and *a*libris, Bibliofind has since been absorbed by Amazon.com, placing its operation within Amazon's efficient, customer-friendly Web site. Its stock of old or rare books, however, has declined markedly in the process.

eBay—The world's best-known Internet auction site generally offers a large selection of golf books, though seldom of the rare or particularly valuable variety.

Some Prominent Golf-Only Book Dealers

Steve Schofield Golf Books—www.steveschofield.com
Springwood House, 29 Nichols Way, Wetherby, West Yorkshire, England LS22 6AD
Tel: 01937 581276

Grant Books—www.grantbooks.co.uk
The Coach House, New Road, Cutnall Green, Droitwich, Worcestershire, England WR9 0PQ
Tel: 01299 851 588

Rhod McEwan Golf Books—www.rhodmcewan.com
Ballater, Royal Deeside, Aberdeenshire, Scotland AB35 5UB
Tel: 013397 55429

George Lewis/Golfiana—www.golfiana.com
PO Box 291, Mamaroneck, New York 10543
Tel: 914-835-5100

Golf Classics
PO Box 250, St. Clair Shores, Michigan 48080
Tel: 313-886-8258

Peter Yagi Golf Books
16149 Redmond Way, #187, Redmond, Washington 98052
Tel: 425-562-6660

Golf Gap
1055 Bay Street, #1109, Toronto, Ontario, Canada M5S 3A3
Tel: 416-485-5316

100 More Bookshops That Focus Heavily on Golf

The following list is culled from a number of worldwide sources and is slanted toward shops maintaining a presence on the Internet. Naturally, a particular outlet's inventory may vary over time, though as a proprietor's specific interests tend to stay constant, most are a good bet to remain well-stocked in the future. Boldfaced entries are known to maintain especially large selections, and a slight bias has occasionally been allowed for purposes of geographic distribution.

Finally, every effort has been made to omit dealers whose golf inventories are made up primarily of contemporary remainders, as such shops will never stock the vast majority of volumes profiled within this volume.

Note: Nearly every shop without an internet address can be contacted via links at abebooks.com.

United States

2nd Look Books – Spokane, WA (www.2ndlookbooks.com)
84 Charing Cross Bookstore – Cleveland, OH (www.84cc.com)
Abracadabra Bookshop & Booksearch International – Rockport, TX
Acorn Books – San Francisco, CA (www.acornbooks.com)
Antique Bookworm – Palatine, IL
Archives Books, Inc. – Edmond, OK (www.archivesinc.com)
Black & White Books – Reno, NV
Booklibrary – Long Beach, CA
The Bookman – Orange & Huntington Beach, CA
   (www.ebookman.com)
BookZone Illinois – Naperville, IL
Book Baron – Anaheim, Fullerton & Long Beach CA
   (www.bookbaron.com)
The Book Center – Oakdale, CA (www.the-book-center.com)
Book Corner – Brandon, FL
Book Gallery – Sand Point, ID
The Book Pantry – Huntington Beach, CA
The Book Store – West Bridgewater, MA
The Book Women – Sumas, WA
Books By The Lake – Bradford, NH
Books Revisited – St. Cloud, MN (www.booksrevisited.com)
The Booksend – Syracuse, NY (www.thebooksend.com)
Connie Popek, Bookseller – Otego, NY
Cordell-Wilson Booksellers – Carthage, MO
Cornwall Discount Books – Cornwall, NY

Craig Hokenson Bookseller – Dallas, TX
Crowfly Books – Peterborough, NH
Dallas Burney Rare Books – Jacksonville, FL
Dave Henson Books – Santa Ana, CA
Dooryard Books – Rockland, ME
Editions – Boiceville, NY
Eileen Serxner Books, Inc. – Bala Cynwyd, PA
Elephantbooks.com – Gilroy, CA
Elliott Bay Books – Seattle, WA
Emerald City Fine Books – Eugene, OR
Frank W. Briscoe, Book Shop – Locust, NC
Frogtown Books, Inc. – Toledo, OH (www.frogtownbooks.com)
Glover's Bookery – Lexington, KY
Harvest Book Company – Ft. Washington, PA
    (www.harvestbooks.com)
Haven Books – Winter Haven, FL
Hermitage Books – Provo, UT
HPFRI – Front Royal, VA
Iconoclast Books – Ketcham, ID
Jacque Mongelli – Warwick, NY
Jay W. Nelson, Bookseller – Austin, MN
King's Books – Tacoma, WA
Koster's Collectible Books – Farmingville, NY
Lew Dabe – Ormond Beach, FL
Madison Avenue Books – Memphis, TN
Manchester By The Book – Manchester, MA
McAllister & Solomon Books – Wilmington, NC
Moody Books, Inc. – Johnson City, TN
Neil Shillington: Bookdealer/Booksearch – Hobe Sound, FL
Old Erie Bookstore – Cleveland, OH
Old Thyme Books – East Lansing, MI
Once Upon A Time Books – Tontitown, AR
Patrica Price, Bookseller – San Bernardino, CA
Peninsula Books – Traverse City, MI
Ronald Purmort Books – Newport, NH
Sea Shell Books – St. Petersburg, FL
Second Time Books – Holiday, FL
Strand Bookstore – New York, NY (www.strandbooks.com)
Third Place Books – Lake Forest Park, WA

Victoria's Books – Arlington Heights, IL
Willis Monie – Books – Cooperstown, NY
Wise Guys Book Shop – Macedonia, NY
Wonder Book and Video – Frederick, MD

Canada

Bibliomania Bookshoppe – Montreal, QC
Book Shop in Penticton – Penticton, BC
Forest House Books – Calgary, AB
Highway Bookshop – Cobalt, ON
John Lord's Books – Stouffville, ON
Tattered Edge Books – Coquitlam, BC

England

Books International, Ltd. – Farnborough, Hampshire
Bookshop Bookfair – Ludlow, Shropshire
Bookzone – Bracknell, Berkshire
Broad Street Books – Hay-on-Wye, Hereforshire
D G & C Books – Glastonbury, Somerset
Hawthorn Books – Westerleigh, Gloucestershire
Internet Bookshop UK, Ltd. – Cambridge, Gloucestershire
   (www.ibukltd.com)
K Books Ltd. – York, North Yorkshire
Lion Books – Bewdly, Worcestershire
Morley Case – Southampton, Hampshire
Old Book Company – Leeds, West Yorkshire (www.oldbook.co.uk)
Peakirk Books – Peterborough, Cambridgeshire
St. Marys Books & Prints – Stamford, Lincolnshire
   (www.stmarysbooks.com)
Stella & Rose's Books – Tintern, Monmouthshire
   (www.stellabooks.com)

Scotland

Archways Sports Books – Edinburgh, Scotland
Brown Studies – Airdrie, Lanarkshire

Pend Books – Newton Stewart, Dumfries & Galloway
   (www.pendbooks.com)

Ireland

Dublin Bookbrowsers – Dublin

Australia

Camberwell Books & Collectibles – Hawthorn East, Victoria
Dee Why Books – Sydney, New South Wales
   (www.deewhybooks.com.au)
Flinders Books – Aspendale, Victoria
Global Village Books – Bundall, Queensland
Jo's Books – Gerringong, New South Wales
Time Booksellers – Frankston, Victoria
   (www.timebooksellers.com.au)
www.BookOz.com – Melbourne, Victoria

New Zealand

Matheson Sports International, Ltd. – Auckland
Tuatara Books – Auckland

South Africa

Africana Book Bargains – East London
Collectors Treasury – Johannesburg

Some Words on Pricing

First and foremost, the reader will recognize that *The Golfer's Library* is in no way intended to serve as a definitive pricing manual. Indeed, the values presented herein are not based upon any sort of official appraisal, but rather represent a sampling of what the book in question can be (or has recently been) purchased for on the open market. Thus as the listed prices are essentially an average of what's "out there," books traded in greater number naturally provide for more accurate estimates. Volumes rarely being sold, on the other hand, present a much smaller statistical sample, leaving us a little less certain of what truly represents an "average" price tag.

It should, of course, be clearly stated as to the quality of books being quoted. That is, these prices represent an approximate value for what I would consider a strong, collectable copy. For volumes of relatively modern vintage, this represents a book in at least Very Good + or Near Fine condition. As a matter of pragmatism, however, we generally must lower the standard to Very Good (or even the occasional Good +) on many older and ancient editions.

Similarly, the quoted price represents what might be called a normal, no-frills copy. In other words, we are ignoring overblown first editions, author signatures, immaculate dust jackets, or any additional extras frequently cited as justification for ridiculously spiked prices. That said, however, it is undeniably true (if not altogether logical) that some editions *do* vary greatly in cost. Consequently, the reader will notice many prices modified with a plus sign (e.g., $200+), a designation indicating that suitable copies are/have been available for the listed number, but that many others may be offered for noticeably higher amounts.

As the price range for less-expensive volumes often isn't very great, I have listed many within the universally affordable designation "Under $25." Also, books still easily found new at the time of this writing (either in stores or available for 24-hour or 2–3 day shipping on Amazon.com) are so noted. Readers will be advised, however, that the "new" price listed represents the book's cover price, a number generally beatable—sometimes by a wide margin—through a variety of discount purchasing channels.

Finally, two closing points. First, on a few rare occasions, reprint editions of a given book are omitted from price listings. This has occurred when copies of this particular edition have not appeared in the marketplace over the last few years and are thus impossible to accurately value. Second, non-American readers will remember that all prices are expressed in U.S. dollars.

Read on.

THE GOLFER'S LIBRARY

SECTION I
ANCIENT VOLUMES

Webster's defines the word "ancient" to mean "having had an existence of many years" and though I suspect that this generally carries with it a connotation of really tremendous age, for *The Golfer's Library* I have chosen to classify as ancient any volume published prior to World War I (1914 or earlier). I select this dividing line based upon its obvious before-and-after contrasts: Before was British competitive dominance, the Great Triumvirate, the gutta-percha ball (mostly), hickory shafts (exclusively), and a game played, at least in America, over generally rudimentary courses. After was Hagen, Jones, and Sarazen, American championship dominance, modernized equipment (they hadn't seen anything yet!), and the greatest era of international golf course design in the game's history.

It seems to me an appropriate line of demarcation.

For the sake of consistency, all profiled books published before 1915 appear in this section, even when—as in the case of several instructional volumes—their content might suggest an alternative location. This seems particularly proper given the commonality of (higher) price these early editions tend to command, though as we shall see, a good many of them are available in less-expensive reprint form.

Advanced Golf • *James Braid*
Methuen, London • 322pp • 1908
1st US edition: George Jacobs c1908

Though Braid had already published *Golf Guide and How to Play Golf* in 1906, *Advanced Golf* remains by far his prized volume, having gone to at least 11 printings in Great Britain and 10 in the United States. What separates this work is the wideness of its scope, for after 14 instructional chapters covering every aspect of playing the game, Braid provides 75 invaluable pages on his background, competitive experiences, and thoughts on the laying out of courses (he built or rebuilt nearly 200). In short, this remains, nearly 100 years hence, the definitive work by and about James Braid.

Never reprinted in the modern era, *Advanced Golf*'s great popularity makes it still relatively easy to find, though better-condition copies are beginning to climb in price.

$75

The Art of Golf • *Sir W.G. Simpson, Bart.*
David Douglas, Edinburgh • 186pp • 1887
1st US edition: G.P. Putnam 1892
Reprinted by the USGA (1982) and Classics of Golf (1992)

The Art of Golf might well be nearly forgotten, at least in America, were it not for the determined efforts of both the USGA and the Classics of Golf to revive it. Dating back to 1887, this book holds several distinctions, not the least of which is that it was the first to employ photographic images in detailing the nuances of the golf swing. Never mind that these shots are grainy and singular (i.e., not the sort of "full-sequence" images utilized today); they include Old Tom Morris, his son Jim, and legendary North Berwick pro Ben Sayers, and thus are of real worth regardless.

But what makes *The Art of Golf* special is Walter Simpson's remarkable writing, done in a breezy, faintly sarcastic style that would find favor (though few equals) among so many modern sportswriters. The opening fifth of the book, in which he addresses the history, color, and attractions of the game, is what really stands out. The remaining instructive pages are of less modern appeal—though we would do well, before skimming, to recall their ingenuity at the time of publication.

An Edinburgh attorney, Simpson was hardly a lifelong golfer/writer in the mold of Darwin or Hutchinson—a great shame, for he clearly was a man who wrote well ahead of his time.

Original: $1,000+ • USGA: (1,900 copies) $150 • COG: New ($39)

The Art of Golf • *Joshua Taylor*
Werner Laurie, London • 161pp • 1912
1st US edition: Outing 1912

Not to be confused with Walter Simpson's timeless volume, this *The Art of Golf* is an instructional tome written by the lesser-known brother of five-time Open champion J.H. Taylor. Though seldom held among the game's elite "how-to" works, it is notable in its focus strictly upon the less-gifted player. For as the author himself explains: "it is extremely difficult for the scratch man to bring himself down to the *thinking* level of the 18 handicap player." Further, "as the better player has been fully catered for in the works of Messrs Vardon, Braid, and my brother, I intend this book solely for those players who find a difficulty in following the advanced theories laid down in the books of these masters."

Note: A single, decidedly anomalous chapter on the evolution of bunkers is contributed by J.H.— probably an astute marketing ploy, but an interesting item for architecture fans. This also represents one of the very few purple golf books ever published.

$175

The Australian Golfer • *D.G. Soutar*
Angus & Robertson, Sydney • 259pp • 1906 (w/1908 2nd edition)

Daniel Soutar was a Carnoustie man who emigrated Down Under, becoming Australia's primary apostle of the Royal & Ancient game and publishing this, his adopted homeland's first known book on the subject. Like many similar volumes produced back in the old country, *The Australian Golfer* is a mix of instruction and more general golfing text. The former occupies 11 of 18 chapters, augmented by the occasional demonstrative sketch. The latter includes material on top Australian players, the rules, and chapters detailing the history of the game in New South Wales, Victoria, and South Australia. A large section of photographs is included, though it is rather curiously segregated at the back of the book.

A volume of obvious historic importance, *The Australian Golfer* has never been reprinted and is virtually impossible to find, outside of a few remaining copies Down Under.

$1,500

The Book of Golf and Golfers •
Horace G. Hutchinson (Editor)
Longmans, Green, London • 316pp • 1899

The Book of Golf and Golfers is the eighth of 14 volumes written or edited by the productive and entrepreneurial Horace Hutchinson, a man who was plainly as good at assembling talent as he was at demonstrating it. For like *The New Book of Golf, The Badminton Library,* and *Golf Greens & Green-Keeping,* this volume is filled primarily with sections penned by all-star guests, with Hutchinson's own contributions representing only an occasional presence.

Subjectwise, this book is a prominent follower of the omnibus approach, featuring chapters on history, technique, equipment, golf in America, ladies golf, and a small bit of greenkeeping, with guest writers that include J.H. Taylor, Harold Hilton, and H.J. Whigham, among others.

If nothing else, Hutchinson believed that golf was for everyone, for in his preface, he addresses Tory political objections to women being on the links by writing: "Their objection, according to their lights, is a perfectly sound one. It is their lights that lead them astray."

Martha Burk, move over.

$325

The Book of St. Andrews Links • *Andrew Bennett*
Innes & Menzies, Edinburgh • 80pp • 1898
Reprinted by Ellesborough (1984)

This diminutive book was one of the first ever written profiling a single golf course and, as far as I can determine, was likely *the* first to do so in a manner consistent with our modern club history volumes. It includes just the sort of historical notes one might expect, plus the R&A rules and profiles of several early St. Andrews golfing clubs. Most noteworthy, however, are the hole-by-hole suggestions on how best to play the three courses then in existence, plus a foldout map of the entire facility.

As only 1,200 copies of this book exist (1,000 originals and 200 reprints), a decent copy will lighten one's wallet considerably.

Original: $4,000+ • Ellesborough: $300+

British Golf Links •
Horace G. Hutchinson
J.S. Virtue, London • 331pp • 1897

A high degree of subjectivity pervades the judging of creative endeavors, but of *British Golf Links* I will state unequivocally: There has never in the history of golf been a book more ahead of its time, for this was without question the game's first coffee-table volume, an oversized, lavishly produced work that, considering its date of publication, seems almost inconceivably clean and attractive.

In short, *British Golf Links* profiles 51 great British courses, plus three in France (Biarritz, Pau, and Cannes), generally utilizing information provided by the club secretaries and other local sources. Each profile runs several large pages and includes hole yardages, descriptions, club history, and lots of evocative touches. This alone is impressive, but what makes *British Golf Links* so utterly remarkable are the pictures: dozens upon dozens of brilliantly clear images that seem to blatantly defy the limited reproduction technology of the time. Adding to the mystique is the fact that a good many of the photographed holes are gone now, making their documentation here nothing short of stunning.

$2,000+

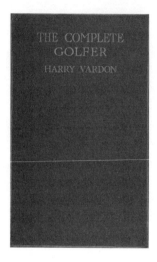

The Complete Golfer • *Harry Vardon*
Methuen, London • 283pp • 1905
1st US edition: McClure Phillips 1905
(w/later edition by Doubleday)
Reprinted by Golf Digest (1977),
Fredonia (2001 PBK), and Alexander
(2003 PBK)

The Complete Golfer was wildly successful in its day, going into at least 20 editions at home and enjoying a similar degree of acclaim overseas. Part of this windfall can be attributed to Vardon's immense personal popularity, of course, as well as his complete dominance of the game in the years prior to the book's release. But ultimately, *The Complete Golfer* sold so well because it was among the most thorough studies of the game yet written by a single author.

It opens with two autobiographical chapters recounting Vardon's youth and his competitive career (bits of which were "borrowed" for his 1933 autobiography *My Golfing Life*), then moves into 16 instructive ones covering every aspect of playing the game. Ultimately, it concludes with three fascinating segments: "The Construction of Courses," "Links I Have Played On," and "Golf in America," each a valuable and historic piece in its own right.

As well-rounded an early edition as one might hope to find.

Original: $200 • Others: Under $25

Concerning Golf • *John L. Low*
Hodder & Stoughton, London • 217pp • 1903 (w/editions through 1906)
Reprinted by the USGA (1987)

John Low secured his position in golf history as a founder of the Oxford & Cambridge Golfing Society, though reaching the final of the British Amateur in 1901 (where he lost to Harold Hilton) surely didn't hurt. More relevant to *Concerning Golf*, perhaps, was his leadership of the R&A's

Rules of Golf Committee which voted in 1902 to ban the new Haskell ball—a recommendation that the R&A as a whole chose to ignore.

Low's traditionalist leanings shine throughout this volume, a manuscript which follows largely the same pattern as standards like *The Art of Golf* and *The Badminton Library*. It begins with a chapter on the character of the game, then runs through a long patch of "suggestions" on technique, finally culminating with sections on courses, weather, match play, style, and temperament. Though the thoughts of so knowledgeable a man are uniformly of interest, few are as well remembered as those dedicated to golf course design ("there is hardly such a thing as an unfair bunker"), making this work timeless in at least that one respect.

Older copies of *Concerning Golf* are often more plentiful than the USGA reprint, though neither is likely to come cheaply.

Original: $150 • USGA (1,900 copies): $125

Famous Golf Links • *Horace G. Hutchinson*
Longmans, Green, London • 199pp • 1891

Not to be confused with the vastly more elaborate *British Golf Links,* the smaller *Famous Golf Links* is actually something of an anthology, composed primarily of course-profile articles authored by Hutchinson for the *Saturday Review.* Predating its illustrious cousin by six years, it covers only 18 courses (plus a section on golf in Canada) and is considerably less spectacular in its illustrations, many of which are simple sketches. It should also be noted that several of the profiles were done by writers other than Hutchinson, one being the fine St. Andrews amateur S. Mure Fergusson.

Perhaps because *British Golf Links* trumped it into oblivion, copies of *Famous Golf Links* are extremely difficult to find.

$1,100+

Famous Scottish Links and Other Golfing Papers •
T.D. Miller
R & R Clark, Edinburgh • 150pp • 1911

Miller, this book's dedication informs us, was a Captain of the R&A and a fairly prominent writer—the latter point deduced by the notation that much of this volume's content had appeared previously "in magazine literature."

A pleasant little volume, *Famous Scottish Links* is filled with profiles of courses, players, and matches dating back as far the middle nineteenth century. In addition to the St. Andrews, Carnousties, and Prestwicks, smaller links such as Montrose, Perth, and Leven also appear, though the course profiles tend to be more general/historical and not of the hole-by-hole sort. Chapters on clubmaker Robert Forgan and the Harry Vardon–Willie Park Jr. challenge match of 1899 are particularly engaging, and Miller's style is straightforward and highly informed.

Another very difficult find.

$1,800+

A Few Rambling Remarks on Golf • *Robert Chambers*
W & R Chambers, Edinburgh • 31pp • 1862 (PBK)
Reprinted by the USGA (1983)

It seems fitting to open with this, one of golf's very earliest recorded publications. Just how far back in the game's history does the printing date of 1862 take us? Well, the book's opening words read: "Golf, or goff, is a pastime peculiar to Scotland"—a revealing chronological statement on at least two counts.

The work itself is fairly basic, explaining, in surprisingly modern English, what the game is, how it's played, its various implements, and some standard fundamentals. The official R&A rules of the day are also included, making this pamphlet-like work a remarkable historic artifact—albeit perhaps a nonessential one for all but the hard-core collector.

The original edition is nearly impossible to find, while the USGA reprint comes paired with *Rules of the Thistle Club,* another similarly sized work and very likely the first attempt at committing the game's history to paper.

Original: $4,000+ • USGA (1,900 copies): $150

F.G. Tait: A Record • *John L. Low*
James Nisbet, London • 304pp • 1900
Reprinted by Classics of Golf (1988)

F.G. Tait: A Record holds the distinction of being the first biography of a golfer ever written, but its quality is such that it would still stand out nicely if produced today. It profiles two-time British Amateur champion and Scottish icon Freddie Tait, a tremendous golfing talent who died at age 30 in South Africa, while fighting in the Boer War. Written by Tait's close friend John Low, it makes excellent use of letters penned by and about the deceased, as well as of his golfing diary, a remarkably extensive career record which is reproduced as an appendix.

With the full support of Tait's family, Low was able to produce a truly detailed and fine biography. Too bad more of the countless golf bios to follow couldn't reach this pioneering standard.

Original: $300+ • COG: New ($29)

The Game of Golf • *William Park Jr.*
Longmans, Green, London • 277pp • 1896
Reprinted by Flagstick Books (2002)

The Game of Golf was the first book ever to be authored by a golf professional, no small achievement in an era when pros were looked upon as little more than common laborers. Park, a two-time Open champion, was uniquely qualified to write it, for he was also a teacher, clubmaker, land developer, and pioneering course architect—perhaps the game's first true renaissance man.

Though seven of the book's 12 chapters are instructive in nature, Park does open with the general "The Game of Golf" and later makes history by becoming, in chapter 10, the first practicing architect to spell out his design principles with "Laying Out and Keeping Golf-Links."

This landmark volume has become extremely difficult to find in recent years, making the Flagstick Books' facsimile a most welcome arrival.

Original: $1,000+ • Flagstick: New ($33)

Golf: A Royal and Ancient Game • *Robert Clark (Editor)*
R & R Clark, Edinburgh • 284pp • 1875 (w/editions through 1899)
Reprinted by E.P. Publishing (1975)

There are many knowledgeable observers who feel that this ancient collection is, quite simply, the most important volume in the annals of golf—and from strictly an historical perspective, how can we argue? For *Golf: A Royal and Ancient Game* represents Mr. Robert Clark's rather remarkable attempt to reprint literally everything that had been written (or, for that matter, sung) about golf prior to the book's initial publication date of 1875. Whether he missed one or two obscure entries we shall likely never know. But the smart money says that we're not likely to care either, as countless historical gems—many of which might have otherwise vanished forever—are recorded herein.

The Goff, the legendary "Heroi-comical Poem in Three Cantos" (reprinted on its own, in 1981, by the USGA) is the logical opener, but what follows is a veritable treasure trove, with ancient records of the R&A and Honourable Company, fifteenth-century Royal proclamations, excerpts from George Carnegie's 1833 *Golfiana*, and much, much more.

Interestingly, copies of the various nineteenth-century editions are easier to locate (at no small cost) than the 1975 reprint, leaving us to wonder how long it will be before some enterprising publisher issues a new-millennium facsimile. Regardless, it is worth noting that much of this material is so removed even from, say, Harry Vardon's era that it can today be viewed as a challenging sort of read. Still, as an historical record of golf's earliest roots, *Golf: A Royal and Ancient Game* is the unquestioned, all-time champion.

Originals (1875–1899): $750+ • E.P.: $75

Golf for Women • *Genevieve Hecker*
Baker & Taylor, New York • 217pp • 1904
Reprinted by Legacy Golf (2001)

Though apparently not the initial American golf book written by a woman, *Golf for Women* likely was the first to find substantial success in the marketplace. As a two-time National Amateur champion, Ms. Hecker certainly had the credentials to author what is almost exclusively a book of instruction, though a couple of chapters on courses and a guest appearance by Irish star Rhona Adair ("Impressions of American Golf") do provide some variety.

An historically notable volume.

$800 • Legacy: New ($23)

Golf Greens & Green-Keeping •
Horace G. Hutchinson (Editor)
Country Life, London • 219pp • 1906
Reprinted by Sleeping Bear (2001)

Without some detailed knowledge of agronomy, one hasn't a clue if the century-old greenkeeping ideas expressed in this book remain sound today. But no matter, for despite likely being the first volume to offer such scientific fare on a large scale, *Golf Greens & Green-Keeping* is included primarily for its architectural aspects that, despite a faintly misleading title, are many.

Indeed, H.S. Colt, Herbert Fowler, James Braid, and Mure Fergusson all provide chapters on the design and upkeep of various types of courses while C.K. Hutchinson ("Formation and Placing of Hazards"), Harold Hilton ("Remarks on the Laying Out of Courses" and "The Championship Courses"), and old Horace Hutchinson himself ("A Few Leading Principles on Laying Out Links") contribute more general architectural fare.

The first book to present such wide-ranging and detailed architectural text, *Golf Greens & Green-Keeping* stands as something of a landmark. Still, the rare and very expensive nature of original editions had rendered it nearly extinct prior to Sleeping Bear's much-needed 2001 reprint.

Original: $1,000 • Sleeping Bear: $100

Golf in America • *James Lee*
Dodd, Mead, New York • 194pp • 1895
Reprinted by the USGA (1986) and Legacy Golf (2001)

This tight little volume holds the distinction of being the very first golfing book ever to be published in the United States. In fact, as a frame of chronological reference, we can quote the opening sentence of the preface—"A new game has lately been added to the list of our outdoor sports"—and proceed from there.

Though perhaps not of Darwinian literary merit, *Golf in America* acquits itself admirably for such a groundbreaker, getting right to the point throughout its five untitled sections. The first covers the origins and spread of the game in the United Kingdom. The second details its move to the United States and Canada, and is especially interesting in that it profiles a number of prominent nineteenth-century clubs. The third and fourth teach the basics of terminology and technique, while the fifth covers etiquette and the rules, also offering a glossary and a list of prominent American clubs and their officers.

Original editions are nearly nonexistent and the limited USGA reprint is expensive, making the Legacy Golf version a most affordable option.

Note: A slightly smaller, unillustrated edition was also released in 1895.

Original: $2,600+ • USGA (1,500 copies): $175 • Legacy: New ($23)

Golf: The Badminton Library •
Horace G. Hutchinson (Editor)
Longmans, Green, London • 495pp • 1890 (w/editions through 1911)
Reprinted by Ashford Press (1987) and Flagstick Books (1996)

Some editions of this classic highlight the Eighth Duke of Beaufort, the impresario responsible for this series of books profiling the popular sports of late nineteenth-century Britain. But not a single word within this volume did His Grace actually pen, that honor falling instead to Horace Hutchinson, with smaller contributions made by Sir Walter Simpson, Lord Wellwood, H.S.C. Everard, Andrew Lang, and the Rt. Hon. A.J. Balfour, M.P.

In its configuration *The Badminton Library* parallels Simpson's *The Art of Golf* greatly, commencing with chapters detailing the game's history and traditions before moving into a broader section of instruction on all aspects of the game. Of course, where Simpson is pleasant and concise, this is a far more detailed affair, serving as an excellent primer for those just learning the game. Also featured are several more eclectic chapters including entries on odds and handicapping, caddies, famous players, golf humor, and what very likely was the first published assess-ment of the great British links.

For a title well over a century old, *The Badminton Library* still reads quite well today. Some revisions and additions were made to the various editions printed through 1911, though both modern reprints are faithful to Hutchinson's original 1890 version—and these are clearly the most affordable option for the average modern reader.

Original: $270 • Ashford: $50 • Flagstick: New ($29)

Golfer's Guide to the Game and Greens of Scotland •
W. Dalrymple (Editor)
W.H. White, Edinburgh • 208pp • 1894

This splendid little volume is rather different from your standard guide-book as its first half is spent profiling dozens of the era's top players, including the Morrises, Allan Robertson, the Kirkaldys, and just about any other nineteenth-century Scottish player you might care to name. The second half then describes over 150 of the nation's top courses in some detail, with 30 of the best supplemented by simple routing maps. Though graphically pedestrian, few guidebooks in the history of the game can match *Golfer's Guide*'s thoroughness and historical value, which perhaps explains why copies are nearly impossible to find.

Note: Several subsequent editions were published (beginning in 1895) under the title *Golfer's Guide for the United Kingdom,* though these too are extremely elusive.

$600

The Golfer's Handbook • *Robert Forgan*
John Innis, Cupar, Scotland • 83pp • 1881 (w/later editions through 1907)

The Golfer's Handbook—not to be confused with the endlessly running annual yearbook of the same title—can reasonably be considered golf's first truly popular book, reaching not less than seven editions over more than 25 years. Essentially it might be seen as a somewhat modernized version of H.B. Farnie's *The Golfer's Manual,* especially since it even managed to appropriate that volume's title for its final three editions.

Contentwise, Forgan's book offered the following five chapters: "Historical Sketch of the Game," "Clubs Employed in the Game," "Hints to Beginners," "History of Golf Balls," and "Champion Golfers." There follows a section entitled Golfiana (which includes a glossary) and a final segment providing both the rules and a listing of prominent UK clubs.

Never reproduced in the modern era, what early copies remain available are predictably expensive.

$2,500+

The Golfer's Manual • *A Keen Hand (H.B. Farnie)*
Whitehead & Orr, Cupar, Scotland • 96pp • 1857 (w/later editions to 1870)
Reprinted by Dropmore (1947) and Vantage (1965)

As it can be fairly argued that this diminutive volume was the first genuine book dedicated solely to the game of golf, its place in history is obviously a grand one. Its subtitle reads "Being an Historical and Descriptive Account of the National Game of Scotland," and in this regard the text is entirely as advertised, featuring chapters entitled "Historical Sketch of the Game," "The Modern Game," "Classification of Clubs," "Golfing Mannerisms," "Choice of Clubs," "Style of Play," "Points of the Game," "Match-playing," and "Conclusion."

Personally, I consider such historic items to be unworthy acquisitions for all but the most dedicated collectors, as the actual content generally represents a rather limited read. In the case of *The Golfer's Manual*, however, where timing and originality make it even more important than Forgan's above-listed entry (and modern reprints make it almost affordable), one might be inclined to think differently. Besides, this volume opens with the splendid words "The origin of the game of golf is hidden in the mists of antiquity."

Even Bernard Darwin would have enjoyed coming up with that one.

Original: $9,000+ • Dropmore: $325 • Vantage: $175

The Golfing Annual • *David S. Duncan (Editor)*
Horace Cox, London • 1887 (w/22 subsequent annual editions)

A veritable institution during the years of the Triumvirate, *The Golfing Annual* was generally a large, well-presented edition that both summarized the state of the game and provided listings of prominent golfing facilities. Earlier editions often feature a somewhat higher writing quality (including such contributors as Horace Hutchinson and Sir Walter Simpson) but later volumes might be preferred for their vastly expanded indexes of courses. Not surprisingly, more descriptive information is provided for British courses than those over the horizon, and the international listings, though impressive in their scope, should in no way be thought of as comprehensive.

Given the *Annual*'s longevity, plenty of copies remain in circulation, with prices varying predictably by age.

$300–$750

The Golfing Pilgrim • *Horace G. Hutchinson*
Methuen, London • 287pp • 1898
1st US edition: Scribner's 1898

The Golfing Pilgrim falls more or less in the middle of Horace Hutchinson's lengthy body of work, both in terms of chronology and quality. It is also one of his more difficult efforts to get a handle on, being—depending upon one's perspective—either wonderfully wide-ranging or terribly ill-defined. The book's subtitle is "On Many Links" and to some extent this *is* a panorama of the turn-of-the-century golfing world. The first several chapters (including the neatly titled "Mecca out of Season") deal with St. Andrews, before the text wanders more freely about, touching upon various other elements of the game.

This rare volume is virtually unillustrated, save for a single page of stick drawings which resemble a golfing version of the logo for Roger Moore's old television show *The Saint*.

$475

Golfing: The Oval Series of Games • *Horace G. Hutchinson*
George Routledge, London • 120pp • 1893
1st US edition ("Golf: A Complete History of the Game"): Penn 1900

This general treatise on the game was one of Hutchinson's earliest works and represents a fine indoctrination for the beginner. It is divided into the following eight sections: "Historical," "Implements," "Educational," "Links," "Golfers and Styles," "Match Play," "Handicapping," and "The Rules and Etiquette of Golf." Though perhaps done better elsewhere in the author's portfolio, this was an important early volume, particularly in America where its 1900 publication (under altered title) enjoyed several subsequent editions.

Hard to find in either country today, these books were decidedly small, with the initial American editions fitting nearly into one's hand.
$125

Great Golfers in the Making • *Henry Leach (Editor)*
Methuen, London • 299pp • 1907
1st US edition: George W. Jacobs 1907
Reprinted by the USGA (1988)

What a fascinating volume!

Leach, an early editor of Britain's ancient *Golf Illustrated* magazine, assembled these 34 chapters as a series of articles, each written by an elite player recounting his beginnings in the game. When put into book form most were revised and extended, allowing these final versions to include, among other things, practical advice geared toward each contributor's specialty (e.g., Willie Park Jr. on putting).

Aside from being an entirely unique concept, *Great Golfers in the Making* stands as a classic because of the astonishing roster of talent assembled. Every great British player of the era participated without exception, as did several legendary old-timers. Even the first great American player, Walter Travis, and two-time U.S. Amateur champion H. Chandler Egan provided chapters.

Original 1907 editions are difficult to find, but USGA reprints of this wonderful collection, though somewhat expensive, are still out there—and very well worth it.
Original: $250+ • USGA (1,500 copies): $130

Great Golfers: Their Methods at a Glance •
George W. Beldam
Macmillan, London • 480pp • 1904

The use of photographs in analyzing the golf swing began in 1887 with Sir Walter Simpson's *The Art of Golf,* so this volume can scarcely be termed pioneering. Yet as far as I can find, this likely was the first to make the photographic dissection of famous golf swings its entire *raison d'etre.*

Though period photography hardly yielded the sort of multi-image swing sequences that we see today, this collection provides multiple pictures for more than 15 elite players, both professional and amateur. Most interesting are the sections on Vardon, Braid, Taylor, Sandy Herd, and Harold Hilton, for in each case the explanatory text was authored by the highlighted player himself. Hilton then takes over the writing in examining the technique of a number of prominent amateurs, including Horace Hutchinson, Johnny Laidley, John Low, long-hitting Ted Blackwell, and others.

An epic of its time, copies of this trendsetting early edition can generally be found—but, once again, at a fairly hefty price.

$325+

The Happy Golfer • *Henry Leach*
Macmillan, London • 414pp • 1914

The Happy Golfer is one of my personal favorites, its subtitle ("Being some experiences, reflections and a few deductions of a wandering player") setting the table for a complete and entertaining survey of early twentieth-century golf worldwide. Indeed, after opening with some history and general thoughts on the game (including chapter five's recounting of the landmark 1913 U.S. Open), we then wander around the globe to all manner of golfing outposts. Stateside readers will particular enjoy Leach's thoughts on the National Golf Links of America before the text moves on to Canada, France (the Riviera, the mountains, Biarritz, and Pau), Italy, and Spain. Eventually we return to the UK for chapters on the greatest of links and "The Old Dignity of London Golf."

As pleasant a read now as then, this hard-to-find volume stands out as an ideal candidate for reprinting.

$450+

Harper's Official Golf Guide 1901 •
W.G. Van Tassel Sutphen (Editor)
Harper's, New York • 332pp • 1901

This earliest of American course guides was a fairly thorough publication, providing detailed listings of established clubs in all of the then-golfing states. In the cases of better-known clubs and tournament venues, hole yardages are frequently listed, along with club officers, general location, and the like.

Indispensable as a turn-of-the-century reference source, this important volume is believed to have spawned a second or third edition, and was the obvious model for the highly successful *American Annual Golf Guide* and *Golfer's Year Book* of later years.

Extremely rare today.

$500+

Hints on the Game of Golf • *Horace Hutchinson*
William Blackwood, Edinburgh • 69pp • 1886
Reprinted by Classics of Golf (1987)

Hutchinson's first work is a brief, often tongue-in-cheek affair that opens with the author's own statement that "For my own part, I have often asserted that 'you cannot learn golf from a book'." That said, the text remains true to its title, offering not a comprehensive dissertation but rather suggestions and "truisms," all divided into sections entitled "Advice to Beginners," "Hints to Golfers of Riper Years," and "The Miseries of Golf." I personally find this volume to be more a pleasant diversion than a classic, but several generations of readers seem to have overridden that opinion.

Later printings of the original can still be found, while the Classics of Golf reprint features both the usual Herbert Warren Wind foreword and an unusual afterword by one J.W. Nicklaus of Columbus, Ohio.

Original: $300 • COG: New (+/−$20)

Historical Gossip about Golf and Golfers •
Golfer (George Robb)
Privately printed, Edinburgh • 58pp • 1863 (PBK)
Reprinted by the USGA (1991)

This tiny and rather disjointed volume is divided into three sections, opening with its most valuable component, a "Historical Sketch." It then profiles the early Bruntsfield Links and closes with an appendix, the contents of which includes some discussion of the French game jeu de mail and the Dutch kolf.

Beyond its great historical significance, I generally consider this to be the least essential of the very early works profiled here. The USGA, however, would disagree, having reprinted it (paired with the J. Gordon McPherson's similarly small *Golf and Golfers, Past and Present*) while bypassing both Forgan's *The Golfer's Handbook* and Farnie's *The Golfer's Manual*.

Original green-wrappered editions are virtually nonexistent.

Original: $9,000+ • USGA (1,500 copies): $200+

A History of the Royal and Ancient Golf Club, St. Andrews • *H.S.C. Everard*
William Blackwood, Edinburgh • 306pp • 1907

If one subscribes to the belief that the earliest sources in a given field tend to be the most desirable, then H.S.C. Everard's history of the R&A immediately becomes *the* volume on the long, long list of St. Andrews stories. Published in 1907, it joins W.W. Tulloch's *The Life of Tom Morris* as a book written as much from personal experience as legend, though it is worth footnoting that much of its content is drawn from articles Everard wrote for *Golf Illustrated*. It was not, apparently, an entirely new manuscript.

Its 28 chapters cover the club's long evolution chronologically, from "Early References to Golf at St. Andrews" (chapter two) to a contemporary account of Old Tom's hiring as Keeper of the Green in 1863, and so on. The book is heavily illustrated with photos and paintings and contains vastly more minutiae than the more general reader may desire. That is just as well, however, as this very difficult-to-find volume ranks high among golf literature's more expensive catches.

$2,550+

How to Play Golf • *Harry Vardon*
Methuen, London • 298pp • 1912
1st US edition: George Jacobs (1912)

Initially published seven years after *The Complete Golfer, How to Play Golf* joined its slightly more expansive predecessor in the bestseller line, also going into at least 20 British editions. Though shorter in overall words, this is a volume of nearly equal thoroughness, covering instruction in 12 chapters, one of which ("Prominent Players and Their Methods") represents entirely new ground in the Vardon portfolio. It also includes chapters on "The Game Abroad" and "Golf Course Architecture," the latter, Fred Hawtree has astutely observed, likely representing the first time the subject was given prime billing in a book written by a prominent player.

Relatively easy to find on both sides of the Atlantic, at widely varying prices.

$65+

How to Play Golf • *H.J. Whigham*
Herbert S. Stone, Chicago • 313pp • 1897 (w/editions through 1903)

Generally considered the first American book dedicated (almost) exclusively to instruction, *How to Play Golf* was written by H.J. Whigham, two-time U.S. Amateur champion and son-in-law of the legendary Charles Blair Macdonald. If we can consider sections on rules and etiquette to be tutorial, then eight of 11 chapters are entirely educational, with three more general closers discussing the building of courses, the development of the game in America, and some great British amateurs. The book is well illustrated with swing photos, plus a few rather incongruous maps of the great British links.

This somewhat rare volume is hardly essential either as instruction or pure history, yet its place in the body of American golf literature is significant.

$275

Inland Golf • *Edward Ray*
Werner Laurie, London • 234pp • 1913
1st US edition: J. Pott 1914

Inland Golf must be among the most enigmatic golfing titles ever chosen, for its famous author grew up every bit a links player on the Isle of Jersey. As the book is primarily instructional, it refers to the post-1900 rise of inland golf courses in Britain, and an apparent need to tailor one's game to their differing conditions. The book is almost entirely instructional, save for the opening chapter ("The Rise of Inland Golf") and several late sections on famous inland courses, Ray's career reminiscences, and the like.

Ray himself makes quite the picture, a large, bearish man outfitted with his customary trilby hat and pipe, and his famously gargantuan lash at the golf ball. Then again, he remains one of only three Britons to win both the U.S. and British Opens and was known to drive it well beyond even Vardon, so who are we to scoff?

Not as strong a book as we might expect from a man of Ray's well-known color, but an interesting read nonetheless.

$175

Ladies' Golf • *May Hezlet*
Hutchinson, London • 336pp • 1904

This popular volume may not have been the first golf book authored by a woman (one Mrs. Edward Kennard having written *The Sorrows of a Golfer's Wife* in 1896) but it does stand among the earliest full-size how-to guides for the UK's distaff players. Like Genevieve Hecker's *Golf for Women* (published in America during the same year) *Ladies' Golf* is a complete instruction guide written by a two-time national champion. It covers everything from technique to the rules, etiquette, and dress, and includes 33 illustrations, nearly all demonstrating the full swing.

Despite its period popularity (which was perhaps due to being billed as a sister volume to J.H. Taylor's *Taylor on Golf*), *Ladies' Golf* is a rather difficult find today.

$250

The Life of Tom Morris • *W. W. Tulloch*
Werner Laurie, London • 334pp • 1908
Reprinted by Ellesborough Press (1982) and the USGA (1992)

The most noteworthy aspect of this volume is simply this: Nearly 100 years after being penned by one of his contemporaries, it remains today as *the* biography of the game's all-time father figure, Old Tom Morris. True, few have ventured forward to challenge it, but this in itself may be the ultimate statement of just how authoritative *The Life of Tom Morris* really is.

The book contains an expansive 28 chapters, recounting the first 87 years of Morris's life with a heavy emphasis on his competitive achievements. Naturally Young Tom's brief-but-wondrous career also comes under the spotlight, making this one of the few legitimate firsthand accounts of golf's first true superstar. Nevertheless, it's Old Tom who remains the primary focus of this story. So much so, in fact, that the book opens with a letter of dedication from the author, offering "this account of your long and honourable life" as a gift on the occasion of Morris's 87th birthday.

A unique and wonderful window into another time.

Original: $800+ • Ellesborough: $200 • USGA (1,500 copies): $175

My Golfing Reminiscences • *Harold Hilton*
James Nisbet, London • 247pp • 1907
Reprinted by Classics of Golf (1998)

Along with possessing one of golf's finest monikers, Harold Horsefall Hilton stands as one of the game's greatest-ever amateurs, which naturally makes this early standard an interesting read. One should, however, take the title literally, for this text centers almost exclusively upon Hilton's own competitive experiences, with only limited biographical info and relatively scant commentary upon his competition, golf courses, the evolution of equipment, etc. Another weakness is that fully half of Hilton's four British Amateur titles and his historic victory in the 1911 U.S. Amateur took place after *My Golfing Reminiscences* was written.

With original editions coming up on the century mark, the Classics of Golf reprint is, as usual, a godsend.

Original: $300+ • COG: New ($29)

The Mystery of Golf • *Arnold Haultain*
Houghton Mifflin, Boston • 151pp • 1908 (limited edition)
Revised 2nd edition: Macmillan, New York • 249pp • 1910
1st UK edition: Macmillan 1910
Reprinted by Serendipity (1965), Classics of Golf (1986), and
Applewood (1988)

One of the strangest yet most engaging golf books of all time, *The Mystery of Golf* probably violates this volume's self-imposed ban on all things metaphysical, philosophizing, as it does, on the many mysteries and quirks of the game. For some its 41 brief chapters babble on, vaguely incoherent; for others these miniessays represent divine truth. I personally tend to fall more toward the former, though I suppose we must heed Herbert Warren Wind who wrote: "In my judgment, no later writer has equaled Haultain's performance." Of course, he later suggests that "you will enjoy Haultain most if you read him in relatively short takes"—which, I suppose, pronounces rather a clear judgment of its own.

Interestingly, Macmillan's revised second edition was expanded substantially from Houghton Mifflin's now-scarce 440-copy first. Having been frequently reprinted, this larger version is now the standard and is not at all difficult to find. Copies of 1908's 151-pager, however, are a genuine catch.

Original (440 copies): $3,000+ • Macmillan: $300 • Serendipity: $40 • COG: New ($33) • Applewood: Under $25

The New Book of Golf •
Horace Hutchinson (Editor)
Longmans, London • 361pp • 1912

As with one or two others in the Hutchinson portfolio, old Horace did little more than write a brief introduction here, with the entirety of the book's text being provided by others. This hardly diminishes the product, however, particularly when Bernard Darwin makes a rare tutorial appearance in an extended section entitled "Elementary Instruction." Aside from a "how to learn" prologue by A.C.M. Croome, the remaining components are "From the Professional's Point of View" (by James Sherlock), "Men of Genius" (C.K. Hutchinson), and "From the Ladies' Point of View" (Mrs. A.E. Ross).

Not Hutchinson's most important entry perhaps, but Darwin's involvement helps make it a worthwhile edition.

$325

Nisbet's Golf Year-Book • *J.L. Low (Editor)*
James Nisbet, London • 1905 (w/nine subsequent annual editions)

Rather like *The Golfer's Handbook* and *The Golfing Annual*, *Nisbet's Golf Year-Book* was one of the game's first volumes to be published yearly. Though only lasting a decade, it was especially notable for the big-name contributors it enticed (the 1906 edition, for example, included Darwin, Harold Hilton, Willie Park Jr., Horace Hutchinson, and all three members of the Triumvirate) as well as the annotated descriptions it provided for many of the better courses throughout the British Empire. American clubs, however, were listed only by name.

Note: John Low was replaced as Editor by one Vyvyan Harmsworth for the final two editions.

$125+

On Many Greens: A Book of Golf and Golfers •
Miles Bantock
Grosset & Dunlap, New York • 167pp • 1901

According to the author, this lighthearted anthology was intended to "while away an hour's railway journey, to cheer a wet day in the club-house, or to raise a laugh among a group of enthusiasts on the club porch." Its many, many entries are largely culled from British and American newspapers, though a fair number of pieces were written by Bantock himself.

Joseph Murdoch singles out one article, "Some Writers Who Golf," as providing valuable information on early American scribes. Beyond this, I'm not certain that this volume is worth its scarcity-driven price to all but the most dedicated.

$350

Practical Golf • *Walter Travis*
Harper's, New York • 225pp • 1901 (w/revised 1903 & 1909 editions)

This was, at the time of its publication, a landmark instructional volume from a man who, despite being born in Australia, was universally hailed as America's first genuine golfing star. Built around a series of articles Travis had composed for *Golf* magazine, it is a full and comprehensive book which attempts to teach the golf swing while also introducing stateside readers to the appeal of what was, in 1901, still rather a fledgling game. All aspects are covered from tee to green, though we note that putting is accorded two full chapters, befitting both its overall importance and Travis's status as an acknowledged genius with the blade.

Architectural fans will note that the second and third editions include "Hazards," an extra chapter dedicated primarily to issues of golf course design.

$250

Reminiscences of Golf on St. Andrews Links •
James Balfour
David Douglas, Edinburgh • 68pp • 1887
Reprinted by Chas A. Dufner (1982) and Classics of Golf (1987)

Few golfing books enjoy the sheer historical standing of *Reminiscences,* partially due to Balfour's later serving as a British cabinet minister, but mostly because this relatively brief volume represents a unique first-hand account of St. Andrews during the mid-nineteenth century. Its seven chapters are basic yet entirely thorough, being titled: "Links," "Balls and Clubs," "Medals," "Players," "Professionals and Caddies," "Incidents in Golf," and "Merits of the Game." Though each section provides a high degree of historical interest and ambience, architecture fans will surely covet the opener that discusses, in great detail, the early permutations of the Old Course.

Though well-conditioned originals are virtually extinct, the Classics of Golf reprint (complete with afterword by Jack Nicklaus) makes this cornerstone volume easily available to everyone.

Note: Joseph Murdoch also lists a 1985 reprint at St. Andrews, though any such edition, like the Dufner 1982 version, is not currently represented in the marketplace.
Original: $4,000+ • COG: New (+/–$20)

The Royal & Ancient Game of Golf •
Harold Hilton and Garden G. Smith
Golf Illustrated, London • 275pp • 1912
Reprinted by Hickory Press (2001)

Here is yet another standard from the early days, an ornate, oversized volume viewing all aspects of the game through the eyes of its all-star cast. The book is divided into 12 sections, the titles (and authors) of which are: "Golf: Its Origin and History" (Garden Smith), "Golf and the Man" (John Low), "Golf: Theoretical and Practical" (Harold Hilton), "The Principal Golf Greens" (Horace Hutchinson), "Some Reflections and Observations" (G.P. Elwes), "Eminent Golfers" (Hilton), "The Gift of Golf" (Low), "Continental Golf: The Riviera and Switzerland" (A.H. Crosfield), "The Game in America" (Hilton), "University Golf—Oxford" (A.C.M. Croome) and "Cambridge" (Bernard Darwin), "Golf Greens on Sand and in Dry Climates" (Martin H.F. Sutton), and "Ode to Golf" (Andrew Lang). A detailed appendix follows, which includes the rules of the game and what quite likely was, at that time, the most extensive golf bibliography yet compiled.

Original editions of this gorgeous production are both scarce and highly expensive, as only 1,000 copies were printed. The Hickory Press edition (limited to 500) is only somewhat easier to locate, but it remains the average reader's obvious choice until the inevitable large-market reprint comes along.
Original: $2,000+ • Hickory: $200

Side Lights on Golf • *Garden G. Smith*
Sisley's, London • 153pp • 1907

Though perhaps not as celebrated as the fruitful and enterprising Horace Hutchinson, *Golf Illustrated* Editor Garden Smith was an important enough literary figure in Victorian golfing circles. This being the last of his three solo books, it includes material at least partially reprinted from several magazines (including the early American publication *Golf*) and thus might be considered at least partially an anthology.

As the title suggests, this book is hardly the standard "how-to" or Triumvirate-oriented tome of the period, its 12 offbeat chapters addressing such subjects as "Historical Side Lights," "Dramatis Personae," "About Waggles," and "The Cheapening of Championships." Though hardly considered essential, this original little volume is nearly impossible to locate today.

$175+

The Soul of Golf • *Pembroke A. Vaile*
Macmillan, London • 355pp • 1912

Hardly a household name today, Pembroke Vaile wrote not less than a dozen golf instruction books between 1909 and 1935. *The Soul of Golf* is likely the best remembered, perhaps because it "assumes on the part of the reader a certain amount of knowledge, and it essays to bring back to the truth those who have been led astray by the false teaching of the most eminent men associated with the game."

Depending upon one's perspective, this is either a minutiae-filled volume reminiscent of Arnold Haultain (who, not surprisingly, is quoted within) or an incisive treatise cutting right to the heart of the matter. Whatever the case, its fundamental notion that a player should sort out the truth in the comfort of his armchair so that he might take an uncluttered mind onto the links seems universal enough.

A somewhat difficult find.

$250+

The Spirit of the Links • *Henry Leach*
Methuen, London • 314pp • 1907

This to me is a most aptly titled volume, for Leach's first book is a pleasant, informative, and well-written overview of the early game. Its eight sections work their way metaphorically through a golfing season, being titled "Spring," "Men and Things," "The Queer Side," "The Wandering Player," "The Sunny Season," "The Professor on the Links," "The Fabric of the Game," and, lastly, "Winter." Each section is subdivided into shorter chapters, with subjects covering all aspects of the game, its venues, charms, and idiosyncrasies.

Though vastly lesser-known than the omnipresent Hutchinson, Leach was comfortably Horace's equal as a writer, helping this book to both profile and sell the game during what were still its formative years.

$375

Taylor on Golf: Impressions, Comments and Hints •
J.H. Taylor
Hutchinson, London • 328pp • 1902
1st US edition: D. Appleton 1902

Like Vardon's *Complete Golfer, Taylor on Golf* might be thought of more as an encyclopedia than a book of instruction, for it genuinely covers the turn-of-the-century game in its entirety. And in true British style, it does so with a pleasant touch of modesty, its preface beginning: "The vast extent and continual growth of the game must be my apology for *Taylor on Golf.*"

Over the course of 41 chapters, the book mixes material on great events, championship courses, the professional life, architecture, and golf in America with a full tutorial, interweaving subjects for a varied and fascinating read. Inherent to the book's charm are several offbeat chapters ("Courses Where the Championship Might Be Played," "The Physical Strain of a Professional's Life," etc.), as well as a full appendix, which includes lists of Open and Amateur champions, a register of leading clubs throughout the UK, and the rules of the game.

That Vardon's book has been contemporarily reprinted and this one has not speaks loudly to the importance of that sixth Open Championship.

$550+

Travers' Golf Book • *Jerome D. Travers*
Macmillan, New York • 242pp • 1913

With one U.S. Open and four U.S. Amateur titles to his credit, Jerry Travers remains one of the more overlooked stars of American golfing history. This volume (his first of three) was published in the year of his final Amateur victory and largely represents the standard biography/

instruction book of the period, beginning with a life story, then expanding into a full-fledged tutorial.

Though perhaps not a truly essential work, it is palpably indicative of early American golf's economic underpinnings when its opening words read: "I started playing golf on my father's country estate . . ."

$200

The World of Golf • *Garden G. Smith*
A.D. Innes, London • 330pp • 1898

Following a brief 1897 effort entitled simply *Golf,* 1898's *The World of Golf* was Garden Smith's second book, and a broad and wide-ranging work at that.

Commencing with a general overview of the game's history, *The World of Golf* then becomes largely as its title suggests: a survey of how and where the game was played toward the end of the nineteenth century. There are chapters on St. Andrews, Prestwick, Hoylake, Sandwich, and clubs around London; then, a bit later, sections on the game in Europe, on three favored Irish links (County Down, Portrush, and Portsalon), and finally in America. Chapters on style and etiquette are inserted near the middle, and a good-sized appendix includes the rules and lists of the leading golf clubs of the UK.

Though seldom mentioned in the same breath as the most famous titles of the period, *The World of Golf* is today a very rare catch.

$300+

SECTION II
HISTORY

In some sense, this is our least-defined genre in that almost any book, if its material has become dated, can be perceived as historical. My own definition, however, tends to run more along the lines of telling a story—that is, any volume chronicling the development of something over an extended period of time. It's a broad definition, yet it seems to apply directly to the great majority of books selected. The exceptions (such as Dr. Quirin's *Golf Clubs of the MGA*) may not follow as clear a chronological timeline, but I dare say that given the nature of their content, few will dispute the general notion that they are, in fact, "historical."

As an aside, several prominent regional volumes are included, the relative value of each to an international audience being largely a judgment call. To my thinking, however, if a book is well-researched, thorough, and covers an important golfing area (e.g., Long Island, Philadelphia, Chicago, etc.), then its inclusion is considerably more worthwhile than another generic "History of Golf" telling us that Tom Morris was Scottish and Jack Nicklaus won a lot. Indeed, I am disappointed that there aren't more such "narrow" volumes to further complicate our decision-making process.

It is also worth noting that a good percentage of this section's books are of a fairly modern vintage, making them both easy to locate and relatively inexpensive.

America's Linksland: A Century of Long Island Golf •
Dr. William Quirin
Sleeping Bear, Chelsea, MI • 279pp • 2002

As the official historian of the Metropolitan Golf Association, Dr. Quirin has done as much research into Long Island's rich golfing past as anyone alive. This beautifully illustrated volume, which was published in advance of the 2003 U.S. Open at Bethpage, represents the fruits of that labor, covering more than 110 years of history in 30 loosely chronological chapters. Many of the chapters are keyed to the development of classic area courses, meaning that extensive coverage is provided for such mainstays as the National Golf Links of America, Garden City, Shinnecock Hills, Bethpage, and C.B. Macdonald's long-lost Lido, as well as so many "lesser" designs that would make the "A" list virtually anyplace else.

Though perhaps not as detailed as certain other regional histories, this book succeeds in covering a great deal of ground in 279 pages, and is a fine addition to several categories of a golfer's library.
New ($55)

Caddie in the Golden Age • *Ernest Hargreaves*
(with Jim Gregson)
Partridge, London • 198pp • 1993

Ernest Hargreaves was all of 16 years old when he caddied for Walter Hagen during the Open Championship of 1929, gaining his own measure of fame when the Haig, in perhaps his grandest-ever gesture, handed the young caddie his entire £100 first-place check. This splendid debut was soon followed by 20+ years working—both on the bag and off—for Henry Cotton, the great British war-era pro who would himself go on to win three Open Championships. Hargreaves wrote this largely overlooked little book as he approached 80, recalling both his own fascinating life and his time with these two most compelling Hall-of-Famers in fine style.

In the case of Hagen, this will likely be the last firsthand account to be written. In the case of Cotton, it will likely be the best.
Under $25

Carry Your Bag, Sir? • *David Stirk*
H.F. & G. Witherby, London • 128pp • 1989

A true golfing library could not be complete without at least one volume chronicling the history of the game's oldest profession—and who better to write it than a noted profiler of golf's earliest roots, David Stirk? *Carry Your Bag, Sir?* begins with the evolution of the word caddie and the first recorded mentions of the trade, then carries its development right on through to the modern era. In addition to profiles of some early Scottish legends, a section on "Caddies Abroad" (frequently barefoot natives) is particularly interesting.

Attractively laid out with many illustrations, *Carry Your Bag, Sir?* manages to effectively capture the seedy essence of golf's most colorful characters.

Under $25

A Centennial Tribute to Golf in Philadelphia •
James Finegan
Golf Association of Philadelphia, Philadelphia • 519pp • 1996

This, I am certain, is the bellwether of regional history volumes, a massive, now-hard-to-find tome that does as thorough a job as humanly possible of covering the people, places, and events of one of America's golfingest areas. Finegan, a retired advertising executive, happens also to be an outstanding writer and researcher, talents that are plainly in evidence here.

Of course, Philadelphia golf's greatest attribute is its grand collection of classic Golden Age courses. Thus in addition to the standard (and wonderfully detailed) historical fare, there are individual profiles of most every course ever to have graced the area, including nearby Pine Valley and, of course, Merion.

Perhaps not every regional golf association merits this majestic a history book, but wouldn't it be great if more of them had the dedication—and a writer like Finegan—to give it a try?

$125

Challenges & Champions: The Royal & Ancient Golf Club 1754–1883 • *John Behrend and Peter N. Lewis*
Royal & Ancient Golf Club, St. Andrews • 280pp • 1998

Commissioned for the 250th anniversary of the R&A, this first of two companion volumes traces the club's almost mythical history from 1754 to 1883. Researched by Lewis (curator of the British Golf Museum) and written by Behrend, it is a comprehensive look, divided into 35 highly-detailed chapters and illustrated with photographs, paintings, sketches, and the occasional map. I find the book somewhat stylistically reminiscent of Everard's *A History of the Royal and Ancient Golf Club* and it is certainly crafted with a similar eye for detail. In fact, the only knock on this obviously important volume is that it may be a bit too thorough for the more general reader.

Designed for the R&A by Grant Books, this initial edition was limited to 1,750 copies, but can still be purchased new at the time of this writing.

One surely cannot have this, Volume I, without . . .

New ($67)

Champions & Guardians: The Royal & Ancient Golf Club 1884–1939 • *John Behrend and Peter N. Lewis*
Royal & Ancient Golf Club, St. Andrews • 286pp • 2001

. . . Volume II.

Published three years after its sibling, *Champions & Guardians* carries the St. Andrews story onward in similar style, highlighting the game's explosive growth and the R&A's ultimate emergence as golf's primary international governing body.

Still available new.

New ($67)

Chicago Golf: The First 100 Years • *Tom Govedarica*
Eagle, Chicago • 286pp • 1991 (PBK)

This inexpensive but uncommon paperback is very well researched and equally thorough, detailing the game's history in one of its earliest American hotbeds. It is arranged chronologically and pays a great deal of attention to both course development and tournaments, making for an invaluable research source. While definitely not a lavishly illustrated coffee-table production, nor a book filled with Darwin-like prose, *Chicago Golf* is a tight, authoritative volume containing a boatload of information.

For anyone interested, it is well worth the hunt.

Under $25

The Chronicles of Golf, 1457–1857 • *Alastair J. Johnston and James F. Johnston*
Privately published, Cleveland • 734pp • 1993

If, as H.B. Farnie suggests, golf's roots are indeed "hidden in the mists of antiquity," then here, for the first time, we have a volume which genuinely begins to cut through that fog. For Alastair Johnston, owner of what is reputed to be the finest privately held golf library in the world, must literally have scoured its depths to produce this massive, mind-boggling record of the game's earliest days.

Piecing things together through all manner of quoted references, Johnston arranges the story chronologically, beginning centuries ahead of what other books have been able to substantially document and running roughly to the point where "accepted" golfing literature takes over. An historic synopsis then ties it all together, followed by a large bibliography which reminds us, in no uncertain terms, of the magnitude of the task.

Is this then the gospel regarding the game's earliest stirrings? We may never know for sure, but with so epic a volume, a good deal more evidence has been placed upon the table. Of course, with only 900 copies produced and no reprint in sight, *The Chronicles of Golf* seems destined to remain a distinctly private party.

$400+

The Clapcott Papers • *Alastair J. Johnston*
Privately published, Edinburgh • 517pp • 1985

The late C.B. Clapcott stands today as rather a mysterious figure in golf writing circles, an historian of rabid fervor who seemed to eschew the notion of having his considerable works published. This collection—assembled by Johnston well after Clapcott's death—includes three sections covering, respectively, the Honourable Company of Edinburgh Golfers, various aspects of golf history, and the evolution of the game's rules. In each case the research is remarkably deep, though nowhere more than in section one, where the details of the Honourable Company's history border on the minute.

With only 420 copies in existence, this truly impressive volume is both rare and, in all likelihood, less than ideal for casual readers.

$325

The Daily Telegraph Golf Chronicle • *Ted Barrett*
Hodder & Stoughton, London • 272pp • 1994 (w/2000 2nd edition)

Though not, as the name might suggest, a volume composed of headlines from the *Daily Telegraph,* this most definitely is a fine general history book, particularly for new or less-devoted golfing readers. Beginning in the 1860s, it does a sharp, concise job of recounting the game's development by recapping, chronologically, its biggest events, stars, trends, venues, and news items. Heavily illustrated (though strictly in black and white), it may be of only limited interest to the very knowledgeable, but more general fans will surely find a great deal of useful information between its covers.

Under $25

Early Golf • *Steven J.H. van Hengel*
Privately printed, Bentveld, Holland • 76pp • 1982 (w/revised 2nd edition 1985)

This relatively rare volume represents the most detailed work ever done on "colf" and "kolf," early Dutch games which may or may not represent the roots of golf as it eventually would be played in Scotland. The book is meticulously researched and reprints many ancient images depicting people playing the game, frequently on ice and often in crowds. It should be noted that most prominent historians consider these to be different games than Scottish golf, a point of view supported by the fact that kolf is still played—on an indoor court—today.

The second edition contains an added chapter on the roots of golf in America.

$70

Early Irish Golf • *William Gibson*
Oakleaf, Naas • 303pp • 1988 (w/PBK)

Written by a career military man, this thorough volume is as compre-hensive a history of the game's roots on the Emerald Isle as might be imagined. Heavily illustrated (exclusively in black and white), it is di-vided into nine highly detailed chapters: "Introduction of Golf to Ire-land (1606)," "Golf in the 18th Century—Scotland, Ireland and the United States of America," "Golf in Ireland (1852–1857)," "Golf in Ireland (1858–1875)," "Scotland's Gift to Ireland," "The Boom Years (1890–1899)," "The Testing Years (1900–1922)," "Golfiana Miscellanea," and "Early Irish Ladies Golf." Though the text is both interesting and highly detailed, more impressive still is a massive appendix detailing the his-tory and evolution of more than 280 early Irish clubs.

Essentially a unique work, *Early Irish Golf* is far more difficult to find than most books of so recent a vintage, especially in hardcover. For the historically minded, however, even a paperback copy is well worth the hunt.

$50

Fifty Years of American Golf • *H.B. Martin*
Dodd Mead, New York • 423pp • 1936
Reprinted by Argosy-Antiquarian (1966)

Among those books from golf's prewar Golden Age that are badly in need of reprinting, few stand higher than the marvelous historical opus *Fifty Years of American Golf.* For here we have a volume penned by Mr. H.B. (Dickie) Martin, golf columnist for the New York *Globe,* prolific author, frequent ghostwriter for Walter Hagen, and a man intimately close to the game's popular explosion on this side of the Atlantic.

The book itself is pleasantly written and remarkably thorough, fea-turing 30 chapters covering some anticipated subjects, but also such novel entries as "Early Commercial Ventures," "Van Cortlandt Park and Public Courses," "Famous Golf Resorts," "Golf Architects and Famous

Courses," and "Golf and the Press." It is, without question, the widest-ranging American historical volume of its era and quite justified, despite the occasional factual error, in its status as a genuine classic.

Copies of both editions are plentiful, but expensive.

Original: $350+ • Argosy: $150

Fifty Years of Golf • *Horace Hutchinson*
Country Life, London • 229pp • 1919
Reprinted by the USGA (1985)

As a two-time Amateur champion, the first Englishman to serve as Captain of the R&A and the author of 14 books, Horace Hutchinson enjoyed a genuinely unique perspective on golf's early development—particularly as that rare writer who had also competed against so many of the stars he was profiling. In this context, I suggest that his grand reminiscence, *Fifty Years of Golf,* must stand as Hutchinson's most important work. For while the timeless *Badminton Library* is undeniably a classic, it is, in the end, primarily an instruction piece. *Fifty Years,* on the other hand, is an account of some of golf's most important people and events, frequently written from an eyewitness standpoint.

The book is quite thorough, running a stout 36 chapters and arranged more or less chronologically. Perhaps of primary interest is the valuable emphasis it places upon the game's formative years in the second half of the nineteenth century. To put this in perspective, the arrival of the Vardon-Taylor-Braid Triumvirate ("The Coming of the Three Great Men") does not appear until more than two-thirds through, at chapter 25.

Though expensive, there are few more useful volumes for the historical section of one's library.

Original: $325 • USGA (1,500 copies): $150

Five Open Champions and the Musselburgh Golf Story •
George Colville
Colville, Musselburgh • 115pp • 1980

This rather thorough volume does, as advertised, profile five Open Champions (Willie Park Sr. and Jr., Mungo Park, Bob Ferguson, and David Brown), as well as the town's legendary links and famous clubmakers. It is an attractive little book and highly informative, though a good deal of its material can be found in John Adams's subsequent work *The Parks of Musselburgh* (1991). Illustrated, but not overly so.

$125

Following the Leaders • *Al Laney*
Ailsa, New York • 169pp • 1991

Following the Leaders appears under the Classics of Golf masthead, making it a rare "new" volume among the Classics' stellar collection of reprints. "New," however, should not be confused with "contemporary" as Laney, longtime correspondent for the late New York *Herald Tribune,* actually wrote the manuscript during the 1970s. Published posthumously, the book profiles great American players from Francis Ouimet to Jack Nicklaus, as seen through the eyes of a lifelong golfing scribe who was there.

Laney's prose may not rival Wind's or some of the great British writers, but his copy is both engaging and reminiscent of an era when, as far as event coverage was concerned, the sportswriter was still king.

New ($29)

The Game of Golf in East Africa • *Richard Hooper*
W. Boyd, Nairobi • 288pp • 1953

Though perhaps not absolutely essential to either US or UK readers, this is one of golf's truly legendary volumes, albeit due more to the decidedly strange circumstances of its existence than any epic literary merit. Basically an account of the game's development in Kenya, Uganda, and Tanganyika (Tanzania), *The Game of Golf in East Africa* was written by a British expatriate and detailed the early clubs, players, and events of a decidedly colonial pastime. Hardly an international best-seller, the volume's modern scarcity stems (according to Joseph Murdoch) from the author's burial of 500 copies in his Nairobi garden before fleeing the Mau Mau uprising. As this account apparently came to Murdoch directly from Hooper himself, we can assume that it isn't apocryphal.

Let the digging begin.

$550+

The Game with the Hole in It • *Peter Dobereiner*
Faber & Faber, London • 142pp • 1970

A high-profile golf writer on both sides of the Atlantic, Peter Dobereiner enjoyed a style that might loosely be described as a cross between traditionally rich British prose and Dan Jenkins. This, his first book, is essentially a general overview of the game, covering its history, players, equipment, courses, and so on. Though relatively brief, it certainly succeeds in capturing some of the game's endless color and variety, and I don't for a moment doubt Dobereiner's introductory claim that "This book is my attempt to give to others something of the pleasure that golf has given to me." But for myself, a chapter entitled "Our Mother, That Sad Old Bitch" fails to make up in humor what it lacks in taste.

Different strokes . . .

Under $25

The Glorious World of Golf • *Peter Dobereiner*
McGraw-Hill, New York • 250pp • 1973

Published three years after *The Game with the Hole in It,* Dobereiner's *The Glorious World of Golf* is a larger, heavily illustrated volume profiling the game in its many worldwide manifestations. Divided into 10 chapters, there are strong doses of history, great courses, the evolution of equipment, and the stars of modern golf here, making this a book well suited to both newcomer and old hand alike. Examining the literature of the time, this work also stands out for being one of the first big-production golf volumes to come along following the doldrums of the 1950s and '60s.

No small claim, that.

Under $25

Golf: An Illustrated History of the Game • *Robert Green*
Willow, London • 208pp • 1987

There have been a great many "history of golf" books published in the modern era, the majority of which have ended up serving the dual function of educating novices and filling bookstore remainder tables around the world. But occasionally one does find a general history volume that is legitimately rewarding, and to me Robert Green's *Golf: An Illustrated History of the Game* is just such a work.

Admittedly this is a subjective judgment, as I doubt that astute readers will discover any startling new perspective or unknown historical facts here. They will, however, find a fairly comprehensive history divided into 16 self-contained chapters, each providing a chronological history of a major event or area of the game. The final three, which cover architecture, great courses, and golf around the globe, add a nice bit of diversity.

Profusely illustrated (mostly in black and white), this is an attractive and useful volume.

Under $25

Golf: A Pictorial History • *Henry Cotton*
Collins, Glasgow • 240pp • 1975
1st US edition ("A History of Golf Illustrated"): Lippincott 1975

This highly visual book likely is no more unique than the entry profiled immediately above, but I've chosen to include it for two fundamental reasons. First, such general histories are usually authored by professional writers, seldom by players—and never by a three-time Open champion like Henry Cotton. Second, it is important to clarify something for American readers: Despite the altered title bestowed upon it by some stateside nitwit, this is in no way a history of the magazine *Golf Illustrated* (either British or American).

Now *that* might be a special volume.

$35 (US title slightly less)

Golf Between Two Wars •
Bernard Darwin
Chatto & Windus, London • 227pp •
1944
Reprinted by Classics of Golf (1985)

Golf Between Two Wars is exactly as the title suggests: an historical account of British golf between 1918 and 1939. It is written with Darwin's usual knowledge and depth and covers all manner of pertinent subjects including great players and tournaments, the beginnings of the Ryder and Walker Cups, changes in equipment, golf architecture, and a good deal more. I personally find that this volume fills a prominent British void, for much has been written about the pre–World War I Triumvirate and post–World War II American dominance, but not so much about the transitional goings-on in between.

Others simply consider it Darwin's best work.

Original: $80+ • COG: New ($33)

Golf Clubs of the MGA • *Dr. William Quirin*
Golf Magazine, New York • 317pp • 1997

Published to commemorate the 100th anniversary of the New York area's Metropolitan Golf Association, this grand volume profiles more than 350 member courses in a truly marvelous collection of regional golfing history. As the MGA's designated historian, Dr. Quirin clearly enjoyed the cooperation of the section's entire golfing community in performing his research, resulting in concise, informative sketches of each club's founding, great moments, famous members, architectural evolution, and so on. A history of the organization itself is naturally included, as are interesting chapters on the many great architects and the famous "lost" courses that have left their mark on this, America's first golfing hotbed.

I doubt that any previous book has provided this depth of information on so many fine courses under a single cover.

$75

Golf: History & Tradition 1500–1945 • *David Stirk*
Excellent Press, Ludlow, England • 344pp • 1998

For anyone thinking that substantial research into the game's earliest days is a thing of the past, this beautifully produced volume stands plainly as a powerful rejoinder. In many ways the culmination of Stirk's several previous works (all with Ian Henderson), this richly detailed text traces the game from its earliest roots, including extensive sections on early clubs, equipment makers, the spread of golf's popularity, its finest players and events, and quite a bit more.

The book is written exclusively from a British perspective—an entirely fair (if not refreshing) approach given that the game's international growth was tied irrevocably to the expansion of the British Empire. Consequently readers searching for stories of the Apple Tree Gang and Charles Blair Macdonald should look elsewhere; the only material concerning areas beyond the United Kingdom involves questions of the early Dutch game Kolven, one section on golf's international growth, and, to a lesser degree, a fascinating chapter titled "Golf in Time of War."

A must for the modern American reader, lest we forget from whence it all came . . .

$100

The Golf History of New England • *Jack Mahoney*
New England Golf, Wellesley, MA • 175pp • 1973 (w/PBK & 1995 Centennial Edition)

Though not as slickly produced as some, this largely unheralded work provides a solid overview of the game as played in New England from its earliest days to the 1970s. Part three, which generally details local stars and events, may not interest the world at large, but parts one and two (which are far more historical) provide a fine supplement to any collection. A sketch of the original Dorset Field Club nine (dated 1886) is particularly notable.

$30

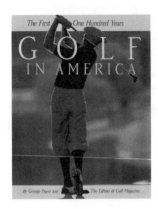

Golf in America: The First One Hundred Years • *George Peper, etc.*
Harry N. Abrams, New York • 304pp • 1988 (w/1994 2nd edition)

This oversized volume is, as advertised, a comprehensive history of golf's first century in America. Though not purely chronological, its 11 chapters do run more or less from start to finish, and offer the bonus of occasionally being written by some highly qualified experts (e.g., "The Course of Architecture" by Tom Doak, "The Chroniclers" by Joseph Murdoch, etc.). It is also somewhat encyclopedic in scope, including sections on "100 Heroes of American Golf," a chronology of important events, records of Major championship winners, and so on.

I'm not certain if knowledgeable readers will find any surprising new facts between these covers but as a thorough, well-produced volume on American golf, it has few modern peers.

$30

Golf in Britain • *Geoffrey Cousins*
Routledge & Kegan Paul, London • 176pp • 1975

Longtime golf writer and author Geoffrey Cousins took a slightly different approach to this mid-1970s book, concentrating primarily upon golf's social role in class-conscious British society. Over 30 chapters he traces the game's evolution, from its humble (and free) Scottish beginnings, through periods of greater exclusivity and finally to the relatively open and accessible game of the modern era. The book is frank and well detailed, and provides both a nice bibliography and an index of clubs specifically mentioned.

For those far removed from British life and history, this book may hold only limited appeal. Yet as golf's worldwide evolution has been tied so intrinsically to its British roots, I find the material to be both interesting and highly relevant.

Under $25

Golf in Canada: A History • *James A. Barclay*
McClelland & Stewart, Toronto • 626pp • 1992

To date, this is *the* history of golf in Canada, a country, lest we forget, whose first real golf club (Royal Montreal) predated America's St. Andrews by a good 15 years. *Golf in Canada,* then, is a grand and comprehensive volume, broken up into six sections ("The Pioneers," "Coast to Coast," "Amateurs Supreme," "The Golden Years between the Wars," "Golf International," and "The Glen Abbey Years") and 42 chapters. Aside from all that is standard and obvious, a number of these chapters are dedicated to interesting sidebar topics, such as "Early Courses and Architects," "Growth and the Public Course," and "The Tide of Commercialism," among many others.

Some 400+ illustrations and a nice set of appendices later, *Golf in Canada* can legitimately be said to capture the entire story in one large, attractive package.

$30

Golf in New Zealand: A Centennial History • *G.M. Kelly*
New Zealand GA, Wellington • 262pp • 1971

There is something very appealing about having a nation's entire golfing history under a single cover, particularly when it's a nation where the game is held in no small esteem. Kelly's work is thorough, yet admirably concise, and devotes nearly 100 of its pages to profiling New Zealand's early clubs. Though not a splashy, image-oriented book, it enjoys a fine ratio of information vs. the amount of space it occupies upon one's shelf.
Under $25

Golf in the Making • *Ian T. Henderson and David I. Stirk*
Henderson & Stirk, Crawley, England • 332pp • 1979 (w/1982 revised 2nd edition)

Though not specifically billed as such, *Golf in the Making* might well be considered a sister volume to the above-listed *Golf: History & Tradition,* for the two books share an author (Stirk), layout, and graphic style, and are of identical dimensions, making them altogether inseparable upon one's shelf. *Golf in the Making*'s scope is a bit more focused, however, concentrating almost exclusively upon 400 years of club and ball development and the Scottish professionals and artisans responsible for it.

Heavily illustrated with photos, drawings, diagrams, and family trees, this extremely well-researched effort broke new ground in detailing the game's roots and represents a veritable encyclopedia of equipment manufacturing through the onset of World War I. With extensive appendices, lists of patent holders, a glossary, and so on, it easily justifies its status as a classic of the genre.

Note: The revised 1982 edition includes added historical notes and a list of prominent British professionals, circa 1906.

$125

The Golf of Our Fathers • *W.K. Montague*
Herald-Review, Duluth, MN • 119pp • 1952 (w/revised 1953 2nd edition)

This relatively minor volume, written somewhat incongruously by a Minnesotan, is a fairly detailed general history of golf in the UK. Divided into 15 tight, well-defined chapters, it starts with the game's earliest development, then moves into balls, clubs, caddies, amateurs, ladies, the evolution of the swing, and the rules. In truth, nearly all of this material has been covered in greater depth elsewhere. What gives *The Golf of Our Fathers* a boost, however, is a final chapter on golf books, a section detailing a fairly extensive list of important early volumes.

Donovan & Murdoch note a supplemental chapter on rules published in 1961, but I should imagine that copies of that are all but extinct.

$125+

Golf: Scotland's Game • *David Hamilton*
Patrick, Kilmacolm, Scotland • 269pp • 1998 (PBK)

This essentially self-published volume is a most interesting one, questioning in several important ways our views of golf's early Scottish history. Well researched and illustrated profusely with paintings, maps, documents, and photos, it traces the game's up-and-down development through seven chapters: "The Links," "The Mysterious Years," "The

Turbulent Century," "Tranquil Times," "The Interlude," "The New Enthusiasm," and, finally, "Our Times."

Aside from its general depth and revisionist conclusions, *Golf: Scotland's Game* is valued for its detailed bibliographies, which are presented at the end of each chapter. Also, though this was primarily a paperback release, 350 hardback copies were produced (the "St. Andrews Edition") and remain relatively findable—for a price.

Hardcover: $225+ • PBK: $35

Golfers' Gallery • *Frank Moran*
Oliver & Boyd, Edinburgh • 196pp • 1946 (w/1949 2nd edition)

Joseph Murdoch singled out Scotsman Frank Moran as being a notably underrated writer, and based upon this excellent little volume I would tend to agree. *Golfers' Gallery* is a collection of historical pieces composed by Moran for his home newspaper, *The Scotsman*, "to provide an escapist corner among the war news." It is ostensibly Moran's recollections of the 40 Open and Amateur championships played between 1920 and 1939, and in this regard only Darwin's superb *Golf Between Two Wars* really covers similar ground.

Of perhaps even greater interest, however, is the book's closing section ("Personalities—Past and Present"), which profiles nearly every great player from Young Tom Morris on through to Walter Hagen and Bobby Jones.

Though obviously involved with the game for many years, Moran only wrote two full-sized golf books. The second, entitled *Book of Scottish Golf Courses,* went into four editions between 1939 and 1949, yet is virtually impossible to locate today.

$30

A History of Golf • *Robert Browning*
J.M. Dent, London • 236pp • 1955
1st US edition: Dutton 1955
Reprinted by Classics of Golf (1985)

There are many who consider this postwar work to be the most comprehensive account of the game ever published, and no less than Herbert

Warren Wind has called it "far and away the finest one-volume history of golf."

Browning, editor of the British magazine *Golfing* from 1910 to 1955, was a constant writer of club handbooks who spent nearly his entire life around the game. But beyond firsthand observance, he obviously knew a thing or two about research, for *A History of Golf* offers a degree of detail not often seen in our golfing milieu. The writing is straightforward and pleasant, keeping things moving at a swift and entertaining pace despite the large amount of material discussed. Presented from a British perspective, the book is divided into 34 neatly categorized chapters and also includes a chronological list of events dating back to 1353.

The original edition is relatively easy to locate while copies of the Classics of Golf reprint (which bear Wind's usual foreword and an afterword by the Scottish writer S.L. McKinlay) are plentiful.

An entry without which no golfer's library is complete.

Original: $150+ • COG: New ($29)

A History of Golf • *Louis T. Stanley*
Wiedenfeld & Nicolson, London • 218pp • 1991

Louis Stanley was not, perhaps, as celebrated a writer as Darwin or Longhurst, but with this volume billed as his 74th (only 18 of which, as far as I can determine, were on golf), he was easily more prolific than the two British giants *combined*. In this context, the dust jacket claim that Stanley "approaches the game with experience gained over many years" must be viewed as one of the bigger understatements in the history of publishing.

Of course, one key to maintaining such output is to waste little time on verbosity, and this volume does manage to move right along. Running over 19 chapters, it is well-illustrated and always to the point, yet it finds the time to profile nearly every important player and include such tidbits as the author's eclectic 18 holes for the British Isles (compiled, we might add, on a challenge from that eccentric old architect Tom Simpson). Offering little in the way of groundbreaking information, this *A History of Golf* may not be as significant as Robert Browning's, but it's not bad.

Under $25

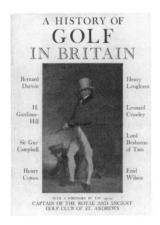

A History of Golf in Britain •
Bernard Darwin, etc.
Cassell, London • 312pp • 1952
Reprinted (abridged) by Classics of Golf
(1990)

Certainly among the more majestic golf books ever undertaken, *A History of Golf in Britain* began life as a well-orchestrated postwar volume, one intended to be *the* comprehensive book about the British game. As such, an all-star roster was assembled to author the following 11 sections: "Then and Now" (Bernard Darwin), "The History of the Rules of Golf" (Dr. Harold Gardiner-Hill), "The Early History of British Golf," "The Development of Implements—Clubs and Balls" and "Links and Courses" (all by Sir Guy Campbell), "Styles and Methods" (Henry Cotton), "1848–1914: From Gutty to Rubber-Core" (Darwin), "1918–1939: Between Two Wars" (Henry Longhurst), "1945–1950: A Fresh Start" (Leonard Crawley), "Women's Golf" (Enid Wilson), and "The Future of the Game" (Lord Brabazon of Tara).

The result, not surprisingly, is a collection of really grand proportion and style, a book that fully lives up to its title and, more importantly, its potential. There is much for readers—British and otherwise—to sink their teeth into here, making this an essential component of any well-rounded library.

Caveat emptor: The Classics of Golf reprint does not include the Gardiner-Hill and Campbell chapters, making for a substantially different (though considerably less expensive) volume.

Original: $200+ • COG: New ($29)

The Illustrated History of Women's Golf • *Rhonda Glenn*
Taylor, Dallas • 343pp • 1991

This, I suspect, is the closest thing to a single title covering the women's game as it exists, beginning with that noted early practitioner, Mary Queen of Scots, and working up to the stars of the modern era. Over 12 chapters it recounts the careers of the top players on both sides of the Atlantic, and also provides an impressively large records section detailing the results of numerous top women's events. Fully illustrated, this is, unquestionably, the definitive volume of its type to date.

Under $25

It Was Good While It Lasted • *Henry Longhurst*
J.M. Dent, London • 342pp • 1941 (w/1945 2nd edition)

One is tempted to omit this Longhurst opus on the grounds that it is not, strictly speaking, about golf, but to do so would deprive our library greatly. Penned during Britain's darkest wartime hours, it represents fond reflections of British life prior to 1939 and does, in fact, venture substantially into many things golfing. Particularly memorable chapters include profiles of St. Andrews, Walter Hagen, and Henry Cotton, and a brief recounting of a 1936 stay at C.B. Macdonald's home during a visit with the Walker Cup team. Throw in Longhurst's candid observations of so many things British and European (including his mid-war assessment of the German mentality) and his usual fine humor and *It Was Good While It Lasted* is simply too entertaining to pass up.

Note: The 1945 edition is a fascinating study in wartime economics. Though the text is unabridged, all photographs were dropped and the copy reconfigured into a lean 192 pages. Neither edition is commonly found today.

$45

The Lonsdale Library: The Game of Golf • *The Earl of Lonsdale (Editor)*
Seeley, Service & Co., London • 251pp • 1931 (w/1 or 2 postwar editions)

Published 41 years after *The Badminton Library, The Lonsdale Library* bears many similarities to its illustrious predecessor beyond just title. It too is an omnibus of golfing information, designed, as part of a larger series, to acquaint beginners with the game by assembling an elite cast to write about its many facets.

Following segments on "The History of the Game" and "The Literature of the Game" by Horace Hutchinson come five instructional chapters by Joyce and Roger Wethered, Britain's legendary amateur siblings. Next are "Match & Medal Play" and "Watching for Profit" by Bernard Darwin, "Ladies' Golf" by Joyce Wethered, and "Middle-Aged Golf" by Darwin. Finally, Darwin adds "Famous Courses" before the noted designer Tom Simpson contributes two chapters on golf architecture and two more on course maintenance.

To my mind a somewhat underrated volume, *The Lonsdale Library* has never been reproduced in the modern era. However, with editions in print until at least 1948, original copies are still fairly accessible to the contemporary collector. This is also among the thickest 250-page books one will ever encounter.

$75

My Golfing Album • *Henry Cotton*
Country Life, London • 248pp • 1959

While a certain degree of hyperbole is always expected on jacket flaps, *My Golfing Album*'s "for here, all golfers will agree, is the greatest golf book ever" must surely rank among the silliest pieces of promotional copy ever written. That said, however, this *is* an interesting volume, arranged rather along the lines of Cotton's earlier work, *This Game of Golf* (see below). It contains 250 short "chapters," a well-rounded group profiling the many people, places, and events of the author's life, plus a number of instructional tips. Arranged more or less at random, this heavily illustrated book is the sort that one can pick up, flip open to any page, and enjoy.

$30

A Passion for Golf • *Laurence Sheehan*
Clarkson Potter, New York • 160pp • 1994

Written by a former managing editor of *Golf Digest,* the subtitle of this smart little volume is "Treasures and Traditions of the Game," and an accurate description this proves to be. Filled more with illustrations than text, *A Passion for Golf* is essentially a collection of images highlighting the game's oldest clubs, collectible and ephemeral items, and traditions, primarily in North America. Interestingly, though profiling aged subjects, it is presented entirely in color, bringing golf's history alive in very much a contemporary manner.

I'm not entirely certain that all of this material falls within the average reader's range of interest, but then I imagine opening it on a cold winter's night—when northern golfers, in particular, have but to dream—and its significance to our library begins to take on a new light.

Under $25

The Perfect Golfer • *H.N. Wethered*
Methuen, London • 246pp • 1931
Reprinted by Flagstick Books (2002)

Contemporary readers who recognize Herbert Newton Wethered will generally do so either as the father of the great amateurs Joyce and Roger or the coauthor (with the colorful Tom Simpson) of *The Architectural Side of Golf.* Neglected then would be *The Perfect Golfer,* a strictly solo project that, I suspect, has been unduly overlooked among the classics of its era.

Essentially this is a rather innovative collection of 12 essays covering The Perfect Champion, Amazon, Links, Style, Temper, Duffer, Critic, Clubs, Shot, Architecture, Golf Book, and, finally, The Imperfect Future—the last taking a cautious view in light of equipment advances, architectural changes, increasing commercialism, and the like.

Wethered, who also authored several additional nongolf books, writes with intelligence and style, making this relatively rare old volume a nice addition to any library. The Flagstick Books reprint is, once again, a tremendous enabler in this regard.

Original: $125+ • Flagstick: New ($29)

The Scrapbook of Old Tom Morris •
Compiled by David Joy
Sleeping Bear, Chelsea, MI • 229pp • 2001

A volume perhaps unique in the annals of golf, *The Scrapbook of Old Tom Morris* is a compilation of ancient newspaper clippings, maps, and photographs chronicling the life of the legendary St. Andrews professional. Guided by small handwritten notations (*not* Old Tom's, for he is reported to have been illiterate), this book is not so much read as studied, for within it lie countless historical nuggets for the student of golf history.

Caveat emptor: Though the clippings and images are both stirring and fascinating, the story here is strictly Old Tom, with just a touch of Allan Robertson. Those hoping to read about Young Tom and other players of the day must look elsewhere.

New ($45)

Sixty Years of Golf • *Robert Harris*
Batchworth, London • 131pp • 1953

Scotsman Robert Harris was a three-time British Walker Cup Captain and an unabashed traditionalist, making this chronicle of change over a 60-year span a very interesting read. Harris addresses this evolution in chapters about clubs, balls, rules, clothing, and golf courses, with several fine extras thrown in. The most interesting of these, I think, is an early section entitled "Old Heroes," which profiles—from Harris's personal experience—every great British player (amateur or professional) from John Laidley right on through to George Duncan.

A rare and much-overlooked primary source, *Sixty Years of Golf* is growing more difficult to find, but is well worth the effort—particularly if one subscribes to the author's sense that with modern equipment "the soul of Golf comes down with a crash."

$65+

South Africa's Wonderful World of Golf • *Paddy O'Donnell*
Don Nelson, Pretoria • 189pp • 1973

A good deal less has been written about South African golf than one might expect, especially given the prominence its players have long enjoyed upon the international stage. This omnibus represented, in its day, a solid attempt at fixing all that, with a good deal of history, in-depth profiles of Bobby Locke and Gary Player, records of national champions, and thumbnail listings of 160 prominent clubs across the country. Indeed, its only real weakness is that it has become dated, with modern stars Ernie Els and Retief Goosen having reached the ripe old age of four at the time of its publication.

Under $25

The Story of American Golf •
Herbert Warren Wind
Farrar, Strauss, New York • 502pp • 1948 (w/revised editions in 1956 and 1975)
Reprinted by Classics of Golf (1995) and Callaway Editions (2000)

Bernard Darwin once wrote that no one "ever had or ever will have a greater genius for hitting a golf ball than Harry Vardon," and while there's a great deal of confidence implicit to such phrasing, I feel equally comfortable in making the following statement: *The Story of American Golf* has been, is, and always will be *the* story of American golf.

It is, in fact, Wind's unquestioned masterpiece, an epic of really tremendous proportion that covers, in the author's highly detailed and literate style, the development of the stateside game from 1888 forward. Without engaging in a needless recitation, suffice it to say that it is *all* here—and "all" has actually grown over the years, as Wind revised both the 1956 and 1975 editions to stay astride of the times.

This volume is a standard, an essential component of any golfer's collection. And while digesting it may not guarantee your knowledge of every pertinent fact in American golfing history, it will absolutely knock the ones you don't know down to a very precious few.

1948: $150+ • 1956: $45 • 1975: Under $25 • COG: New ($33) • Callaway: New ($35)

Unplayable Lies • *Fred Corcoran*
Duell, Sloan & Pearce, New York • 274pp • 1965

Fred Corcoran was a bona fide legend in professional golfing circles, a masterful promoter who ran the PGA of America, served as business manager to numerous stars, and generally promoted professional golf with an unparalleled zeal and color. This volume, which bears a few biographical elements, is essentially a collection of stories from a career spent rubbing elbows with celebrities and athletes. Given Corcoran's great personality and almost unparalleled entrée into many famous lives, it is a highly entertaining read.

Under $25

The World of Golf • *Gordon Menzies (Editor)*
BBC, London • 224pp • 1982

The companion book to a seven-part BBC series presented by Peter Alliss, *The World of Golf* is a well-written overview of the game featuring seven chapters provided by a particularly well-qualified roster. The entries are: "Royal and Ancient" (Pat Ward-Thomas), "Spreading the Gospel" (Peter Dobereiner), "America Gets the Bug" (Ross Goodner), "The Ladies" (Lewine Mair), "The All-Time Greats" (Michael McDonnell), "Golf Is Big Business" (Renton Laidlaw), and "St. Andrews Is Still the Mecca" (Michael Williams).

Though not the sort of volume that offers stunning revelations, this is a succinct, attractively illustrated account of a long and detailed story.

Under $25

The World of Golf • *Charles Price*
Random House, New York • 307pp • 1962
1st UK edition: Cassell 1963

Somewhat overshadowed by Herbert Warren Wind, American golf writer
Charles Price was himself quite the craftsman and, as an excellent amateur player, a most experienced and knowledgeable one as well. *The
World of Golf* is certainly his grandest work, a large, well-illustrated
volume covering the game's history and evolution over six centuries. It
is divided into five broad sections—"The Game," "The Pioneers," "The
Shotmakers," "The Masters," and "The Parbusters"—and generally covers things chronologically, featuring the great players and events, and
numerous notes of history and humor.

In its day, *The World of Golf* was groundbreaking in that no such
comprehensive a volume had previously been produced. Numerous books
have adopted a similar approach since, but few can match Price's writing style and overall knowledge of the game.

Highly recommended.

$30

SECTION III
ANTHOLOGIES

It is a curious quirk of golf literature that few among the game's elite writers have actually written many full-sized, honest-to-goodness books on golf. This statement may seem bizarre at first glance but consider, for example, Henry Longhurst. This great character's name appears on no less than 22 volumes published between 1935 and 1988, but only one (1937's *Golf*) is a full-length manuscript, authored completely by Longhurst and dedicated more than tangentially to the game. In Herbert Warren Wind's case, the ratio differs little. Wind's name appears on at least 18 books overall, but looking beyond anthologies, autobiographies that he assembled for others, and one short work of fiction, the landmark *Story of American Golf* represents his single original, full-sized golfing manuscript. And then there is the Dean, Bernard Darwin. Darwin's ever-present name graced more than 35 volumes over a spectacular half-century career, yet perhaps only seven of these could truly be considered new and complete works authored exclusively by the Master himself.

What these and many other fine writers left us, of course, were anthologies; large collections of articles originally composed for various newspapers or magazines, gathered together some years after the fact. In most cases these represent a nice sampling of a broader career. In others (especially the timeless Darwin) they form a massive body of work documenting countless events, issues, and personalities, filling in so much of the fabric of golf's past.

I believe that nearly every golf writer of genuine distinction is represented here, some, of course, more than others. It should be noted that in the cases of the most productive, special attention has been paid to identifying the sources of each book's content so as to aid the collector in avoiding the acquisition of duplicate material. For Darwin in particular, this has been no easy task.

The American Golfer • *Charles Price (Editor)*
Random House, New York • 241pp • 1964
Reprinted by Classics of Golf (1987)

The Depression killed this country's two finest golf magazines, *Golf Illustrated* and *The American Golfer,* both really excellent publications offering an eclectic menu far beyond today's steady stream of "How to Cure Your Slice." In this easy-to-find compilation, the talented scribe Charles Price draws together 75 of the latter magazine's best articles, a wide-ranging selection capturing many aspects of American golf from 1920 to 1936.

What makes this volume special, I believe, is not merely the information contained in the articles but rather the remarkable sense of period ambience that the collection evokes. Bernard Darwin, O.B. Keeler, and a number of high-profile players appear, but so do Grantland Rice, Ring Lardner, and Rube Goldberg, only occasional writers of golf but giants of the Roaring Twenties American sporting scene. This volume reads like a time capsule; it's enough to make one wish that Damon Runyan had written, at least once or twice, about the Royal & Ancient game.

$30 • COG: New ($39)

Around Golf • *J.S.F. Morrison*
Arthur Barker, London • 246pp • 1939

This largely overlooked collection of prewar British writings was assembled by John Morrison, best known as the last surviving partner of H.S. Colt's legendary architectural firm, but who was also a fine and experienced player in his own right. The anthology is a pleasingly eclectic affair, featuring such pieces as "Watching Golf" (Bernard Darwin), "The Oxford & Cambridge Golfing Society" (C.H. Alison), "A Comparison of British and American Golf" (Henry Longhurst), "My Most Thrilling Matches" (Joyce Wethered), and "St. Andrews and Golf" (Sir Guy Campbell), plus additional material on caddies, several famous courses, and so on.

Though surprisingly unknown, *Around Golf* has plenty to recommend it. As such—and having never been reprinted—it stands today as a somewhat expensive catch.

$150+

Bernard Darwin and Aberdovey • *Bernard Darwin*
Grant, Droitwich • 81pp • 1996

As the faithful well know, Aberdovey held a special place in Bernard Darwin's life, causing the old Welsh links to appear frequently within his writing. This volume is a collection of 23 essays from *Country Life* and the *Times* that related directly to the course, supplemented by period photos and a bit of modern scene-setting. For the avid Darwin reader only a handful of these pieces will be new, with most having appeared in other anthologies. But oh, those tantalizing few . . .

Compiled by Geoffrey Piper and Peter Burles, and still available new.

$50

Bernard Darwin on Golf • *Bernard Darwin*
Lyons, Guilford, CT • 414pp • 2003

That Darwin's work is still being repackaged some 43 years after his death is impressive, and this large volume (which contains 77 essays) clearly represents the easiest way for contemporary newcomers to discover his vast portfolio. Darwin veterans will not be surprised to find that the great majority of these pieces have appeared in previous collections, yet even such hard-core types will be pleased with a pair of "new" Golden Age articles ("A Little Too Much Massy" and "Aces of Clubs") as well as something really interesting: five 10–12 page essays originally produced for the *Atlantic Monthly* between 1928 and 1954.

Compiled by Jeff Silverman.

New ($25)

The Best of Henry Longhurst • *Henry Longhurst*
Golf Digest, Norwalk, CT • 206pp • 1978
1st UK edition: Collins 1979 (w/PBKs)

The writings in this occasionally disjointed volume are culled from all manner of Longhurst works, ranging from his pieces for the *Sunday Times* and *Golf Illustrated,* to excerpts from his various books (golfing and nongolfing), to miscellaneous articles written for magazines like *Golf Digest* and *Esquire.* As such it is an ideal collection for a newcomer to the Longhurst library, offering a thorough sampling and great variety. It does, however, lack some of the focus inherent to his single-source anthologies.

Under $25

The Complete Golfer • *Herbert Warren Wind*
Simon & Schuster, New York • 315pp • 1954
1st UK edition: Heineman 1954
Reprinted by Classics of Golf (1991)

There are anthologies and there are *anthologies*—and in the world of golf, this remarkable collection stands high atop the italicized category. Assembled by Wind as a by-product of his research for *The Story of American Golf*, it is divided into six varied sections: "Short Stories," "Cartoons," "The Spirit of the Game," "Great Players, Historic Moments," "The Masters' Voices," and "Golf Course Architecture."

What makes *The Complete Golfer* so special, I think, is its high level of sophistication; that is, these excerpts are hardly drawn from general volumes aimed at beginners, but come instead from all manner of fascinating, erudite, and occasionally obscure sources. Graphically it is severely limited (though the architecture section includes eight color maps drawn by Robert Trent Jones) but as we hop from a P.G. Wodehouse short story, to the history of the Hong Kong Golf Club, to Darwin writing about the great Triumvirate, and onward through some 60 more equally varied entries, one hardly seems to notice. This is truly a sampling of golf's wide range of writing at its very finest.

The late Joseph Murdoch, golf book collector nonpareil, stated that this was the volume that got him started. Reading it may not inspire everyone to pursue several thousand more titles but if you're not sent scurrying after a good few dozen, either you already possess an expansive collection or it's time to consider tennis.

Under $25 • COG: New ($39)

Darwin on the Green • *Bernard Darwin*
Souvenir, London • 240pp • 1986

The second of several posthumous Darwin anthologies, *On the Green* collects 50 articles written for *Country Life* over a quite remarkable span of 53 years. It is arranged chronologically and includes at least one selection from each year in which Darwin contributed to the magazine, thus providing a rare glimpse at the stylistic evolution of a golf-writing institution. Not incidentally, a good deal of this collection has not been anthologized before or since.

Under $25

The Darwin Sketchbook • *Bernard Darwin*
Classics of Golf, New York • 384pp • 1991

This 1991 volume is primarily a collection of player profiles, culled from a variety of Darwin's books and articles. It begins with ancient heroes such as Young Tom Morris and Douglas Rolland and stretches as far as a 1953 *Country Life* piece on Ben Hogan, visiting virtually every great player of the intervening 80 years—American and British—en route. Excerpts from Darwin's three autobiographical works close things out.

   Though avid Darwin readers will likely own much of this material dispersed among its original sources, taken as a whole (and with the beginner prominently in mind) it remains an excellent collection.

New ($33)

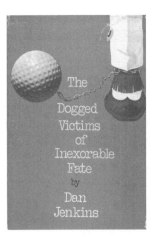

The Dogged Victims of Inexorable Fate • *Dan Jenkins*
Little Brown, Boston • 298pp • 1970 (w/PBKs)
Reprinted by Classics of Golf (1985)

Arguably Dan Jenkins's finest golf book, this is a collection of a dozen essays that initially ran in *Sports Illustrated* before, in the author's words, being "expanded and embellished" for their crossover to hardcover. The subjects vary nicely, from an historical piece on the U.S. Open to Hollywood golf at Riviera, with a lot of ground covered in between. Beyond all the satire and sarcasm—which stands always near the forefront—Dan Jenkins definitely knows golf.

Original: Under $25 • COG: New ($29)

The Essential Henry Longhurst • *Henry Longhurst*
Willow, London • 320pp • 1988 (w/1990 PBK)

From 1954 to 1969 Longhurst supplemented his weekly *Sunday Times* columns with fortnightly pieces on subjects entirely of his choosing for the British magazine *Golf Illustrated*. This anthology represents a stout 130 of these articles as selected by contemporary *GI* contributor Chris Plumridge. It is arranged in the following 10 sections: "Theory and Practice," "I Was There," "Fairway and Hazard," "Club and Ball," "Games We Play," "Great Players and Great Characters," "The World of True Golf," "Committee Man," "Traveller's Tales," and "Professional Qualities."

 The adjective in the title is appropriate.

Under $25

Every Idle Dream • *Bernard Darwin*
Collins, London • 254pp • 1948

True enough, *Every Idle Dream* is really not a golf book, and its one golf-oriented piece, the melancholy "Giving Up the Game," is reprinted in both *The Darwin Sketchbook* and *Mostly Golf*. But this collection of 29 widely varied essays ("A Day in Bed," "In the Cotswolds," "Portrait of a Dog of Character," etc.) is well worth having as definitive proof of the oft-stated notion that Darwin was not a great golf writer, but rather a great writer who happened, most frequently, to write about golf.

 Widely available.

Under $25

Fairways and Greens • *Dan Jenkins*
Doubleday, New York • 247pp • 1994 (w/PBK)
1st UK edition: Collins Willow 1995 (w/PBK)

This collection of Jenkins's work primarily features material published previously in *Golf Digest* or *Sports Illustrated,* though, in the author's own words, "there is quite a bit of fresh material here, either in the form of essays or what I would call a combination of transplants or face-lifts." There is a total of 33 pieces, all bearing Jenkins's irreverent yet

highly knowledgeable style. Any way you look at it, no golfer's library is complete without a solid dose of this Texas-born institution.
Under $25

Following Through: Herbert Warren Wind on Golf •
Herbert Warren Wind
Ticknor & Fields, New York • 414pp • 1985 (w/PBKs)
1st UK edition: MacMillan 1986

Following Through is, to my eyes, the more cohesive of Wind's two self-penned anthologies (see *Herbert Warren Wind's Golf Book,* below), undoubtedly because all of its 27 selections were culled from a single source, the *New Yorker.* The resulting consistency of essay length and style gives the book a very solid, reliable feel—almost as though one is opening different chapters of a single, unified volume. And as far as the writing is concerned, let us simply call this as fine a collection of golf essays as has ever been published by an American, and leave it at that.

Note: Four pieces ("The Women," "Rule 38, Paragraph 3," "North to the Links of Dornoch," and "The Third Man: Venturi") also appear in *Herbert Warren Wind's Golf Book.*
Under $25

For the Love of Golf • *Peter Dobereiner*
Stanley Paul, London • 256pp • 1981
1st US edition ("The World of Golf"): Atheneum 1981

Dobereiner was a regular contributor to a variety of newspapers and major golfing publications, leaving a substantial body of written work as a result. This particular collection, which contains over 70 articles, is divided into six sections: "What It's All About," "Around the World," "Inside the Ropes" (which profiles competitions), "On the Tee" (profiling players), "Tomorrow It Will Be Better" (highlighting the game's difficulties), and "Deeming, Dropping and Devil Worship" (pieces involving the rules). Obviously a fine sampler, this volume also includes one of my personal Dobereiner favorites, a 1978 *Golf Digest* article profiling the 50 best golf courses outside of North America.
Under $25

Fresh Fairways • *Louis T. Stanley*
Methuen, London • 220pp • 1949

The remarkable Louis Stanley, amidst writing several lifetimes' worth of books on golf, automobile racing, and popular figures, was also the golf correspondent for the noted British magazine *The Field*. This collection, which was actually a follow-up to his first such work, *Green Fairways* (see below), features 45 wide-ranging pieces from the magazine, demonstrating that beyond his superhuman output, Stanley was also quite capable of creating a fine golfing atmosphere with his prose.
$40

A Friendly Round • *Bernard Darwin*
Mills & Boon, London • 142pp • 1922

Published in 1922, *A Friendly Round* is, by my calculation, the third Darwin anthology to reach the marketplace. It is also among the shortest, comprising only 24 essays, all culled from the *Times*. *A Friendly Round* is today a tough find, but those pursuers whom it has thus far managed to elude can take some solace in the fact that 16 of its 24 pieces rather inexplicably are duplicated in 1930's *Second Shots*. This leaves only eight ("An Inspiration for the New Year," "A Little Abstinence," "Through the Looking Glass," "The Golfing Winds," "Summer Holidays," "In the Garden," "The Looker-On," and "Short Putts") as being unique to this now-expensive volume.
$350+

Golf à la Carte • *Peter Dobereiner*
Stanley Paul, London • 219pp • 1991
Lyons & Burford, New York • 219pp • 1991 (w/PBK)

Published 10 years after *For the Love of Golf, Golf à la Carte* represents another collection of Dobereiner's best work, culled from *Golf Digest, Golf World* (UK), the *Guardian,* and the *Observer.* Covering a wide range of topics, it will certainly appeal to anyone fond of Dobereiner's unique brand of golf writing.
Under $25

Golf: A Turn-of-the-Century Treasury •
Mel Shapiro (Editor)
Castle, Secaucus, NJ • 467pp • 1986

This very enjoyable volume is a collection of 48 magazine articles that originally appeared in various American publications between 1895 and 1909. Their scope is suitably wide, including all manner of instruction, etiquette, and state-of-the-growing-game pieces, plus a fascinating series of articles profiling the top courses in 13 major cities or regions. Though many of the writers are entirely unknown today, such luminaries as Horace Hutchinson, J.D. Dunn, Harold Hilton, H.J. Whigham, Findlay Douglas, Van Tassel Sutphen, Walter Travis (on putting), John Reid (on St. Andrews), and even Harry Vardon appear.

Taken as a whole, *A Turn-of-the-Century Treasury* paints a rich and vivid picture of early American golf. I'm amazed that it never spawned a second volume.

Under $25

The Golf Book • *Michael Bartlett (Editor)*
Arbor House, New York • 282pp • 1980

As golf anthologies go, this is a fairly broad collection, encompassing a diversity of writers ranging from Darwin, Longhurst, and Pat Ward-Thomas to Dan Jenkins, Ian Fleming, and the incomparable P.G. Wodehouse. The selections are drawn from a real variety of sources (Ward-Thomas's "Elements of Greatness—A Classic Course," for example, comes from *The World Atlas of Golf*) and are divided into four main sections, "The Spirit of the Game," "The Drama of the Game," "The Secret of the Game," and "The Fun of the Game." A fifth segment, "The Record of the Game," is a simple ledger of important tournament results.

A solid entry.

Under $25

Golf from the Times • *Bernard Darwin*
The Times, London • 141pp • 1912

This early collection is subtitled "A Reprint, revised and re-arranged, of some articles on golf, by The Times Special Contributor." I find this at least somewhat curious, however, as the entire book contains only 10 articles, making each considerably longer than the newspaper norm. Of course, this expansiveness also serves to justify the book's back cover, which reads: "The Times treats the game of golf in a more comprehensive way than any other newspaper."

The toughest find among Darwin anthologies, but an important one as all 10 essays are unique to this volume.

$850+

Golf Mixture • *Henry Longhurst*
Werner Laurie, London • 203pp • 1952

The earliest of Longhurst's anthologies, *Golf Mixture* includes 95 pieces, nearly all of which had previously appeared in the *Sunday Times* or *Country Life*. Owing to having been written during Britain's austere postwar years, the great majority are relatively short (often less than 700 words), yet no less readable for their brevity.

As is always true of Longhurst, the subject matter is varied and humorous, while the implicit commentary touches on items well beyond the confines of golf. The closing piece, a portrait of Ben Hogan, stands out nicely, as does the author's suggestion that among on-course monuments commemorating famous shots, there should somewhere lie "a succession of plaques zigzagging round the right of the green and marking the erratic progress by which the victim socketed his way into golfing history."

There was only one Henry Longhurst.

$30

The Golf Omnibus • *P.G. Wodehouse*
Barrie & Jenkins, London • 467pp •
1973 (w/PBKs)
1st US edition: Simon & Schuster 1973
Reprinted by Wings Books (1991 &
1996) and others

As stated in the introduction, *The Golfer's Library* mostly ignores books of humor because they generally strike me as (a) not knowing a great deal about golf, or (b) not being terribly funny. One fantastically obvious exception, however, is the timeless work of the great P.G. Wodehouse.

Wodehouse, an all-around talent with a pen, published two books of golfing stories during the 1920s, *The Clicking of Cuthbert* and *The Heart of a Goof* (respectively retitled *Golf without Tears* and *Divots* by some genius in the United States). One could—and probably should—own both of those volumes, though for the sake of economy we shall instead highlight *The Golf Omnibus*, an affordable modern anthology which includes the entirety of both early books, plus an additional dozen stories to boot.

Easy to find and even easier to read, this definitive Wodehouse collection will make even the most serious of golfers howl.
Under $25

Golf: Pleasures of Life Series • *Bernard Darwin*
Burke, London • 222pp • 1954
Reprinted by Flagstick Books (2000)

This engaging volume was part of a unique postwar series highlighting the more appealing aspects of British life. Beyond *Golf,* other titles include *Drink, Food, Gardens, Clothes, Cricket, Theatre,* and, splendidly enough,

Women (the author of which, one C. Willett Cunnington, could not possibly have held so keen an understanding of his topic as Darwin did of his).

Though frequently considered (and thus classified as) an anthology, *Golf* is actually composed largely of new Darwin writing, augmented extensively by quotations drawn from other historically prominent golfing books. Its 11 chapters profile various aspects of the game such as "The Links," "Some Great Matches," "Caddies," "Cures," "Architectural," "Golf As It Is Not," and so on, and are particularly interesting in their demonstration of who else's writing Darwin himself was enamored with.

All told a fine, thorough and highly literate overview, the likes of which few other sports can boast.

Original: $85+ • Flagstick: New ($29)

Golfer-at-Large • *Charles Price*
Antheneum, New York • 241pp • 1982

Charles Price spent several decades writing regular columns first for *Golf* magazine (where he also served as editor), then later for *Golf Digest*. This collection is drawn from the former, though the jacket notes are a bit ambiguous as to whether they have all appeared previously, and some apparently were revised for this edition. There are 27 pieces included, with subjects ranging from player and tournament profiles to more diverse items like "How to Tell a Golf Club from a Country Club," "California Casual," and "Golf's Great Walks."

As the only anthology of Price's writing ever published, this makes for a fine and inexpensive addition.

Under $25

The Golfer's Bedside Book • *Donald Steel (Editor)*
Batsford, London • 240pp • 1965

The Golfer's Bedside Book "is *not* an anthology" emphasizes editor Donald Steel in his brief introduction, an essentially true statement as the vast majority of this volume's entries were created specifically for it. Steel managed to assemble a truly first-rate cast of 1960s British writers including Henry Longhurst, Henry Cotton, Geoffrey Cousins, Leonard Crawley, Sam McKinlay, Frank Moran, Frank Pennink, Pat Ward-Thomas, and Ben Wright, resulting in a full volume rich with variety and texture.

Given that so little of its content appears elsewhere, this frequently overlooked gem (at least in America) becomes a rather desirable addition to the collection.

Under $25

The Golfer's Bedside Book • *Donald Steel (Editor)*
Batsford, London • 240pp • 1971

Six years after his first successful anthology, Steel returned with this sequel, an entirely new collection primed to confuse everyone with its repetition of title. Rest assured, however, that while similar in style, this is a completely separate entry with different writers—but well worth having in its own right.

Under $25

The Golfer's Companion • *Peter Lawless (Editor)*
J.M. Dent, London • 498pp • 1937

This is one of those splendid little volumes of a type so common in prewar Britain, bringing together all manner of star writers and players in broad, highly intelligent profiles of the game. Here an initial chapter on "The Pleasures of Golf" (by Bernard Darwin) is followed by detailed sections on the game's history (Robert Browning) and techniques (Henry Cotton). Then, among other interesting items, comes a bit more Darwin, Open champion Alf Padgham on equipment, Lawless on "Courses of the British Isles," O.B. Keeler on "Golf in the United States," and Lawless, once more, discussing the game as it is played around the world.

Beyond these cornerstones, two additional sections immediately grab one's attention. The first is a rather unique 170-page "Golfer's Anthology," a luxurious compilation (assembled by Lawless) featuring excerpts from the game's greatest writers on a variety of golfing subjects. The second, toward the book's end, is a 13-page "Golfer's Bibliography," undoubtedly the most detailed ever published up to that time.

Thankfully, this largely forgotten gem had enough copies printed to remain relatively available today, though almost exclusively in the UK. $80+

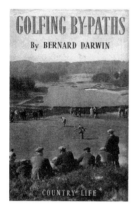

Golfing By-Paths • *Bernard Darwin*
Country Life, London • 203pp • 1946

Golfing By-Paths was the last anthology to be published during Darwin's lifetime, though in 1946 the material was relatively contemporary as all but one of the 58 articles had been penned for *Country Life* during World War II. The rare Darwin collection that includes illustrations (30 photographs), it is an especially valuable acquisition in that all but one of its entries (1942's "My First Open") are, I believe, unique to this volume. Easier to locate than nearly all of its prewar siblings.
$85+

Green Fairways • *Louis T. Stanley*
Methuen, London • 204pp • 1947

This was the first golf book published by *The Field* correspondent Louis Stanley and features 50 articles culled directly from the magazine. Commercially it must have done well as it spawned a follow-up, *Fresh Fairways*, and paved the way for the 17 more golfing volumes. Stanley likely deserves greater modern recognition, particularly in America. But there were always Longhurst and Darwin . . .
$40

The Happy Golfer • *Bernard Darwin*
Flagstick, New York • 264pp • 1997

One of the great charms of the *American Golfer* magazine was that Darwin was a regular contributor to it, cabling in articles on all manner of golfing subjects from 1922 until the magazine's demise in 1936. This collection presents, chronologically, 80 of Darwin's best offerings, beginning with his famous comparison of the Lido, Pine Valley, and the National and ending with a piece on Saunton which begins, "The other day I made a brief raid into Devonshire . . ."

Of particular interest to British readers, for whom most of this material will be new.

New ($33)

Herbert Warren Wind's Golf Book • *Herbert Warren Wind*
Simon & Schuster, New York • 317pp • 1971
1st UK edition ("The Lure of Golf"): Heinemann 1971

The first of two anthologies of Wind's legendary essays, this fine collection draws material from a variety of sources. Of the 29 selected pieces, nine come from the *New Yorker* and six from *Sports Illustrated,* with the remainder drawn from odd magazine pieces, Wind's collaborative book efforts with Gene Sarazen, Ben Hogan, and Jack Nicklaus, and one or two additional works of his own. The material is quite sweeping and, as expected, superbly written, making this another required acquisition.

Under $25

An Introduction to the Literature of Golf •
Herbert Warren Wind
Ailsa, New York • 274pp • 1996

This is rather a unique sort of book, representing a compilation of Wind's forewords to the first 37 Classics of Golf reprints, which were produced between 1986 and 1994. Naturally the reader learns a great deal about each of the individual volumes, but what makes these entries special, I believe, is their sense of context. For Wind remains forever the master of tying the subject of a piece to all manner of golfing history, weaving perhaps better than anyone the lush tapestry that is this colorful game.

Aside from making one wish to acquire nearly every book in the Classics of Golf series, these miniessays provide an uncommonly rich overview of some very fine golfing literature. Tough to find used, but still available new at the time of this writing, this is a collection well worth having.

New ($29)

The Long Green Fairway • *Pat Ward-Thomas*
Hodder & Stoughton, London • 192pp • 1966

A former RAF pilot and POW in Germany, Pat Ward-Thomas was a
fixture among the game's finest and most prominent post–World War II
writers. *The Long Green Fairway* is a collection of 59 of his articles, nine
from the *Guardian* (his regular beat) and 50 from *Country Life,* where
he split the prestigious golf commentary role with an aging Bernard
Darwin beginning in 1957. The book is divided into four sections—"The
Conquerors," "The Contestants," "The Courses," and "Contempla-
tions"—making for a suitably wide-ranging retrospective of golf on both
sides of the Atlantic.

    Ward-Thomas once wrote that his goal was to avoid the "magnifi-
cation of the trivial" and simply "write about the games themselves, the
way they were played and their settings." As this volume demonstrates,
few postwar correspondents have done so in a more pleasant, less ego-
tistical manner.

Under $25

Mostly Golf • *Bernard Darwin*
A&C Black, London • 198pp • 1976
Reprinted by Classics of Golf (1986)

Edited by Peter Ryde, Darwin's successor as golf correspondent for the
Times, Mostly Golf was the first of several posthumous Darwin anthologies, originally published on the centenary of his birth in 1976. The
selection of material is broad and, as the title suggests, occasionally ventures beyond the fairways. Once again, hard-core Darwin fans will own
a fair amount of this collection already, though several of the decidedly
nongolf pieces (e.g., an excerpt from his biography of cricketer W.G.
Grace) will likely fall beyond even their dedicated holdings. A special
bonus is Ryde's expansive foreword, a fascinating profile of Darwin
that in itself adds nicely to any golfer's library.

Original: $50 • COG: New ($33)

Never on Weekdays •
Henry Longhurst
Cassell, London • 182pp • 1968

The sister volume—with an identical format—to *Only on Sundays* (see just below).
Under $25

Only on Sundays • *Henry Longhurst*
Cassell, London • 259pp • 1964 (w/1989
PBK)

Only on Sundays was the first collection of
Longhurst's weekly pieces for the *Sunday
Times* to be assembled in anthological form—
and it quickly proved itself a best-seller. Over
70 of the best specimens are included here,
and without any subject-oriented arranging
they simply rise up one after another, each a
random jewel to be discovered. For older
British readers there will be a great deal of
nostalgia here. For the younger and/or inter-
national crowd you will soon understand why that British icon, Lord
Brabazon of Tara, claimed always to begin his Sunday mornings by opening the *Times* and seeking out Longhurst.
Under $25

On the Tour with Harry Sprague • *Herbert Warren Wind*
Simon & Schuster, New York • 94pp • 1960
Reprinted by Classics of Golf (1996)

Substantially different from Wind's standard fare, this brief volume is comprised of a decidedly fictional set of letters composed by one Harry Sprague, an unsophisticated Massachusetts golf pro struggling to make it on the PGA Tour. Written between 1958 and 1960, these creatively humorous notes originally ran in *Sports Illustrated* (how times have changed!), presumably as a supplement to the author's regular golf coverage.

On the whole, this book might be considered nonessential by some, yet it still reads today as an engaging work—and a unique diversion within the otherwise-serious Wind repertoire.

Original: Under $25 • COG: New ($29)

Out of the Rough • *Bernard Darwin*
Chapman & Hall, London • 336pp • 1932

Here again we have a mix of 49 pieces culled from the *Times* and *Country Life,* with the pleasant added bonus of six "character sketches" (including Sarazen, Arthur Croome, Great Men of Hoylake, the Triumvirate, Ouimet, and Walter Travis) written specifically for this volume. I believe that only one entry, 1929's "The Knot in the Handkerchief," appears in a later anthology, making this very hard-to-find prewar collection another important piece of the grand Darwin puzzle.

$125+

Playing the Like • *Bernard Darwin*
Chapman & Hall, London • 246pp •
1934
Reprinted by the Sportsman's Book Club
(1952) and Flagstick Books (2001)

This 1934 anthology stays the course of collecting pieces from the *Times* or *Country Life,* with a few notable exceptions. The opening seven profiles of Tait, Vardon, Taylor, Hilton, Braid, Herd, and Ball, for example, were originally written for American readers and made their British debut here. Similarly, articles on St. Andrews, Deal, and Sandwich were created especially for this volume.

Once again Flagstick books has done us a service, for the original is rare and copies of the Sportsman's reprint are not exactly plentiful.

Original: $300+ • Sportsman's: $50 • Flagstick: New ($33)

A Round with Darwin • *Bernard Darwin*
Souvenir, London • 223pp • 1984

The second posthumous anthology of the great man's work, *A Round with Darwin* includes 50 essays drawn from five previous volumes: *Tee Shots and Others, Out of the Rough, Mostly Golf* (itself a posthumous collection), *Rubs of the Green,* and *Life Is Sweet Brother.* Though perhaps entirely duplicative for the inveterate Darwin collector, it may, in fact, be invaluable for everyone else. This is because *Out of the Rough* and *Rubs of the Green* are among the very hardest Darwin works to locate, and fully 28 and 13 of their respective *Times* and *Country* Life pieces are reprinted here.

Compiled by Margaret Hughes.

Under $25

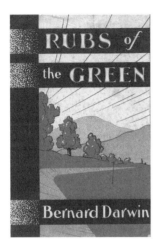

Rubs of the Green • *Bernard Darwin*
Chapman & Hall, London • 260pp • 1936

Sticking with the time-honored formula, here we have 39 more pieces from the usual *Times* or *Country Life* sources, plus six additional essays prepared specifically for this collection. Of the recycled 39, 13 appear in the above-listed *A Round with Darwin*. Three of those 13 ("A Musical Cure," "The Evening Round," and the splendidly named "An Attack of Socketing"), plus a fourth, "Hydes and Jekylls," were also duplicated years later in *Mostly Golf.* Like most prewar Darwins, this too is a very tough find.

$175+

Scottish Golf and Golfers • *Sam McKinlay*
Ailsa, New York • 211pp • 1992

Scottish Golf and Golfers is another "new" book published by the Classics of Golf, though its content is in fact a collection of columns written for the *Glasgow Herald* between 1956 and 1980 by the not-well-enough-known Sam McKinlay. A fine player himself, McKinlay's writing quality is self-evident (he counted Herbert Warren Wind among his biggest fans) and the book's content is nicely varied, arranged chronologically within sections titled "People," "Places," and "Things." Though published previously, the material will, on the whole, be fresh to readers outside of the UK, and perhaps even to a fair number of Britons (those not residing near Glasgow, at any rate) as well.

New ($33)

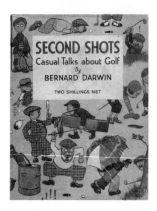

Second Shots • *Bernard Darwin*
George Newnes, London • 178pp • 1930

This time we have 34 pieces, all from the *Times*. As mentioned above, fully 16 of them appeared previously in 1922's *A Friendly Round,* with the rest apparently unique to this collection. Among prewar Darwin anthologies this is comfortably the easiest to find, though by no means at bargain prices.
$150+

Strokes of Genius • *Thomas Boswell*
Doubleday, Garden City, NY • 240pp • 1987 (w/PBK)

Boswell, longtime writer for the *Washington Post,* is perhaps best known for his coverage of baseball, but this anthology serves to demonstrate his capabilities in the golfing realm as well. Composed entirely of pieces previously published in either the *Post* or *Golf* magazine, it paints a fine picture of life on the PGA Tour during the Nicklaus-dominated late 1970s and 1980s. This is strictly contemporary material (often in the form of *Post* dispatches clipped chronologically together) and makes little attempt at venturing beyond its period boundaries.
Under $25

Talking about Golf • *Henry Longhurst*
Macdonald, London • 150pp • 1966

A bit less easy to find than some other Longhurst collections, *Talking about Golf* is also rather unique. Its 48 articles were, in fact, answers to specific questions posed each issue by the editors of *Golf Illustrated.* As such, they represent a wide range of subjects, including many technical and pragmatic concerns. For a lesser writer the publication of such material might seem gimmicky or even exploitive. With Longhurst, however, it represents an alternative sampling of a special talent.
$40

Tee Shots and Others • *Bernard Darwin*
Kegan Paul, Trench, Trubner, London • 271pp • 1911
1st US edition: David McKay circa 1911
Reprinted by the USGA (1984)

This early volume was only Darwin's second book (after 1910's *The Golf Courses of the British Isles*) and the first of his many published anthologies. It is composed primarily of his very earliest writings, weekly columns for the *Evening Standard* newspaper which he began contributing to in 1907 under the pseudonym "Tee Shots." Though perhaps less refined than his later copy, this is especially worthwhile as a revealing look at the formative stages of the Master's work.

Original editions are nearly impossible to find, with the USGA reprint (which includes a moving introduction from an aged Joyce Wethered) only slightly easier.

Original: $400+ • USGA (1,500 copies): $150+

Vardon on Golf • *Herbert Warren Wind and Robert Macdonald (Editors)*
Classics of Golf, New York • 187pp • 1989

In his foreword to *Vardon on Golf,* Wind writes that "Vardon looms as an intensely fascinating figure," and for the uninitiated, this modern collection represents the perfect entry point to the renowned Greyhound's life and writings. Essentially it draws material from each of Vardon's four books, thus resulting in a volume both biographical and instructive. Parts one and five represent the former, reprinting a combined total of 11 slightly abridged chapters from 1933's *My Golfing Life.* Parts two through four cover the latter, being drawn from *The Complete Golfer, How to Play Golf,* and *Progressive Golf,* respectively.

For hard-core types who already own Vardon's four original works, this book is largely superfluous. For those less familiar with perhaps golf's greatest legend, however, it is ideal.

New ($29)

SECTION IV
TOURNAMENTS AND TOURS

When one considers the disproportionate significance that a handful of golfers playing professionally enjoy relative to millions upon millions of amateurs, it seems surprising to find so few really good books chronicling their celebrated exploits, particularly in the modern era. One reason for this may be the scarcity of contemporary writers willing to leave the friendly confines of the press tent, reducing their coverage to little more than extrapolations based on interview quotes. Another, perhaps, is that as golf's lone mass-market aspect, the professional tours are the only area of the game subject to the sort of superficial, hero-worshiping drivel that more frequently appears on the bookshelves of other sports. And finally, we might surmise that in our modern era, live television coverage has minimized the need for cogent, knowledgeable writing about professional golf in the first place, as most avid fans will choose to see an event in the present rather than read about it in the past.

Or perhaps it is something else entirely.

In any event, a fairly thin list, but not without some important entries.

The Amateur • *John Behrend*
Grant, Droitwich • 255pp • 1995

This comprehensive history of the British Amateur was published to mark the event's 100th playing and provides a detailed recounting of the championship year-by-year, plus all relevant statistics. It is easy for modern observers (particularly in America) to dismiss the Amateur as an event of secondary importance, but when one reads of the early years— of Hutchinson, Laidley, Tait, Hilton, and the great John Ball—it doesn't take long to recognize that Bobby Jones's 1930 win represented the end of a long and splendid era, not the event's high watermark.

A limited edition (975 copies) that is still available new at this writing.

New ($59)

Augusta National & The Masters •
Frank Christian
Sleeping Bear, Chelsea, MI • 207pp • 1996

This book is largely a visual one, not surprising given that its author and his ancestors have served as official photographers for Augusta National since 1933. There are many better sources if one is searching purely for Masters Tournament information but the many images of the club and golf course as they once were still make for an interesting read.

New ($45)

Augusta Revisited: An Intimate View • *Furman Bisher*
Oxmoore, Birmingham, AL • 186pp • 1976

Given his venerated status within Southern sportswriting circles, one rather *assumes* that Furman Bisher would have some cachet at the Masters, making this book something of a no-brainer. And it is indeed an attractive and interesting volume, blending the tournament's wonderful aesthetic with a wide range of material on players, the course, and the traditions and inner workings of the event itself. Also offering some historical perspective on both the club and Bobby Jones, it represents an all-encompassing profile of golf's most famous tournament.

A must for those who ignore professional golf until April.

Under $25

The Bogey Man • *George Plimpton*
Harper & Row, New York • 306pp • 1968
1st UK edition: Andre Deutch 1969

Plimpton made his name by participating, as a rank amateur, in professional sporting events, then writing books about his experiences. *The Bogey Man,* his venture into golf, recounts his playing in the 1966 Bing Crosby, Lucky International, and Bob Hope Desert Classic. Of course, Plimpton was either a far more dedicated golfer than he lets on or a man who really does his homework. For despite occasionally wandering in some odd directions, the book succeeds nicely in mixing a realistic portrayal of the life and color of the PGA Tour with a good dose of history and humor.

Or perhaps I just find undue amusement in people hitting the ball sideways.

Under $25

The British Open • *Francis Murray*
Pavilion, London • 224pp • 2000
1st US edition: Contemporary 2000

Among modern books chronicling the Open Championship, this strikes me as the strongest entry, offering detailed year-by-year coverage dating to the beginning of the last century. That the previous 40 merit only a one-chapter overview might bother the historically minded but a compensatory touch is the inclusion of maps for every venue, past and present, each as it was at the time of its last hosting (e.g., Prestwick in 1925, Musselburgh in 1889, and so on).

An effective and attractive volume.

New ($35)

The Dawn of Professional Golf • *Peter N. Lewis*
Hobbs & McEwan, Tunbridge Wells • 176pp • 1995

Written by the curator of the British Golf Museum, *The Dawn of Professional Golf* examines the expansion of professional golf in Britain between 1894 and 1914. Astute readers will note these dates, respectively, as the years of J.H. Taylor's first Open Championship and Harry Vardon's sixth, but this volume is about far more than just the Great Triumvirate. A section detailing the period's many great challenge matches might be the most interesting, while statistical breakdowns on the careers of the era's best players—largely unavailable elsewhere—are invaluable to those wishing to make the "how great was Vardon, really?" comparisons.

$40

Gettin' to the Dance Floor • *Al Barkow*
Atheneum, New York • 282pp • 1986 (w/PBK)
1st UK edition: Heinemann Kingswood 1986

Gettin' to the Dance Floor represents a unique entry in our collection, for it is not so much a written volume as an oral history, chronicling the joys and rigors of life in the early years of the professional golf tour. Barkow tracked down 24 players from that bygone era, committing their stories to paper more or less verbatim and creating, in the process, a wonderfully atmospheric piece. One of the book's charms is the diversity of those interviewed, as legends like Nelson, Snead, and Sarazen are mixed with second-tier stars (Runyon, Melhorn, Cooper, etc.), pioneers (Bill Spiller, Patty Berg, and Betsy Rawls), and several rather colorful lesser-knowns. Another nice touch are the two photographs of each player, one during their prewar heyday, the other as Barkow found them in the 1980s.

A fun and unique history.

Under $25

A Golf Story • *Charles Price*
Atheneum, New York • 161pp • 1986
Reprinted by Triumph (2001)

Here is rather a versatile entry, one classified amidst Tournaments and Tours but just as easily positioned as a Biography, Club History, or General History sort of book. It is the talented Charles Price's weaving of three stories—those of Bobby Jones, the Augusta National Golf Club, and the Masters Tournament—into a single chronological narrative covering nearly 100 years. Though not specifically intended as such, this might, in many ways, be considered the ideal history of Augusta National.

Caveat emptor: The original 1986 edition includes a color photographic insert (showing all 18 holes) omitted from the 2001 reprint.

Original: $35 • Triumph: New ($20)

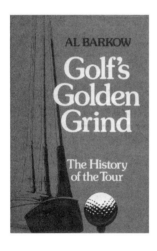

Golf's Golden Grind: The History of the Tour • *Al Barkow*
Harcourt Brace Jovanovich, New York • 310pp • 1974 (w/PBK)
Reprinted by Burford (2000 PBK)

Twelve years before documenting professional golf's prewar years with *Getting' to the Dance Floor,* Al Barkow wrote this detailed history of the PGA Tour, *Golf's Golden Grind.* Tracking American professional golf from its earliest nineteenth-century competitions right into the Jack Nicklaus/Johnny Miller days of the early 1970s, this enjoyable read focuses not only on the elite events and players but also upon the game's growth in a much wider context. More importantly, it is richly atmospheric, capturing the historic ambience of several golfing eras, each rather more colorful than today.

All told, *Golf's Golden Grind* manages to offer a relatively rare one-two punch: It is a highly detailed, very well-researched volume, yet its easy prose and pleasant style make it read more like an interesting novel than a dry textbook.

Under $25

AN INSIDE VIEW OF THE PRO TOUR

golfers' gold

TONY LEMA WITH GWILYM S. BROWN

Golfers' Gold • *Tony Lema*
(with Gwilym S. Brown)
Little Brown, Boston • 248p • 1964 (w/ PBKs)
1st UK edition ("Tony Lema's Inside Story of the Professional Golf Tour"): Foulsham 1964
Reprinted by Classics of Golf (1987)

Perhaps because of Lema's tragic death in a 1966 airplane crash, this colorful volume is somewhat overlooked in the world of golf literature. It is, as its UK title indicates, Lema's inside view of the PGA Tour, circa 1964, and as such includes the standard profiles-of-the-stars and "how-I-won" material that all such stories must. But in addition it highlights many less obvious aspects of the Tour life as well as detailing Lema's own climb from hotheaded rookie to bona fide Tour star, painting for the reader an uncommonly clear picture of the focus and discipline necessary at the game's highest levels.

Many have lamented that Lema's untimely death deprived the golfing world of more great victories, but *Golfers' Gold* clearly illustrates that it lost a sharp, funny, and talented man off the course as well.

Original: Under $25 • COG: New ($29)

The History of the PGA Tour • *Al Barkow*
Doubleday, New York • 298pp • 1989

A strong argument can probably be made that given the presence of Barkow's two above-listed history-of-the-Tour volumes, the inclusion of this 1989 work is unnecessary. Fair enough. But in addition to covering 15 more years than *Golf's Golden Grind,* this Tour-copyrighted effort offers a unique 70-page statistical section that includes year-by-year player rankings (beginning in 1916), overall rankings from six different eras, and statistical player bios (including full listings of events won) for 100 all-time greats.

Under $25

The Hole Truth • *Tommy Bolt (with Jimmy Mann)*
Lippincott, Philadelphia • 187pp • 1971

This book's subtitle is "Inside Big-Time Big-Money Golf" and it represents the ever-honest Bolt's look into life on the PGA Tour, circa 1970. Utilizing an offbeat Q&A format, it is told in Bolt's own folksy words and thus to some degree resembles Al Barkow's oral history of the Tour, *Gettin' to the Dance Floor.*

Typical Tommy: "The PGA considers the pioneers of the organization the officials who never missed a payday in their lives, not the struggling players who put up their own cash to provide the show."

Why isn't this book better remembered?

Under $25

The Making of The Masters • *David Owen*
Simon & Schuster, New York • 290pp • 1999 (w/PBK)

The question of just how many books one might require concerning the Masters seems a valid one, but this modern volume succeeds in offering some genuinely new and novel material. This is very likely due to Owen's being granted access to the Augusta National Club archive, a rare treat and one which, not surprisingly, bore real fruit. For presented here (albeit on too small a scale) are a number of never-before-seen photos of the golf course from 1935, a 1932 Olmsted Brothers map of the club's master plan, and more material on the legendary dictator Clifford Roberts than has ever previously made it to print.

One might have assumed that there would be little left to discover about the most covered venue in golf, but as that noted philosopher Felix Unger once said, "When you assume . . ."

Under $25

Massacre at Winged Foot • *Dick Schaap*
Random House, New York • 226pp • 1974

The 1974 U.S. Open was perhaps the toughest of the modern era, with Winged Foot's brutal West course yielding a remarkable winning score of +7. In assembling this entertaining volume, veteran reporter Dick

Schaap relied (we imagine) upon a variety of stringers in order to report events from all over the property on a minute-to-minute basis. The result is a chronological account of the Open that remains relatively unique, revealing much about the lives, challenges, and humor of touring professionals as well as the grand logistical undertaking that is the Open.

This was not, we should note, Schaap's first try at this format, but *Massacre at Winged Foot* is noticeably more detailed and engaging than his 1970 effort, *The Masters*.

Under $25

Masters of Golf • *Pat Ward-Thomas*
Heinemann, London • 257pp • 1961

The first of Ward-Thomas's four books, *Masters of Golf* profiles both the era's top players and some of Britain's lesser stars, all through the author's well-seasoned eyes. I find myself among the many who are enamored with his writing style, appreciating the honest insights he provided in so literate and gentlemanly a manner. As such, his pieces on men like Hogan, Locke, Thomson, Cotton, Snead, Palmer, Nelson, Nicklaus, and Player still hold great interest to this day.

It should be noted that many of these were reprinted in the Classics of Golf 1990 volume *The Lay of the Land,* a Ward-Thomas sampler that offers no new material but also includes excerpts from *The Long Green Fairway* and *Not Only Golf.*

$30

The Ryder Cup • *Colin M. Jarman*
McGraw Hill, New York • 400pp • 1999

Given the rather tasteless, jingoistic money grab that the American and European PGAs have turned the Ryder Cup into, it is tempting simply to ignore it altogether within *The Golfer's Library.* Still, I suppose that some representation is required and Jarman's thorough volume (subtitled The Definitive History of Playing Golf for Pride and Country) seems as good a choice as any, recapping, as it does, every individual match played since the event's onset in 1927.

Still available new.

New ($25)

The Snake in the Sandtrap • *Lee Trevino (with Sam Blair)*
Holt, Rinehart & Winston, New York • 166pp • 1985

Ostensibly a sister volume to Trevino's 1982 autobiography *They Call Me Super Mex,* this entertaining little book recounts stories and incidents from all over the golfing globe. It might not be the most essential entry in the library, but the combination of Trevino's career record and his nontraditional golfing background have always made his perspective an especially interesting one. Besides, any man who writes "I knew with a name like Juan Rodriguez he damn sure wasn't Irish" is probably worth reading on entertainment value alone.
Under $25

Teed Off • *Dave Hill (with Nick Seitz)*
Prentice-Hall, Englewood Cliffs, NJ • 217pp • 1977

This controversial tell-all book about life on the PGA Tour made a big splash in its day, and a good deal of its material remains highly relevant today. Divided into 18 chapters, it candidly addresses virtually every aspect of professional golf, from cheating and gambling to sex, Major championships, golf architecture, and Jack Nicklaus. The chapter entitled "The Field," in which Hill analyzes 40 of his biggest-name contemporaries, must surely have made for some chilly receptions on the practice tee.

    Calling Hazletine a cow pasture was just the tip of the iceberg.
$40

The U.S. Open: Golf's Ultimate Challenge •
Robert Sommers
Atheneum, New York • 350pp • 1987 (revised 2nd edition 1996)
1st UK edition: Stanley Paul 1987
Reprinted by Classics of Golf (1989)

It is important that we have at least one volume chronicling the history of the U.S. Open, and thus far this is the Cadillac of the field. Sommers, a former editor of the USGA's defunct *Golf Journal,* provides something well beyond a generic year-by-year recap, instead weaving a substantial text that captures the event's people, places, and results in genuinely high detail.

The book is broken into large chronological sections, each of which is then divided into several smaller chapters. There are two inserts of black and white photos and the necessary appendices of results, but in the end it's Sommer's fine writing and intrinsic grasp of history that make this *the* U.S. Open volume worth having.

Original: Under $25 • COG: New ($33)

SECTION V
ARCHITECTURE

This is perhaps my personal favorite category as I am one who believes strongly that golf's greatest feature is the uniqueness of its playing fields, the inherent variety of which is unmatched by any other sport. Consequently books which outline the philosophies or profile the work of the game's great architects are of strong interest, particularly when so many of the better ones involve designers of the game's pre–World War II Golden Age.

Selection criteria for this genre are thus relatively obvious, but two specific points are worth mentioning. First, books which are transparently self-serving (i.e., loaded with material designed primarily to attract future commissions) are omitted, as most big-name architects get more than enough public relations help from the golfing media as it is. Second, I have chosen to include several genre-straddling books written by legendary architects (e.g., C.B. Macdonald's *Scotland's Gift—Golf*) simply because such men are thoroughly identified with the design field and somehow seem out of place anywhere else.

Though the architecture category has seen fewer reprints than some other genres, those that have been produced are of tremendous value as many original editions are extremely scarce and terribly expensive.

The Anatomy of a Golf Course • *Tom Doak*
Lyons & Burford, New York • 242pp • 1992

It seems only appropriate to commence our architectural section with this book, a modern classic in the field and an excellent primer for the less initiated. Over the course of 15 chapters Doak guides the reader through virtually every aspect of course design and construction, including routing, esthetics, psychology of design, style and placement of hazards, and much more.

One of the book's great charms is its ability to blend the philosophies of the great Golden Age architects (from whom the author's own design work draws so much) into a modern, state-of-the-art text. Another is the many diagrams provided by former Doak associate Gil Hanse, all of which attractively illustrate the author's instructive points.

Few modern golf volumes are as detailed, or read as well.

New ($23)

The Architects of Golf • *Geoffrey S. Cornish and Ronald E. Whitten*
HarperCollins, New York • 648pp • 1993

Penned by venerable architect Geoffrey Cornish and *Golf Digest* Architectural Editor Ron Whitten, *The Architects of Golf* is actually a greatly expanded second version of the duo's 1981 groundbreaker *The Golf Course* (see below)—though the expansion is so grand as to make the link purely a matter of common formats.

This heroic work opens with 183 pages (divided into 12 chapters) on the history and evolution of golf course design. Next come 254 remarkable pages of architect profiles, providing biographical info and lists of design credits for every substantial designer in history, and then some. Finally we have a master list (arranged alphabetically) of literally thousands of courses worldwide, with cross-references to their various creators.

This increasingly rare volume is more a textbook than a collection of flowing prose, and so enormous a research effort seldom fails to produce some inaccuracies. But for anyone interested in the who, what, where, when, and whys of golf course design, there can be no more desirable an acquisition.

$140+

The Architectural Side of Golf • *H.N. Wethered and Tom Simpson*
Longmans, London • 210pp • 1929
Reprinted by Sportsman's Book Club (as "Design for Golf")
(1952), Grant Books (1995), and Flagstick Books (2002)

Long heralded as an architectural work of great importance, *The Architectural Side of Golf* is a collaboration between the patriarch of a legendary British golfing family (Wethered) and one of the game's more colorful architects (Simpson).

Given such divergent personalities, it hardly seems surprising that the book carries something of a schizophrenic character. To wit: The first seven chapters are a concise group that addresses a fine range of architectural issues. They are supplemented by Simpson's hole maps and sketches, functional, instructive images that today may seem a bit stilted but reportedly held great sway in their day. But if one senses that most everything has been covered to this point, there will be little surprise in finding that the final 11 chapters wander about rather curiously, in some cases scarcely seeming to relate to golf, much less course architecture.

There is no doubt much in this volume to merit its time-honored status, but my own preference leans more toward the more focused Golden Age efforts of Thomas, MacKenzie, or Hunter.

Original: $1,750+ • Grant: $175 • Flagstick: New ($33)

The Art of Golf Design •
Michael G. Miller and Geoff Shackelford
Sleeping Bear, Chelsea, MI • 191pp •
2001

The Art of Golf Design represents a bit of a wild card in this collection, a compilation of splendid landscapes by America's finest golf painter intermingled with essays on various aspects of course architecture. The overall package is attractive and the essays, old and new, are certainly thought-provoking. But in the end it is Mr. Miller's grand and colorful landscapes of so many famous golfing grounds—from Winged Foot to Kingston Heath—that make this a book worth having.

Full disclosure: I myself contributed a very minor essay here, though the project managed to succeed regardless.

New ($65)

Aspects of Golf Course Architecture 1889–1924 •
Fred Hawtree (Editor)
Grant, Droitwich • 170pp • 1998

The value a reader finds in this modern collection of old architectural writings will depend largely upon the depth of their previous devotion to the subject. That is to say that the avid collector may well own a number of the books from which many of these pieces are drawn, such as Vardon's *The Complete Golfer,* Braid's *Advanced Golf,* J.H. Taylor's *Taylor on Golf,* and so on. Then again, Dr. MacKenzie's treatise, "Military Entrenchments," is quite a bit less common, as are contributions by H.S. Colt, Herbert Fowler, Sir Guy Campbell, and others.

There are a total of 16 worthwhile essays here—and anybody dedicated enough to previously own them all hardly needs advice in building a library.

Still available new.

New ($76)

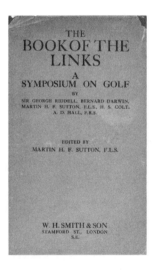

The Book of the Links: A Symposium on Golf •
Martin H.F. Sutton (Editor)
W.H. Smith, London • 212pp • 1912

Sutton's preface to *The Book of the Links* suggests that the volume was assembled to include ". . . all the points upon which golf secretaries, green committees, and green-keepers desire instruction." To accomplish this, many areas of design, construction, and up-keep are covered, frequently in the form of essays contributed by such luminaries as H.S. Colt ("The Construction of New Courses" and "Golf Architecture") and Bernard Darwin ("The Influence of Courses upon Players' Styles"), among others.

Beyond such architectural material, the remainder of the book is primarily agronomical, making it at least somewhat outdated today despite having enjoyed great prominence in its time. Though perhaps less relevant to the modern era than its later sister volume (see *Golf Course, Design, Construction & Upkeep* below) and never reprinted, *The Book of the Links* is today an elusive and expensive catch.
$500+

Bury Me in a Pot Bunker • *Pete Dye (with Mark Shaw)*
Addison-Wesley, Reading, MA • 241pp • 1995 (w/PBK)

This is an appealing book, and one manifestly different from the standard architect-generated fare. For after providing several chapters of biographical and historical context, Dye recounts, one to a chapter, the building of 14 of his most famous courses. All of the biggest names are here (PGA West, Teeth of the Dog, Harbour Town, Oak Tree, Kiawah, etc.) and the various stories do provide great insight into the thoughts and methods of modern golf design's undisputed King. What's missing, unfortunately, are graphics, for not a single sketch, routing map, or photograph breaks up the entertaining text.

In the end, *Bury Me in a Pot Bunker* is likely the most we're going to get from Dye, a genuine shame given his critically important position in the evolution of his chosen field.
Under $25

The Captain • *Geoff Shackelford*
Captain Fantastic, Santa Monica, CA • 207pp • 1996
Reprinted by Sleeping Bear (1997)

This engaging biography of the legendary West Coast designer was a quiet landmark, sparking, as it did, the valuable rush of new-millennium architect bios (Ross, MacKenzie, Macdonald, etc.) soon to follow.

Captain Thomas was truly a renaissance man and his various achievements—military hero, champion dog trainer and rose breeder, world-class fisherman—make for interesting reading. But above all Thomas was a superlative creator of strategic golf courses, and it is in this area that *The Captain*, with its many maps and period photos, ultimately excels. Fans of Thomas's famous Los Angeles Triumvirate (Riviera, Bel-Air, and the Los Angeles Country Club) will find the expansive coverage of these layouts especially interesting—but also somewhat distressing in its revelation as to just how much the virtuoso's work has been altered.

Original: $100+ • Sleeping Bear: New ($35)

Classic Golf Hole Design • *Robert Muir Graves and Geoffrey Cornish*
John Wiley & Sons, Hoboken, NJ • 323pp • 2002

This decidedly modern volume focuses upon a simple premise: the study of ancient, classic holes and their reproduction throughout the history of golf course design. Thorough to the point of covering decidedly more than its stated ground, the book is divided into seven chapters: "Architecture and Art: The Nature of Golf Course Design," "The History of Golf Course Architecture," "Golf Holes Are Compositions," "The Tradition of Replicating Classic Holes," "Broad Criteria for Classic Golf Holes," "Specific Features of Classic Golf Holes," and, finally, "The Classic Golf Holes."

Aside from being copiously illustrated, the book contains numerous interesting tables and sidebars, ranging from the earliest courses in 36 golfing countries to a breakdown of the 18 holes (and their inspirations) at the National Golf Links of America. Also included are extended lists of notable replica holes worldwide, countless routing maps, an extensive and detailed bibliography, and much more.

Indeed, the only negative to this information-laden volume might be the computerized nature of some of its graphics, a look which seems faintly at odds with its distinctly classic subject matter.

New ($65)

Colt & Co. • *Fred Hawtree*
Cambuc Archive, Oxford • 214pp • 1991

This increasingly rare volume is in fact a biography of one of golf design's great pioneers, Harry Shapland Colt. As such it is unquestionably successful, highlighting first his "Life and Times," then later "Colt's Legacies" (primarily his writings and design techniques). But in between lies a particularly fascinating section: 60 pages reprinting 12 years' worth of letters (1939–1951) exchanged amongst the firm's principals, Colt, C.H. Alison, and J.S.F. Morrison. These correspondences are amusing, revealing, and particularly late in life and during wartime, quite poignant. They stand as a splendid documentation of a unique era and a talented cadre of men.

Though an enclosed booklet manages to catalog more than 300 projects undertaken by the firm (including those of early partner Dr. Alister MacKenzie), this book should not be construed as a guide to Colt & Co.'s golf courses. That, sadly, is a volume we are still awaiting.

$150+

The Course Beautiful • *A.W. Tillinghast*
TreeWolf, Short Hills, NJ • 120pp • 1995

The Course Beautiful, the first of TreeWolf's magnificent A.W. Tillinghast trilogy, is a collection of the legendary architect's magazine columns (written primarily for *Golf Illustrated*) as selected by Tillinghast Association founders Rick Wolffe and Bob Trebus. Though the theme of the subsequent volumes would vary (see *Reminiscences of the Links* and *Gleanings from the Wayside* below), this book focuses primarily upon architectural issues, providing a virtual textbook on all aspects of course design and construction.

As it happens, the largely uneducated Tillinghast was a notably skilled writer, making these pieces every bit as entertaining as they are instructive. Period photos and course maps (most of which did not accompany the original articles) supplement the text, making for a highly rewarding package.

New ($35)

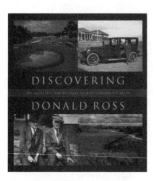

Discovering Donald Ross •
Bradley S. Klein
Sleeping Bear, Chelsea, MI • 367pp •
2001

Though an intensely interesting task, attempting to wrap one's arms around the massive golfing life of Donald Ross is, to say the least, challenging. How, for starters, does one cover the verifiable design of roughly 400 golf courses?

In this, the first real Ross biography, Bradley Klein addresses the dilemma by highlighting a large number of featured courses, all within a semichronological approach to the prolific Scotsman's life. In addition to a fine mix of old and new photos, readers will be delighted by a large number of previously unpublished routing maps, copious material on Pinehurst, several letters (including one received, in 1942, from A.W. Tillinghast), an updated listing of Ross courses, and numerous additional items of interest.

Several late chapters on restorative issues take the book in a slightly different direction but on the whole, we must be impressed by the thoughtful and wide-ranging portrait this large volume paints.

New ($85)

Eighteen Stakes on a Sunday Afternoon • *Geoffrey Cornish*
Grant, Droitwich • 218pp • 2002

This limited-edition volume (700 copies) represents a general North American architectural history as narrated by the author, extensively utilizing written comments extracted from all manner of sources. It is chronological, concise, and eminently interesting, sweeping the reader through 100+ years of development with great variety and ease. The book's greatest value, I suppose, lies in the vast diversity of sources mined for the excerpts. Numerous old magazine articles—many from nongolfing publications—are cited here, demonstrating a knowledge of subject and depth of research that is not easily matched.

Not surprisingly, *Eighteen Stakes* also provides one of the stronger architectural bibliographies in recent memory, a major plus.

New ($79)

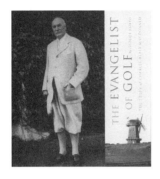

The Evangelist of Golf •
George Bahto
Clock Tower, Chelsea, MI • 280pp •
2002

Like most contemporary biographies of Golden Age architects, *The Evangelist of Golf* is centered less upon the life and more upon the golf-design works of the game's first great American advocate, Charles Blair Macdonald. That said, it succeeds in featuring detailed profiles of every course laid out—wholly or in part—by Macdonald, with special attention paid to his two masterpieces, the National Golf Links of America and the long-deceased Lido. A large and well-illustrated book, *The Evangelist* also includes a number of course maps, an intriguing timeline of Macdonald's career (along with that of his protégés, Seth Raynor and Charles Banks), and the most detailed listing to date of their combined design credits.

Considering the relative paucity of Macdonald material over the years, this is an important and useful volume.

New ($85)

Gleanings from the Wayside • *A.W. Tillinghast*
TreeWolf, Short Hills, NJ • 160pp • 2001

The third in TreeWolf's Tillinghast trilogy (see *The Course Beautiful* and *Reminiscences of the Links*), *Gleanings* boasts an interesting mix both of architectural writing and stories of Tilly's Depression-era cross-country travels on behalf of the PGA of America. Among the highlights are profiles of Oakland Hills (pre–Trent Jones), Pinehurst No. 2, Baltimore C.C., and Winged Foot's West course, the latter in the form of a hole-by-hole preview of the 1929 U.S. Open. Also included are Tillinghast's reports on his wanderings through California, Texas, and Mexico and a large number of maps and aerial photos covering some of his famous (and not so famous) designs.

For architectural aficionados in particular, the entire trilogy is a must.

New ($40)

The Golden Age of Golf Design •
Geoff Shackelford
Sleeping Bear, Chelsea, MI • 211pp •
1999

For fans of classic golf design, and especially those relatively new to the genre, this richly illustrated volume represents an indispensable acquisition. Essentially it is an overview of the field's remarkable pre–World War II era, though a more detailed survey would be difficult to imagine.

Shackelford's approach seems basic enough: Divide the volume into various schools of architectural thought, then briefly profile each major designer, their philosophies, and their most important works. This is all very well done, of course, but what makes *The Golden Age* sing is the quality of its illustrations, an especially varied lot that include numerous seldom-seen photos, hole drawings, aerial photos, and routing maps. Even the devoted architectural reader can learn a lot from this volume, which delivers a great deal of bang for its buck.

New ($65)

Golf Architecture •
Dr. Alister MacKenzie
Simkin, Marshall, Hamilton, Kent,
London • 135pp • 1920
Reprinted by Classics of Golf (1987)

Dr. MacKenzie's fabled work is very likely the most famous of Golden Age architecture books, and this celebrity does not come without reason. It is, in fact, a fairly concise volume featuring a total of four chapters: "General Principles of Economy in Golf Construction and Green-Keeping," "Some Further Suggestions," "Ideal Holes," and "The Future of Golf Architecture."

While each is interesting in its own right, the first and last are probably of greatest significance. In the former, MacKenzie details his famous 13 "essential features of an ideal golf course," while it is near the end that he recounts theories on camouflage techniques as gleaned from his experiences in the Boer War. Though less illustrated than either George Thomas's or Robert Hunter's books, *Golf Architecture* does include 16 period photos (several demonstrating construction techniques) and six MacKenzie drawings.

Original copies are rare and very expensive. The Classics of Golf reprint, on the other hand, is readily available and includes both the 1928 prospectus for Cypress Point (complete with MacKenzie's original routing map) and a wonderful Herbert Warren Wind foreword covering both the Doctor's life and the prominent architectural books of the period. For most, it's the obvious choice.

Original: $1,800+ • COG: New ($33)

Golf Architecture: A Worldwide Perspective Volume 1 •
Paul Daley
Full Swing, Victoria • 242pp • 2002

Here is a book that truly lives up to its title, incorporating 42 essays from literally the world over on all aspects of the theory and practice of golf course architecture. Names like Pete Dye, Donald Steel, Rees Jones, Tom Doak, and Gil Hanse all appear here, so the volume does have star appeal. But what really makes it noteworthy is both the vast range of subjects covered and the many fine photos (old and new) and diagrams that bring it to life.

Volume II, which was published in late 2003, is an absolute sibling, offering a good deal more of the same.

New ($50)

Golf Architecture in America: Its Strategy and Construction •
George C. Thomas Jr.
Times-Mirror, Los Angeles • 342pp • 1927
Reprinted by the USGA (1990) and Sleeping Bear (1997)

Seventy-five years after its initial publication, there are many who still consider *Golf Architecture in America* to be the finest book of its type ever written—and I must unabashedly count myself among them.

To begin with, it is comprehensive, with 13 chapters covering everything from "The Strategy of Golf Courses" and "The General Plan for the Property" to "Actual Construction" and "Remodeling Old Courses." Further chapters on "Beauty and Utility" and "Adapting the Course to the Ground" remain especially relevant (if not altogether practiced) today while a late section titled "Arbitrary Values," which advocates an altered system of scoring, remains offbeat food for thought.

Perhaps more central to the book's greatness, however, are its illustrations, an amazingly varied collection of photographs, drawings, routing maps, and even period scorecards, which can be studied *ad infinitum* by historians and architects alike. Part of this graphic variety is due to the author's myriad sources, for he, unlike the average writer, was able to solicit contributions from fellow designers like Tillinghast, Ross, and MacKenzie—one heck of a supporting cast.

In short, I cannot imagine having an interest in golf architecture and not securing a copy of this endlessly fascinating volume.

Original: $800+ • USGA (1,500 copies): $150+ • Sleeping Bear: New ($85)

The Golf Course • *Geoffrey S. Cornish and Ronald T. Whitten*
Rutledge, New York • 320pp • 1981

Something of a landmark in the genre, *The Golf Course* offers the same three-section format as its imposing successor, *The Architects of Golf* (see above). This includes an extensive history of golf design, profiles of numerous important architects (complete with design credits), and a master list of courses worldwide.

An important volume at its time of publication, *The Golf Course* has only fallen from the limelight because of the thoroughly trumping, *tour de force* nature of *The Architects of Golf.*

$35+

Golf Course Architecture: Design, Construction, and Restoration • *Dr. Michael J. Hurdzan*
Sleeping Bear, Chelsea, MI • 406pp • 1996

Really more a textbook than a book of lyrical prose, *Golf Course Architecture* largely represents a how-to guide for the modern design field. It does possess some interesting historical notes and photos, and cannot be accused of denying the master designers of the Golden Age their just due. But at its heart this is a technical volume built to highlight contemporary design, construction, and agronomical techniques.

Extremely valuable for modern computer-aided architects and greenkeepers, I'd imagine, but less so for fans of classic design.
New ($85)

Golf Courses: Design, Construction and Upkeep • *Martin H.F. Sutton*
Simpkin Marshall, London • 152pp • 1933 (w/revised 1950 2nd edition)

As with his earlier *The Book of the Links,* Martin Sutton brought in several high-profile guests to contribute architectural essays here, all of which once again surround a central section on agronomy. This time the ringers include Bernard Darwin (Introduction), MacKenzie Ross ("The Scottish Golf Links: Their Influence on World Golf Course Architecture"), Tom Simpson ("The Design and Construction of a Golf Course"), a young Robert Trent Jones ("Golf Course Architecture in the United States"), C.H. Alison ("Golf Courses Overseas"), and C.K. Cotton ("Golf Club Management").

The cynical among us might suggest that as the largest seed merchant in Great Britain, Sutton recognized an opportunity to attractively package his product when he saw it. Very well, but this volume—which I find a bit more engaging than its sister—stands up quite nicely even if one skips the agronomical sales pitches completely.

Relatively available, but definitely not cheap.
Original: $600+ • 1950: $425+

The Golf Courses of James Braid • *John E. Moreton*
Grant, Droitwich • 126pp • 1996

For a relatively small book, this limited-edition effort packs a remarkable amount of information within its 126 pages. It is essentially a chronology of Braid's design work (covering a stout 185 courses), though a number of salient biographical facts are blended in along the way. The individual course entries vary somewhat in depth and are interspersed with photographs and the occasional routing map. Much like the next volume profiled below, this book is far more for serious students of architecture and history than for browsing at bedtime.

Foldout maps of Braid's plans for Royal Blackheath and 36 holes at Gleneagles are included.

$135

The Golf Courses of Old Tom Morris • *Robert Kroeger*
Heritage, Cincinnati • 360pp • 1995

In no way to be confused with a general coffee-table tome, this limited-edition work (1,975 copies) borders on the scholarly, profiling the life and works of Old Tom without benefit of thumbnail descriptions or sprawling color plates.

The first section examines his life biographically, including his skills as a tournament competitor, his general approach to golf design, and, rather interestingly, his relationships with (and impact upon) 19 future architects of distinction. The second section then covers 57 of Old Tom's designs in splendid detail, often reprinting nineteenth-century hole descriptions as well as period photographs. As many have been altered substantially, further information is often provided as to the status of the remaining Morris holes. All in all a captivating volume—and one rather remarkably left for an American to write.

$50

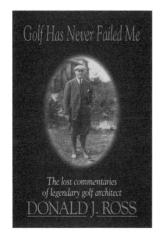

Golf Has Never Failed Me •
Donald Ross
Sleeping Bear, Chelsea, MI • 258pp •
1996

The subtitle to this book—"The lost commentaries of legendary golf architect Donald J. Ross"—pretty well sums it up. Ross, who was far less prolific as a writer than a course designer, apparently prepared much of this manuscript with an eye toward publication shortly before World War I. Never finalized, it was discovered decades later, then supplemented with some additional Ross material and polished by *Golf Digest* Architectural Editor Ron Whitten.

The end result is 95 vignettes (varying in length from five pages down to 21 words) addressing Ross's views on most every aspect of golf course design and construction. The photographs and maps that support the text are, on the whole, quite interesting and the concluding list of Ross design credits is more accurate than several other published ledgers.

New ($30)

Golf's Magnificent Challenge • *Robert Trent Jones*
(with Larry Dennis)
McGraw-Hill, New York • 287pp • 1988

This large, heavily illustrated volume really is two books in one: a lavish coffee-table affair filled with bright color photos and a serious text detailing Trent Jones's theories on golf design. The text is divided into eight chapters, which first profile both the game and Jones himself, then sort through many aspects of design and construction. Refreshingly absent is a self-promoting "list of the author's courses" and it must be noted that a large percentage of the illustrations are of courses *not* built by Jones.

The author's place in the history of golf design may generate some controversy among traditionalists, but *Golf's Magnificent Challenge* remains a thorough, honest, and attractive overall effort.

$30

Grounds for Golf • *Geoff Shackelford*
Thomas Dunne, New York • 300pp • 2003

This neatly laid out volume (subtitled "The History and Fundamentals of Golf Course Design") serves as a much-needed modern primer on the increasingly popular subject of golf architecture. Though Tom Doak's 1992 *The Anatomy of a Golf Course* may represent the contemporary standard with regard to the strategies and nuances of hole design, *Grounds for Golf* paints a broader canvas, covering the great architects and their work, but also aspects of the modern design trade, its evolution and business aspects.

Divided into 18 chapters/holes, *Grounds* is extensively illustrated with photographs (primarily black and white) and numerous highly detailed hole drawings penned by talented architect Gil Hanse. Also laced with countless golf-related quotations, *Grounds for Golf* is an ideal book for the newly interested while also offering much of value to the well-seasoned.

New ($27)

Hazards • *Aleck Bauer*
Rubovits, Chicago • 61pp • 1913
Reprinted by Grant (1993)

The original edition of this quirky little volume featured brief excerpts of Dr. MacKenzie, Ted Ray, H.S. Colt, and others writing on the subject of hazards, followed by detailed studies of 12 legendary British holes notorious for their bunkering. The Grant Books reprint spices things up considerably by adding detailed introductions by Peter Thomson and Fred Hawtree and closing pieces by Peter Dobereiner and historian Philip Truett. Thus the often-elusive modern version is preferred—a convenient state of affairs as the limited-edition original may well be extinct.

Original: $1,500+ • Grant: $100

The Life and Work of Dr. Alister MacKenzie • *Tom Doak, Dr. James S. Scott, and Raymund M. Haddock*
Sleeping Bear, Chelsea, MI • 231pp • 2001

As the first full-fledged biography of the celebrated Dr. MacKenzie, this book is one that automatically grabs our interest. Naturally, like most bios of long-ago architects, it is relatively light in its portrayal of the good doctor's early life—but then how does one locate substantial day-to-day material on a man born, relatively anonymously, in 1870?

Much stronger, of course, is its presentation of his courses, perhaps because Doak may well be the only person ever (including MacKenzie himself) to see all of them. Extensive space is allocated to the usual high-profile classics, but many readers may find more interesting the material on less-seen gems like Crystal Downs, the University of Michigan, or the Valley Club of Montecito. MacKenzie's visits to Australia and South America are also covered, as are his partnerships with Perry Maxwell, Alex Russell, Robert Hunter, and, of course, H.S. Colt and C.H. Alison. A full list of MacKenzie's worldwide designs concludes the proceedings. **New ($65)**

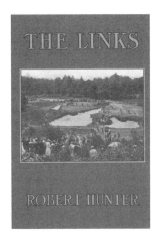

The Links • *Robert Hunter*
Scribners, New York • 163pp • 1926
Reprinted by the USGA (undated), Flagstick (1998), and Sleeping Bear (2000)

Few entries in this collection have been reprinted more frequently, which must say something regarding the quality and desirability of Robert Hunter's epic work. Hunter, of course, was one of golf's more curious characters, an academician and avowed socialist who married into wealth and lived like a king. Interestingly, he wrote this volume without, as far as we know, having ever actually built a golf course—and he did so *before* becoming partners with the legendary Dr. Alister MacKenzie, an equally intriguing point.

Not surprisingly *The Links* carries a more scholarly tone in its examination of architecture with fully half of its eight chapters devoted to the importance of greens and the value and placement of hazards. It is also revered for its many fine period photos and diagrams, though George Thomas's 1927 *Golf Architecture in America* would clearly usurp it in this regard. Still, an unquestioned classic of the genre, and one that remains constantly in demand.

Original: $800+ • USGA (1,500 copies): $175 • Flagstick: New ($39) • Sleeping Bear: New ($55)

Links Golf: The Inside Story • *Paul Daley*
Pelican, Gretna, LA • 160pp • 2000

Despite a title suggesting the presence of some vast conspiracy of which we were previously unaware, this fine volume represents an informative profile of the oldest and most sacred form of golf, that played on genuine seaside linksland. More than a simple traveler's guidebook, it includes sections on hazarding, blind shots, caddies, the geographic conditions and playing skills necessary for links golf, and quite a bit more. It is also heavily illustrated, though primarily in black and white.

While I suspect that little in here will come as news to the golfers of Great Britain and Ireland, it remains a useful rundown for the rest of the golfing world.

New ($35)

Masters of the Links • *Geoff Shackelford (Editor)*
Sleeping Bear, Chelsea, MI • 241pp • 1997

Masters of the Links represents the first time that a broad body of writings on the subject of golf course architecture, both old and contemporary, has been assembled under one cover. The book is divided into five sections: "St. Andrews and Links," "Architecture," "Planning, Construction and Maintenance," "Hazards and Holes," and "Contemporary Design," each of which contains topical writings by some of the game's finest architects.

It is notable that excepting C.B. Macdonald's piece entitled "Architecture" (which is drawn from *Scotland's Gift—Golf*), not a single entry comes from a previously published book. Among the old, they are drawn from period magazines such as *Golf Illustrated*, *The Fairway*, and *Game and Gossip* or, in the case of William Langford's article on hazard placement, from a rare promotional brochure. The contemporary section (which includes contributions from Pete Dye and Ben Crenshaw) includes only pieces written specifically for this volume.

New ($25)

The Missing Links: America's Greatest Lost Golf Courses and Holes • *Daniel Wexler*
Sleeping Bear, Chelsea, MI • 222pp • 2000

It is not easy to comment objectively upon one's own work, so I shall simply state the basics of this volume and leave it at that.

The Missing Links profiles a number of America's finest lost golf courses—that is, topflight layouts that were long ago plowed under by airports, shopping malls, and the like. Twenty-seven of the very best are featured at length, with hole-by-hole tours, old photos, and color maps. The general relevance of such a project might miss some contemporary readers, but the book does succeed in documenting numerous courses (e.g., the Lido, Timber Point, Deepdale, etc.) that would rank among the nation's elite were they still in existence today.

For those who enjoy the concept, a sister volume, *Lost Links: Forgotten Treasures of Golf's Golden Age,* features 74 more courses, as well as lost holes from a number of America's most famous layouts.

New ($35)

Reminiscences of the Links • *A.W. Tillinghast*
TreeWolf, Short Hills, NJ • 160pp • 1998

The second of TreeWolf's three Tillinghast volumes (see *The Course Beautiful* and *Gleanings from the Wayside*), *Reminiscences,* with its largely historical content, might well be the most indispensable of the lot. Strange, you might say, given that Tillinghast's fame rested far more on his design skills than his status as a raconteur. But the timing of Tilly's life, at least in golf terms, was spectacular, allowing him to witness countless important people and events from an era of American golf sadly under-recorded: the pre–World War I years.

Within *Reminiscences,* we find eyewitness accounts of legends like Old Tom Morris, Harry Vardon, Willie Anderson, and Johnny McDermott, the reporting of early championships generally seen only as numerical records today, and bonuses such as Tilly's 1939 all-time ranking of golfers (Vardon first, Jones second, Hagen third). Once again, the maps and photographs, though generally not associated with the original articles, are of great interest on their own, making this a truly valuable acquisition.

New ($35)

Scotland's Gift—Golf •
Charles Blair Macdonald
Scribners, New York • 340pp • 1928
Reprinted by Classics of Golf (1985)

Being the story of a man who might rightfully be called the father of golf in America, *Scotland's Gift—Golf* is certainly one of the game's seminal volumes. It is, in fact, an autobiography, though Macdonald tends to balance his own life story against the broader story of golf—not surprising, one supposes, since according to many contemporaries he viewed the two as being of essentially equal importance.

But whatever pomposity the author might possess, *Scotland's Gift* remains a treasure trove of golfing history, told by the man most central to the American end of it. It recounts Macdonald's years at St. Andrews (where he attended the university), his founding and development of the Chicago Golf Club, his leadership in forming the USGA, and his victory in the first official U.S. Amateur Championship (made so after C.B.'s own protests nullified two previous events, both of which he had lost).

Macdonald's biggest impact, however, was likely as America's first true course architect, and *Scotland's Gift* details both his groundbreaking philosophy and his building of this nation's architectural template, the National Golf Links of America. A chapter discussing his work on three other classics, the Lido, Mid Ocean and Yale, as well as his relationship with protégé Seth Raynor is also included.

Some readers may find the minutiae of early USGA business a bit tedious (imagine the organization actually being so concerned with equipment advances today!) but in the end, *Scotland's Gift* is both a fascinating read and a cornerstone to any American golfing library.

Original: $800+ • COG: New ($39)

Scotland's Golf Courses • *Robert Price*
Aberdeen University, Aberdeen • 235pp • 1989 (w/PBK)

This is a unique edition among architecture volumes.

The author, a professor of geography, examines 425 Scottish courses from the perspective of their landforms, teaching us much along the way about golfing environments, why courses are built where they are, and so on. Included are numerous charts and geographic maps—items which, at a glance, may appear dry but on second look (and many thereafter) become quite fascinating. Also valuable is a detailed appendix listing each course's vital information, including its date of establishment, land type, and style of vegetation (e.g., links, parkland, moorland, etc.).

Neither a coffee-table book nor a volume reliant upon stunning prose, *Scotland's Golf Courses* is not the easiest to find, but represents an intriguing addition to our architectural list.

Under $25

Some Essays on Golf Course Architecture •
H.S. Colt and C.H. Alison
Country Life & George Newnes, London • 69pp • 1920
Reprinted by Grant Books in hardcover (1990) and PBK (1993)

Universally acclaimed as one of the first important architectural books, this brief but to-the-point volume was created at least partially to help revive Colt's design firm following the doldrums of World War I. Most of the essays are penned by Colt himself and are arranged as follows: "Golf in the Nineties" (by Alison), "The Modern Course—Framework," "The Placing of Bunkers," "Construction," "Financial Considerations," "Labour-Saving Machinery and the Cost of Construction" (by then-partner Dr. Alister MacKenzie), "Golf in Belgium," and "Other Opinions."

Why Alison, with one essay contributed, gets coauthor billing while MacKenzie (with the same) doesn't is only slightly more mysterious than the need for a chapter on the sleeping giant that is Belgian golf.

Original 1920 editions are virtually impossible to find while the 1990 reprint (which includes an introductory Colt bio from Fred Hawtree) isn't far behind. The paperback duplicate, however, can generally still be located.

Original: $2,000 • Grant: $250+ • Grant PBK: $35

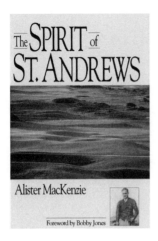

Alister MacKenzie

Foreword by Bobby Jones

The Spirit of St. Andrews •
Dr. Alister MacKenzie
Sleeping Bear, Chelsea, MI • 269pp •
1995 (w/PBK)

The great Peter Alliss probably said it best in his jacket notes for *The Spirit of St. Andrews* when he wrote: "Perhaps the discovery of this manuscript written in the doctor's own fair hand was not quite as dramatic as Lord Caernarvon discovering the burial ground of Tutankhamen, but for lovers of golf it must run it damn close."

For this book is a genuine time capsule, a manuscript laid out by Dr. MacKenzie perhaps a year prior to his death—and promptly lost for six decades thereafter. Presented with only minimal editing, it is far wider-ranging than the doctor's 1920 classic *Golf Architecture,* featuring sections on the game's history and technique (MacKenzie's having shown dramatic improvement late in life) in addition to architectural chapters on general concepts, construction, and ideal holes around the world. A period foreword written by Bobby Jones adds a nice touch, as does MacKenzie's 1934 obituary from the *Santa Cruz Sentinel.*

In short, this is *Golf Architecture* and then some.

New ($25)

The Toronto Terror • *James A. Barclay*
Sleeping Bear, Chelsea, MI • 207pp • 2000

The Toronto Terror covers the life of famous Canadian architect Stanley Thompson, designer of such classics as Banff, Jasper Park, and Cape Breton Park's Highlands Links. Though not as highly illustrated as many such books, it is a well-researched document that is divided into two primary sections (The Thompson Family and Stanley Thompson, Golf Course Architect) followed by an appendix (General Thoughts on Golf Course Design) and an annotated list of Thompson's courses worldwide. Strictly a black and white production, *The Toronto Terror* is also that rare architectural work that offers not a single map of any of its subject's many celebrated courses.

Thompson, however, was a talented and eccentric individual, making this a beneficial volume despite its lack of grandeur.

New ($35)

Section VI
Courses and Travel

This is at once both our most wide-ranging category and yet also our most limited, for while the world represents a nearly limitless playing field, very few really great books have been produced in this genre. A similar paradox exists in the fact that volumes covering "Great Golf Courses of the World" are generally spread too thin to provide more than superficial profiles while more detailed regional works pose the obvious question: Does so narrowly defined a work deserve one of our precious 400 spaces? Judgment calls all.

At any rate, I've attempted to provide a high degree of diversity here, with books specific to the United States, Canada, the United Kingdom, Australia, Southeast Asia, and Southern Africa all included, as well as a healthy mix of coffee-table volumes and more serious literature, newer books and time-honored older ones. This, then, is surely a genre of uncommon broadness—but it's a big world out there.

100 Greatest Golf Courses—And Then Some •
William H. Davis, etc.
Golf Digest, Norwalk, CT • 279pp • 1982

Published eight years after *Golf Digest*'s earlier *Great Golf Courses of the World* (see below), this colorful book is part sibling, part second edition to its popular predecessor. Featuring slightly more modern graphics, it again tours the world region-by-region, this time examining 50 top American courses in relative depth before covering the rest of the planet on a more superficial level. Of note is the fact that the American, Canadian, British, Australian, and Japanese sections are based on the magazine's rankings of the period—always an interesting (if inherently silly) list to compare to the present.

Extra features here include Davis's opening essay on modern architecture, profiles of top public, collegiate, and estate courses, and a closing gazetteer highlighting odd and fascinating courses the world over.

Though hardly on par with the seminal *World Atlas of Golf,* this nonetheless remains a fun title.

Under $25

The 500 World's Greatest Golf Holes • *George Peper*
(with the Editors of Golf *Magazine)*
Artisan, New York • 442pp • 2000 (w/PBK)

One of the grander undertakings in the history of golf publishing, this huge and colorful volume does indeed feature 500 famous holes, drawn from all six golfing continents. Divided into four sections, it highlights a top 18, a top 100, and then the overall 500 (the latter section partitioned by region) before closing with an enjoyable 57-page gazetteer offering a variety of "best of" lists. Despite one or two prominently reversed images, it is an attractively illustrated and well-researched work that clearly took a bit of time and effort.

The fact that one might personally disagree with a number of the holes selected is, I suppose, half of the fun.

New ($60) • PBK: ($30)

America's Greatest Golfing Resorts • *Richard Miller*
Bobbs-Merrill, Indianapolis • 239pp • 1977

Somewhat different from the standard "Great Resorts of . . ." volume, *America's Greatest Golfing Resorts* is an understated affair written from a refreshingly historical perspective. Illustrated solely in black and white, it profiles 20 famous properties with an eye not simply toward golf but also toward their glamorous pasts, featuring famous guests and stories as well as current amenities. Obvious choices like Pinehurst, the Homestead, and Pebble Beach appear as do a number of modern favorites. But with venerable names like Banff, the Cloister, La Quinta, and the Broadmoor aboard, it's really the old gems—and their decades of lore—that set this work apart from the generic coffee-table crowd.

Under $25

Australia's Finest Golf Courses • *Darius Oliver*
New Holland, Sydney • 160pp • 2003

At first glance, *Australia's Finest Golf Courses* might seem nonessential if one already possesses a copy of Tom Ramsey's earlier *Great Australian Golf Courses* (see below). However this contemporary work, which highlights 67 of Oz's elite, is well worth acquiring in its own right for two compelling reasons. First, it is vastly more up-to-date, featuring not less than 25 courses that have opened in the interceding 13 years. And second, it is notably attractive, offering over 125 color plates by the talented David Scaletti.

Aside from providing short-but-highly detailed histories of each layout, *Australia's Finest* also offers a gazetteer of sorts, rating the nation's courses in all sorts of architectural categories. It also scores bonus points for profiling media magnate Kerry Packer's private Ellerston Golf Course, a spectacular Greg Norman design seldom seen by plebian eyes.

New ($45)

Blasted Heaths and Blessed Greens • *James Finegan*
Simon & Schuster, New York • 286pp • 1996

This splendid little book is a beautifully crafted golfer's tour of Scotland, guided by an exceptional writer who has visited Great Britain and

Ireland more than 35 times. Very much in the tradition of Darwin's *Golf Courses of the British Isles,* it wanders to and fro, commenting at varied lengths on both the world-famous courses and the hidden gems. As it is essentially unillustrated and hardly a new concept, browsers might easily overlook both this and its sister volumes on Ireland and England—but that would be a great mistake indeed.

This armchair recounting is a truly transportive experience. Enough so, in fact, to leave one wishing that retired ad man Finegan had spent more of his life writing about golf, and thus given us a much larger body of work.

New ($21)

The Book of Irish Golf • *John Redmond*
Gill & Macmillan, Dublin • 159pp • 1997

Written by a former golf correspondent for Irish Press Newspapers, this attractive book represents a fairly thorough overview of golf on the Emerald Isle from its earliest days to the present. It is divided into eight sections—"The Origins of Golf in Ireland," "Ireland's Great Courses," "Great Occasions in Irish Golf," "Ladies' Golf in Ireland," "Players," "Great Moments in Irish Golf," "19th Hole," and "Ireland's New Golfing Gems"—each of which is filled with color photos and easy-to-read text.

Not quite a classic, but pleasing enough.

New ($40)

The Championship Courses of Scotland • *Sandy Lyle*
(with Bob Ferrier)
Windmill, Kingswood, England • 288pp • 1982

Covering Carnoustie, Royal Troon, Turnberry, Muirfield, Gleneagles, and, of course, St. Andrews, this generously proportioned volume literally takes the reader around these hallowed links shot by shot. For each hole there are photos, paintings, maps, and comprehensive prose, explaining, in uncommon detail, the strategies and demands of playing these timeless layouts.

Ideal reading in advance of an Open Championship.

Under $25

Classic American Courses • *Mike Stachura*
Carlton, Kansas City, MO • 224pp • 2003

A neatly arranged volume, *Classic American Courses* profiles 50 layouts "whose import and wonder cannot be argued," each, rather mechanically, over four pages with three color photos. Entries include a featured hole, a table of historic milestones, and some brief (600 words) prose to provide a bit of context. Despite lacking any sort of maps, this is a functional and highly attractive volume, though I doubt it offers much new material to the more educated reader.

Incidentally, the use of the word "classic" in the title should not necessarily suggest Golden Age, as 14 of the selected courses post-date World War II. Lest purists be offended by the inclusion of places like Bellerive and Firestone, however, the author provides quotations from the likes of Dan Jenkins and Jack Nicklaus that essentially categorize these places as tough but dull.

Fair enough.

New ($35)

Classic Golf Links of England, Scotland, Wales & Ireland • *Donald Steel*
Pelican, Gretna, LA • 224pp • 1992

As both a writer and longtime golf architect, Donald Steel is eminently qualified to examine the great links of the UK and Ireland, and this volume certainly lives up to its titular billing. All told, Steel examines 75 courses throughout the region, many ultrafamous but many others relative sleepers, at least on the international stage. The book is divided into nine geographical zones, with each course's write-up including championship yardages and a simple-but-accurate routing map. The profiles are thorough, well-written, and appropriately historical while the numerous color photographs do a fine job of capturing the unique ambience of the links.

It can be reasonably argued that this is the finest book on seaside British courses since the days of Hutchinson and Darwin. Now if only Steel would do a sister volume on the heathlands!

New ($40)

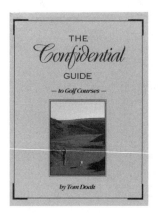

The Confidential Guide • *Tom Doak*
Sleeping Bear, Chelsea, MI • 361pp • 1996

Few books have caused more of a stir in the decidedly staid world of golf course architecture than this one, and even fewer represent as entertaining a read. For here the ever-opinionated Doak rates and candidly comments upon over 800 courses on five continents, ruffling feathers while informing (and amusing) the reader to no end. Thirty-one of the author's favorites are profiled in greater depth up front but even more interesting is The Doak Gazetteer, a deluxe appendix of bests, worsts, toughests, and the like from around the world.

Critics—and there have been a few—would do well to remember that nobody has studied architecture or visited the world's great courses more than Tom Doak. And besides, for those who may find some of this volume's commentary overly harsh, be advised that you are reading the *softened* version, an even more forthright edition having been privately published two years earlier.

New ($45)

The Continental Golf Yearbook
Guides Plumon, Paris • 1926 (w/approx 18 subsequent annual editions) (some PBK)

This thick and highly informative annual covered golf throughout Europe, profiling courses in every continental country (thus not the UK). What makes it special is the remarkable depth of its information as hundreds of clubs are highlighted, each with course specs, photographs, a routing map (some relatively detailed), and, frequently, hole-by-hole playing descriptions. With railways maps included, this was, during its time, *the* guide to European golf.

First published in 1926, it existed in some form as late as 1950, though later editions were a bit less elaborate and predominantly in French. Perhaps because its soft covers made *The Continental Golf*

Yearbook's earlier editions less durable, copies of this splendid period guide are virtually nonexistent today.

$150

Discover Australia's Golf Courses • *Tom Ramsey*
Dent, Melbourne • 231pp • 1987

As golf course guidebooks go, this is about as attractive and thorough as it gets. Penned by Australia's leading golf writer, *Discover Australia's Golf Courses* tours the sprawling country state by state, highlighting over 200 of Oz's finest courses and also providing a comprehensive listing in the form of a "Travellers' Guide." The book is heavily illustrated with both color photos and detailed area maps, and the course profiles frequently provide significant historic and architectural background.

An admirably complete volume.

$30

Emerald Fairways and Foam-Flecked Seas • *James Finegan*
Simon & Schuster, New York • 287pp • 1996

The perfect sister volume to *Blasted Heaths and Blessed Greens* (see above), *Emerald Fairways and Foam-Flecked Seas* matches its sibling in size, style, and overall quality, this time in covering the courses of Ireland. A more recent entry, 2003's *All Courses Great and Small,* follows the same formula in visiting England and Wales, closing out Finegan's memorable and comprehensive British Isles trilogy.

Sadly, books like these seldom get written anymore.

New ($21)

Emerald Gems: The Links of Ireland •
Lawrence Casey Lambrecht
Lambrecht Photography, Westerly, RI • 209pp • 2002

Likely the largest volume in anyone's collection, this (very) oversized book profiles 49 Irish links in both words and pictures. The words are ably provided by regional types like Dermot Gilleece, Pat Ruddy, and

David Feherty, but it is Lambrecht's genuinely stunning imagery that makes *Emerald Gems* stand out. Indeed it can be reasonably argued that this is the finest album of golfing photography ever assembled, a collection that lovers of golf—especially the links variety—will gaze over time and time again.

One large and very sturdy coffee table not included.

New ($99)

Famous Fairways • *Peter Allen*
Stanley Paul, London • 164pp • 1968

I must admit to having been thoroughly surprised upon discovering that Peter Allen was not a professional golf writer, for his lyrical descriptions of the game and its courses can absolutely hold their own with anyone's. Instead, Allen (who was actually Sir Peter, his OBE being modestly omitted from the title page) was the Chairman of Royal Dutch Shell and a lifelong golfer who got around, playing on five continents and at one time being Augusta National's only non-American member.

Famous Fairways represents his portrayal of more than 80 of the world's best-known courses, descriptions he laces with personal recollections, historical footnotes, and, on several occasions, some perspective from golfing luminaries. That the serious golfer will be familiar with the vast majority of his selections is, I believe, irrelevant. For Allen has the ability—like Darwin and Longhurst and Wind—to draw the reader back again and again, wishing to once more live vicariously through his lucid and colorful prose.

FYI: New World readers will happily note that 26 of his selections lie in North America, and include nearly all of the household names. Also, photos are strictly black and white, and rather limited.

$40

Following the Fairways • *Nick Edmund (Editor)*
Kensington West, London (annual publication since 1986)

Though undeniably a commercialized affair, *Following the Fairways* remains a very fine annual, reading more like an independent book than an annual tour guide. Covering all of Great Britain and Ireland, it provides comprehensive course lists on a county-by-county basis, plus in-depth profiles and up-to-date contact information for many famous links.

Be advised that the course maps are rudimentary, other images are generally golf-oriented paintings or photos of advertising hostelries, and the copy changes little from year to year. But for a golfer traveling to Britain or Ireland, this is a tough volume to beat.

New/Under $25

Frank Pennink's Golfer's Companion • *Frank Pennink*
Cassell, London • 311pp • 1962

As a Walker Cup player, writer, and well-known golf course architect, Dutch-born Frank Pennink knew a thing or two about the finer layouts of Great Britain and Ireland. This small (but certainly not thin) volume highlights 128 of the elite, both seaside and inland, making it an ideal book to slip in one's glove compartment and travel with. Though essentially unillustrated, it remains a highly detailed work, with each course's vital specs and yardages provided, and their histories and layouts described. Naturally, 40 years' time has rendered some information (e.g., greens fees) obsolete, but if today's golfers play only the courses profiled herein, I doubt they should lose much sleep worrying about the modern omissions.

Though surprisingly difficult to find, Pennink's 1976 book, *Frank Pennink's Choice of Golf Courses,* is of a similar ilk.

$30

Golf Addict Visits the USA • *George Houghton*
Museum, London • 85pp • 1955

Joseph Murdoch has labeled George Houghton "the most prolific contributor to the library of golf," an assessment that I am not prepared to question. In fact, I only mention it here because this brief book is included principally as a representative of a body of work too large (some 30 volumes in total) to be altogether ignored.

Houghton's formula was to create a fun and amusing portrait of golf in the 1950s, visiting clubs and recounting stories of players and courses. There's no doubt that this approach—illustrated only with simple cartoons—was a successful one, though reminiscent of Darwin or Longhurst it wasn't.

Under $25

Golf, as It Was in the Beginning • *Michael Fay*
Universe, New York • 224pp • 2002

While its premise (the profiling of 18 great Open Championship holes) is hardly unique, this slickly produced volume still offers much to recommend it. The selection of holes is agreeably eclectic (the Alps in, the Road Hole out) but what really sells the book are its many added historical touches and a good deal of excellent photography.

Intelligent eye candy.

New ($40)

Golf Courses • *Getmapping*
HarperCollins, London • 128pp • 2002

Getmapping is a leading British aerial photography company whose entrepreneurial sense is aptly demonstrated by the production of this book. Only 128 pages in length it is, very simply, a collection of contemporary aerial images of 50 well-known golf courses throughout the United Kingdom. Purists may scoff at the omission of several classic layouts (apparently to make room for some much blander newer ones) and the descriptive information accompanying each image is limited at best. But oh, the quality of the photographs!

For fans of golf course aerials, an absolute must.

New ($25)

The Golf Courses of the British Isles • *Bernard Darwin*

Duckworth, London • 253pp • 1910 (w/revised 2nd edition)
1st US edition: Appleton 1911
Reprinted (as "Historic Golf Courses of the British Isles") by Duckworth (1987), Classics of Golf (1988), and others

The golfer/poet Patric Dickinson once wrote that "There is nothing new to say about St. Andrews, just as there is nothing new to say about Shakespeare," and one is sorely tempted to apply such deft phrasing in describing this, one of golf's all-time classic volumes. For really, what *is* there new to say?

Very simply, *The Golf Courses of the British Isles* is Darwin's 1910 tour of his homeland's finest layouts, written in his uniquely evocative hand. Divided into 14 chapters, it attacks this formidable task on a regional basis and includes a chapter on Ireland to go along with England, Scotland, and Wales. The text is supplemented by a now-famous set of watercolors produced by New Zealander Harry Rountree—paintings which tend to show precious little of their chosen courses but are considered an absolutely essential part of the mix by most.

Happily, the 1988 Classics of Golf reprint has made this otherwise prohibitively expensive landmark accessible to all. Sadly the 1925 second edition (retitled *The Golf Courses of Great Britain*) remains highly evasive, an unfortunate circumstance given its substantial expansions, revisions, and—in the case of the Irish chapter—deletions.

A foundation of any golfer's library.

Original: $1,400+ • 1925 Revised: $425 • Duckworth: Under $25 • COG: New ($49)

The Golf Courses of New Hampshire • *Bob Labbance and David Cornwell*

N.E. Golf Specialists, Stockbridge, VT • 183pp • 1989 (PBK)

New Hampshire is a relatively small golfing market to be sure, but I've chosen this book to represent Labbance and Cornwell's New England trilogy, which includes sister volumes *The Maine Golf Guide* and *Vermont Golf Courses*. All three are paperbacks of limited size, carry a highly localized feel, and are illustrated strictly in black and white. Yet taken as a whole, they are a wonderful collection for travelers, historians, and architecture buffs, amply covering the backgrounds of the many Golden Age layouts that remain, often unaltered, throughout the region's endless scenic reaches. Interesting extras include profiles of prominent area architects, listings of courses that no longer exist, and a variety of routing maps, some accurate, some rough.

Thorough stuff.

Under $25

Golf: New Horizons • *Gene Sarazen (with Peter McLean)*
Thomas Y. Crowell, New York • 276pp • 1966 (w/expanded 2nd edition 1968)

This famous little volume is subtitled *Pan Am's Guide to Golf Courses Round the World,* and as it surely is not among the game's elite guidebooks, its inclusion may well raise some eyebrows. I've chosen it, however, as a sentimental entry, for aside from being quite popular, it represents a romantic period in golf's international development, when jet travel was opening up new markets and Pan Am reigned supreme. Admittedly the individual course listings contain little vital information but the photos (mostly stills from *Shell's Wonderful World of Golf*), the regional descriptions, and the endpapers sporting Pan Am's worldwide route map make this a small but tasty piece of golfing history.

Under $25

Great Australian Golf Courses • *Tom Ramsey*
Weldon, Sydney • 384pp • 1990

Where *Discover Australia's Golf Courses* (see above) represents a comprehensive survey, *Great Australian Golf Courses* serves instead to highlight the very best. Featuring 48 elite layouts from Down Under, this lavish work provides a wealth of historical and design information for each facility, as well as countless color photos that serve to capture nicely the vast and varied Australian landscape. The courses are arranged alphabetically, with profiles generally running between six and 12 pages, and it is doubtful that the reader will find any genuinely important club missing.

For the more deeply interested, Ramsey also wrote 1981's *25 Great Australian Golf Courses*, another well-illustrated volume which includes shot-by-shot advice for every hole.

$30

Great Donald Ross Golf Courses You Can Play •
Paul Dunn and B.J. Dunn
Derrydale, Lanham, MD • 279pp • 2001

This modern, oversized volume profiles over 100 public or public-access courses in 18 states, all believed (at least at press time) to have been designed by the prolific Donald Ross. Though executed on a distinctly grander scale, it essentially follows the pattern of Labbance and Cornwell's three New England books, providing a great sense of each facility's historical and architectural background in addition to simply highlighting current holes. Not surprisingly, Ross's "home" states of Massachusetts, North Carolina, and Florida are the best represented here, and the inclusion of places like French Lick, George Wright, Seaview, the Sagamore, and, of course, Pinehurst makes for valuable reading.

We must note, however, that of Ross's genuinely elite designs, only Pinehurst isn't private, meaning that the vast majority of his top-shelf work must be studied elsewhere.

New ($50)

Great Golf Courses of Canada • *John Gordon*
McGraw-Hill Ryerson, Toronto • 237pp • 1991 (w/1993 rev. 2nd edition) (PBKs)

One of the better books of its type, this large volume features 38 Canadian courses from Nova Scotia to British Columbia, as profiled by one of the nation's leading golf writers. Gordon's text carries an historical flavor while also profiling each course's best holes but, as with most such coffee-table books, it is the graphics that grab one's attention. Multiple photos appear for each layout along with a color routing map of reasonable quality, allowing the flavor of each facility to be captured in no small measure.

It is well worth mentioning that the 1993 second edition was revised to an uncommon degree, with 22 of the original 38 courses being replaced with newer selections. It makes for an interesting choice between classic and modern design, and results in what very nearly might be considered two separate volumes.

Under $25 (both editions)

Great Golf Courses of Ireland • *John Redmond*
Gill & Macmillan, Dublin • 164pp • 1999

Though perhaps not as grand as some regional "Great Golf Course" volumes—and certainly nothing like Larry Lamprecht's dazzling *Emerald Gems*—this engaging book features 35 of Ireland's finest as profiled by noted writer John Redmond. The photos are solid but more importantly, each course comes complete with scorecard, routing map, and a healthy measure of odds and ends regarding club traditions, trophies, players, and the like.

A tight, informative work.

New ($40)

Great Golf Courses of the World • *William H. Davis, etc.*
Golf Digest, Norwalk, CT • 278pp • 1974

More than a quarter-century after its publication it is interesting to reflect on what a groundbreaking volume this was, for rather amazingly, no previous American book had ever profiled a large number of elite courses so graphically. Though plainly trumped by subsequent works, this old favorite highlights 22 American and seven British courses in some detail before surveying the rest of world in a more general, but highly colorful, manner.

Several interesting extras are offered including frequently reproduced maps of Augusta National, St. Andrews, Pine Valley, Pebble Beach, and Cypress Point, an annotated 900-course "Where to Play" section, and the unquestioned highlight, Herbert Warren Wind's 15-page essay profiling the great architects of the Golden Age.

Under $25

Guide to Southern African Golf Courses • *Grant Winter*
Struik, Cape Town • 278pp • 1996 (PBK)

A softcover-only regional guidebook, the *Guide to Southern African Golf Courses* profiles 111 choice layouts in South Africa, Namibia, Botswana, Zimbabwe, Zambia, and Swaziland. Each is written of at some length and the volume is nicely illustrated with maps and lots of color photos. This is a satisfying, useful, and relatively inexpensive edition, though it can be most difficult to find in the United States or Europe.
$30

Historic Golf Courses of America • *Pat Seelig*
Taylor, Dallas • 192pp • 1994

This rather unique volume is built around the premise of a National Historic Register for golf, a concept that might send certain high-profile modern architects who call themselves "restorationists" running for the door. The book features 50 layouts of obvious historic importance, the choices being fairly straightforward save for a handful of interesting wildcards (e.g., Van Cortlandt Park and the TPC Sawgrass). The profiles are relatively brief and the illustrations—both old and new—are of a decidedly mixed variety.

There's little doubt that most of these courses have been covered in far greater depth elsewhere, but the purpose and tone of this volume make it palpably worthwhile nonetheless.
Under $25

Legendary Golf Clubs of Scotland, England, Wales & Ireland • *John de St. Jorre*
Edgeworth, Wellington, FL • 312pp • 1998

This lush and expansive effort is somewhat unique in modern golf literature, for it is not a study of legendary courses per se but rather legendary clubs, profiling memberships, artifacts, traditions, and general ambience at 12 highly noteworthy facilities. Though predictably one sees little of the golf courses, the book succeeds admirably in providing a glimpse of an affluent, yet not particularly overbearing way of life that dates back to the days of Queen Victoria. For the record, the featured clubs are the R&A, Prestwick, Royal Liverpool, Royal St. George's, Rye, Sunningdale, Swinley Forest, Royal Worlington & Newmarket, Royal West Norfolk, Royal Porthcawl, Royal County Down, and Portmarnock.

Equally for the record, though it is difficult to imagine comparable American clubs—who often confuse overbearing exclusivity with greatness—providing such intimate access, a sequel, *Legendary Golf Clubs of the American East,* was published in late 2003.

New ($65)

Play the Best Courses: Great Golf in the British Isles •
Peter Allen
Stanley Paul, London • 264pp • 1973 (w/PBK)

When reading Allen's *Famous Fairways* (see above), one cannot help thinking that any Englishman who'd played so many great courses abroad must surely have experienced a good deal more than the 50 or so British layouts profiled therein. Sure enough, written five years after *Famous Fairways, Play the Best Courses* proves that hunch to be entirely accurate.

For in this somewhat longer volume, Allen weaves his descriptive magic over 104 famous courses in the UK and Ireland, painting each from the perspective of a good (but not great) amateur player. Once again, it is his overwhelming love and knowledge of the game that shine through, allowing for uncommonly vivid descriptions of so many hallowed playgrounds, often laced with real historical and literary perspective.

Illustrations are once again sporadic but well-chosen, and this time the occasional color shot does appear. Note: there is a bit of duplicate material relative to *Famous Fairways,* though hardly enough to really matter.

$30

Round in Sixty-Eight • *Henry Longhurst*
Werner Laurie, London • 174pp • 1953

We must concede up front that this delightful volume is far more about travel than golf, the title referring to a 68-day trip around the world and not a career-best round. The trip does begin golfingly enough, however, with Longhurst's coverage of the 1951 Ryder Cup matches at Pinehurst.

But from there it's on to San Francisco, Hawaii, New Zealand, Australia, and Ceylon (Sri Lanka), occasionally teeing it up but mostly viewing a remarkable collection of people and places through Henry's famously British eyes.

For those who enjoy *Round in Sixty-Eight*, 1949's *You Never Know Till You Get There* is of a similar ilk, covering trips to the Middle East, Asia, Hong Kong, Northern Africa, and the Bahamas.

$40

A Round of Golf Courses • *Patric Dickinson*
Evans Brothers, London • 159pp • 1951 (w/1990 PBK)

Patric Dickinson was a poet and, by reputation, a bit of an eccentric. But he was also a golfer (the positions hardly being at odds) and, having played at Cambridge, evidently a fairly good one. Most importantly for us, however, he was a superb writer—and the observant reader will note that "superb" is not a word I have thrown about too loosely.

The premise of this volume is simple: These are descriptions, essentially hole by hole, of 18 famous British courses, with a few photos, scorecards, and rudimentary hole sketches or routing maps thrown in. What makes it sing is Dickinson's remarkable skill with the English language, for his ability to describe familiar subjects in wholly new ways, and to convey the particular ambience of distant places, is genuinely impressive. As Bernard Darwin writes reverently in his foreword, "I feel rather like the man who admired Shakespeare: 'Things come into his head that would never come into mine'."

Truly a joy to read, *A Round of Golf Courses* disappoints only in whetting our appetites for a golf-writing career that never was. For rather inexplicably, this was the frequently published Dickinson's only book on the Royal & Ancient game.

$65

The Sandbelt: Melbourne's Golfing Heaven • *Paul Daley and David Scaletti*
Plus Four, Victoria • 140pp • 2001

Though Daley, Nick Faldo, Ian Baker-Finch, and Tom Doak lead a small cast of brief essay contributors, this beautiful effort is, without question, a picture book. Indeed Scaletti's many images of such classics as Royal Melbourne, Kingston Heath, Huntingdale, Yarra Yarra, etc. are enough to make any golfing foreigner consider making the interminably long flight.

No scorecards, routing maps, hole-by-hole descriptions, or greens fee information here. Just page after page of large color photos, the crispness of which provide an almost visceral sense of the unique golfing experience that is the Sandbelt.

New ($65)

The Scottish Golf Book • *Malcolm Campbell*
Sports Publishing, Chicago • 224pp • 1999

Similar in style to John Redmond's *The Book of Irish Golf,* this colorful volume serves as both a history book and travel guide to the game's ancestral home. It opens with a suitably detailed recounting of golf's beginnings, then profiles great Scottish players from Allan Robertson to the present. What comes next is the heart of the deal, three attractive chapters entitled "Scotland's Historic Courses" (eight in total), "Scotland's Classic Courses" (16), and "Scotland's Hidden Gems" (24), all of which are well illustrated, historical, and informative. Finally, we have detailed profiles of nine of Scotland's toughest holes, a chapter highlighting great championship events, and a meticulous chronology dating back to 1457.

One may find individual areas of this book covered in greater depth elsewhere but taken as a whole, this is an agreeable effort.

New ($35)

A Season in Dornoch • *Lorne Rubenstein*
Simon & Schuster, New York • 242pp • 2001 (w/PBK)

The subtitle of this innovative entry is "Golf and Life in the Scottish Highlands," which right away suggests something a bit out of the ordinary. Chronicling a summer spent by Rubenstein and his wife in the remote North Sea town that gave us, among other things, Donald Ross, it isn't so much about playing the celebrated links as it is the game's role in everyday Scottish life. There is lots of history and local lore here but it's fed to us pleasantly, within the natural flow of the narrative. In fact, *A Season in Dornoch*'s greatest charm might be that it wanders through golf's homeland in a meaningful manner without ever resorting to the sort of tired clichés that one has come to expect in a volume of this type.

Particularly for those suffering the modern, hyper-commercialized American golf industry, this is a refreshing reminder of the game's time-honored values in the very land that spawned it.

New ($23)

South African Golf Courses: A Portrait of the Best •
Stuart McLean
Struik, Cape Town • 144pp • 1993

Where Grant Winters' *Guide to Southern African Golf Courses* (see above) covers the big picture, this highly attractive volume profiles 25 of South Africa's finest clubs in much greater detail. Each course is examined both historically and on a hole-by-hole basis, and reasonably accurate color routing maps are included. What makes this title so special, however, are its pictures, a really gorgeous collection that serves admirably to illustrate the stunning beauty of the great South African landscape.

Though well worth acquiring, this already-rare title is seldom found very far from the Cape.

$45

South East Asia Golf Guide • *Alan Clarke and*
Neil Ffrench-Blake (Editors)
Priory, Brackley, England • 143pp • 1995 (PBK)
1st US edition: Pelican 1996

This small but thorough work is one of the few paperback-only editions to make our list, a surefire indication that no comparable hardcover book has yet been written. A highly functional guide to golf in Indonesia, Malaysia, the Philippines, Singapore, and Thailand, it features comprehensive lists of each country's courses and individual profiles of the region's 250 best. These write-ups are short but detailed, and are heavily illustrated with color photos and area maps.

Ideal for the traveler, as hotel and sightseeing prospects are included.

Under $25

Sports Illustrated's the Best 18 Golf Holes in America •
Dan Jenkins
Delacorte, New York • 160pp • 1966

This was Dan Jenkins's first-ever book, its genesis being a two-part *Sports Illustrated* article in which the chosen 18 holes were selected. As such it may not sound like the sort of material that makes for a full-fledged volume (especially for those who might disagree with several of the stranger selections) but Jenkins makes it so by profiling far more than just the golf holes themselves. His insightful forays into places like Merion, Pine Valley, and Seminole are in fact fairly unique, and go a long way toward making this oversized entry decidedly worthwhile.
Under $25

The Sunley Book of Royal Golf • *Sir Peter Allen*
Stanley Paul, London • 160pp • 1989

The last of Sir Peter's three books on golf (we note that his OBE finally makes the masthead here), this somewhat smaller volume profiles the various clubs that have received Great Britain's "Royal" designation, both at home and abroad, over some 150+ years. Though this might not strike some as vital reading, the histories of these far-flung courses are generally quite interesting, as is the longstanding connection between royalty and golf. And then there is Allen's writing, which remains, here as always, among the very best.
Under $25

Town & Country Book of Golf • *Richard Miller*
Taylor, Dallas • 216pp • 1992

Town & Country magazine was covering the game of golf in America well before the turn of the last century, making this volume's essential mission—the profiling of five of the magazine's time-honored society "golf capitals"—particularly fitting. The chosen locales (the Hamptons, the Carolina Sandhills, Palm Beach, Palm Springs, and Pebble Beach) will appeal to any golfer, as will the book's access to some highly private golfing grounds. Where else, for example, might the reader visit

Maidstone, Seminole, and the late Walter Annenberg's private estate course under a single cover?
Under $25

The World Atlas of Golf •
Pat Ward-Thomas, etc.
Mitchell Beazley, London • 280pp • 1976
(w/editions through 2002)
1st US edition: Random House 1976

Among volumes profiling the world's greatest courses, there can be nothing to compare with *The World Atlas of Golf,* which has recently embarked on its fifth edition at the time of this writing. One attraction of this book is its scope, covering, as it does, some 170+ courses on six continents and 43 countries. Another is its obvious beauty, particularly the full-color aerial-view paintings of 70 featured layouts. But above all, this classic stands out for the quality of its writing—no great surprise with a roster of Ward-Thomas, Herbert Warren Wind, Charles Price, and Peter Thomson, and a foreword by Alistair Cooke.

Though including several modern courses of dubious quality, *The World Atlas* covers nearly all the genuine greats in admirable, if not unparalleled, detail. Subsequent volumes have updated numerous photographs and yardages, and the inclusion of contemporary sidebars keeps the book relevant to recent tournament play. Yet through it all, the basic text, authored nearly 30 years ago by some blue-chip talents, essentially remains faithful to the first edition.

Alas, *The World Atlas* is certainly not perfect; several of the newer aerial paintings don't match the style of their predecessors, multiple maps in the large Gazetteer section are badly flawed, and the occasional historical inaccuracy has been discovered over time. But no real golfer's collection can afford not to have at least one of these editions, and I suspect that a good many may include two or three.

Original: Under $25 • Recent Editions: New ($25)

The World Atlas of Golf Courses • *Bob Ferrier*
Hamlyn, London • 208pp • 1990 (w/1991 2nd edition)
1st US edition: Mallard 1990

Judged on its own merit, *The World Atlas of Golf Courses* is an attractive and worthwhile volume, profiling 66 of the planet's finest layouts in words, maps, and pictures. Its problem, of course, is that in its selection of courses, style, and even a title, it has made itself rather a poor man's copy of the above-listed *World Atlas of Golf*. Indeed, not one of the 66 selected courses fails to appear in Pat Ward-Thomas & Company's enduring classic, whose maps, layout, and writing quality are substantially grander. If money or shelf space is an issue, it makes for an easy choice.
Under $25

The World's Best Golf • *William H. Davis*
Pocket Books/Golf Digest, New York • 312pp • 1991

The third of *Golf Digest* founder Davis's books highlighting the world's best courses follows the successful formula of its predecessors (see *Great Golf Courses of the World* and *100 Greatest Golf Courses—and Then Some*) pretty closely. Though lacking most of their interesting sidebar features, it does offer a higher level of photography, some concise thumbnail descriptions, and a large coffee-table presence.

Far from essential, but undeniably colorful.
Under $25

SECTION VII
INSTRUCTION

Far—and I mean *far*—more books have been written about instruction than any other area of golf. The catch, of course, is that most come from writers we've never heard of, and offer either little new material or something too over-the-top to be taken seriously. In fact *The Golfer's Library* probably awaits a sister volume profiling 400 of the most "interesting" instructional books of all time, though I certainly won't be the one writing it.

In any event, my own approach to the instructional genre is simple. Those time-honored books hailed as classics naturally are included, as are a handful of avant-garde or cult favorites and several volumes written by acknowledged giants of the teaching profession. Beyond this, however, I, like most golfers, am particularly interested in the methods employed by the game's greatest players, past and present. Therefore, included here are all manner of works penned by or about the game's elite, detailing styles, techniques, and swing theories, essentially from the time of Harry Vardon forward.

I find impressive the degree to which so many of these volumes (even the older ones) continue to be reprinted, reminding us yet again of how consistently instruction books sell—and sell, and sell.

All About Putting • *Golf Digest*
Golf Digest, New York • 191pp • 1973
1st UK edition: Kaye & Ward 1973

As the title says . . .
This book is essentially a compilation of material from *Golf Digest* dedicated solely to putting. Broken into four sections ("The Great Putters," "Proven Principles of the Great Putters," "Special Putting Techniques," and "Practice, Rules and Equipment"), it features all manner of analysis, tips, and techniques.
A popular and well-rounded work.
Under $25

Bobby Jones on Golf • *Robert Tyre (Bobby) Jones*
Doubleday, New York • 246pp • 1966 (w/PBKs)
1st UK edition: Cassell 1968
Reprinted by Golf Digest Classics (several editions)

This was the last full-size golf book that Jones wrote, though in reality its contents largely were culled from numerous magazine and newspaper pieces that he authored before 1935. As the title suggests, it is a volume wide in scope, covering virtually every aspect of playing the game over 15 chapters, each of which is further subdivided into multiple subsections.
As Jones's other important books, *Golf Is My Game* and *Down the Fairway*, are only partially dedicated to instruction, this (along with 1969's brief *Bobby Jones on the Basic Golf Swing*) represents the best how-to material authored by one of the game's all-time legends. As Charles Price reminds us in his foreword, "there is no more rewarding reading in the whole library of golf."
Original: $65 • Golf Digest: Under $25

Bobby Jones on the Basic Golf Swing • *Bobby Jones*
(with Anthony Ravielli)
Doubleday, Garden City • 63pp • 1969
Reprinted by Classics of Golf (1990)

Though some may argue that this diminutive volume is really just an elaborate retread, it is, in many ways, one of golf's more innovative efforts. The project was the brainchild of Anthony Ravielli, scratchboard artist extraordinaire who first came to the attention of golfers by illustrating Ben Hogan's seminal *The Modern Fundamentals of Golf* in 1957. Here, Ravielli created similarly detailed drawings to complement what is essentially a paired-down version of *Bobby Jones on Golf,* with Jones himself having done much of the editing.

Divided into 10 chapters covering the entire swing, *The Basic Golf Swing* obviously adds little to what Jones had previously told us—but it certainly manages to *show* us things in an entirely new and attractive light.

Original: $50 • COG: New ($33)

Bobby Locke on Golf • *Bobby Locke*
Country Life, London • 196pp • 1953
1st US edition: Simon & Schuster 1954

Like such early classics as *Taylor on Golf* and Vardon's *The Complete Golfer, Bobby Locke on Golf* is a book more encyclopedic in scope than purely instructive. It is divided into four sections: "My Golfing Life," "How I Play Golf," "The Psychology of Golf," and "Courses and Players." The instructive component, though perhaps faintly outdated, is thorough—and probably worthwhile simply for Locke's thoughts on putting, his universally acknowledged forte. "Courses and Players" includes detailed descriptions of the four-time Open Champion's favorite 18 holes, his impressions of courses worldwide, and his choices for the world's best player with each club (putter: Ben Hogan!).

They don't write 'em like this anymore.

$65

Building and Improving Your Golf Mind, Golf Body, Golf Swing • *Michael Hebron*
Smithtown Landing CC, Smithtown, NY • 420pp • 1993 (PBK)

Something of a cult favorite, this enormous volume was written and compiled over many years by longtime PGA pro Mike Hebron, author of *See and Feel the Inside Move the Outside, Golf Swing Secrets and Lies,* and *The Art and Zen of Learning Golf.* Essentially it is a complete teaching manual, covering the mental and physical components of a sound, repeating golf swing, from beginning to end. Though hardly built for casual readers, it does feature hundreds of photos and diagrams (many depicting the game's all-time greats) as well as a vast amount of ancillary material on physical and mental preparation.

Though hardly on the order of *The Golfing Machine* (see below), this comprehensive book must surely be referred to in doses.

Still findable new, mostly via the Internet.

New ($35)

Bunker Play • *Gary Player (with Mike Wade)*
Broadway, New York • 160pp • 1996

As the Black Knight may well be the finest bunker player of all time, who better to author this thorough and well-illustrated treatise on escaping the sand? This volume was billed as a part of something called "The Golf Masters Series" though as far as I can ascertain, only one other entry, Seve Ballesteros's *Trouble-Shooting*, ever came to fruition.

Under $25

The Complete Short Game • *Ernie Els (with Steve Newell)*
Broadway, New York • 144pp • 1998

Coming two years after its sister volume on the full swing (see *How to Build a Classic Golf Swing*, below), *The Complete Short Game* is an attractive and easy-to-read book covering the entire arsenal of shots around the greens. I'm not certain that this is the best among contemporary short game books but paired with its excellent sibling, it makes for an impressive overall blueprint on how to play the game.

New ($28)

Dave Pelz's Putting Bible • *Dave Pelz (with James A. Frank)*
Doubleday, New York • 394pp • 2000
1st UK edition: Aurum 2000

A former NASA physicist, Dave Pelz is contemporary golf's unquestioned guru of the short game, developing its study to an unprecedented degree by mixing scientific application with technique, practice regimen, and common sense. This comprehensive volume might well be considered putting's "Good Book," covering every element of the subject that you've ever considered, and plenty more that you haven't.

Rather dry, somewhat technical, and absolutely essential.
New ($30)

Dave Pelz's Short Game Bible • *Dave Pelz*
(with James A. Frank)
Broadway, New York • 429pp • 1999

See the above listing, substituting "short game" for "putting."
Equally essential.
New ($30)

The Elements of Scoring • *Ray Floyd (with Jaime Diaz)*
Simon & Schuster, New York • 173pp • 1998

Early in chapter one Floyd writes: "If somehow I was given your physical game, and we had a match, I would beat you 99 times out of 100. Because I know how to play the game better than you do."

Thus this is a volume concerned not with method, style, or distance, but simply with how to use one's brains and skills to get the ball in the hole in the fewest number of strokes. Probably more important to the average golfer than any two books on technique.
Under $25

Faldo: A Swing for Life • *Nick Faldo*
(with Richard Simmons)
Viking Penguin, New York • 224pp • 1995 (w/PBKs)
First UK edition: Weidenfeld & Nicholson 1995

Skeptics will say that to learn Nick Faldo's swing, one need only study the various writings of David Leadbetter. Such claims may have some truth to them, I suppose, but to miss out on the many personal aspects presented here by one of the most precise ball-strikers ever to play would be a shame. This volume is thorough, covering every aspect of the long and short games, plus a good deal of mental ground. Chapter five, "Working the Ball," will be of particular interest to more capable players.

Under $25

Five Lessons: The Modern Fundamentals of Golf • *Ben Hogan (with Herbert Warren Wind)*
A.S. Barnes, New York • 127pp • 1957 (w/countless reprints & editions, some PBK)
1st UK edition ("The Modern Fundamentals of Golf"): Kaye & Ward 1957

Arguably the landmark golf instruction book of all time, *The Modern Fundamentals of Golf* first appeared as a series of articles in *Sports Illustrated*, with Hogan's words converted to prose by Herbert Warren Wind, and accompanying drawings prepared by artist Anthony Ravielli. Following an introductory section entitled "The Fundamentals," each original "lesson" becomes its own chapter: "The Grip," "Stance and Posture," "The First Part of the Swing," "The Second Part of the Swing," and "Summary and Review."

Rather than wax lyrically with several lines of superlatives, suffice it to say that nearly all of the Hogan theory one has heard over the last half-century—grip, swing plane, hips initiating the downswing, supination, and so on—emanate from this volume. I doubt if any instructional book has ever been studied more.

Original: $60 (but still available new: $24)

From 60 Yards In • *Ray Floyd and Larry Dennis*
Harper & Row, New York • 172pp • 1989 (w/PBK)

Ray Floyd's credentials as a "scorer" are renowned, and this crafty little book leads one through the areas of golf where so very many strokes are shaved. Floyd opens with his belief that today's stars aren't nearly the shotmakers of yesteryear but boast superior short games, then presents a thorough course on every aspect of pitching, chipping, and putting.

A well-conceived and valuable volume.

Under $25

The Fundamentals of Hogan • *David Leadbetter*
(with Lorne Rubenstein)
Sleeping Bear and Doubleday, New York • 133pp • 2000

Leadbetter analyzes Hogan, utilizing recently discovered photos originally taken during the preparation of the latter's *The Modern Fundamentals of Golf*. It is true, I suppose, that one might be more interested in Hogan's thoughts on Hogan's swing than the musings of an outsider. But anytime one of the game's elite teachers spends 100+ pages breaking down the game's all-time most studied swing, how can we not be interested?

New ($28)

Getting Up and Down • *Tom Watson (with Nick Seitz)*
Random House, New York • 192pp • 1983 (w/PBKs)
1st UK edition: Hodder & Stoughton 1983

Once upon a time Tom Watson got the ball up and down as well as any man alive, knee-knockers included. This volume covers all aspects of the short game, beginning with detailed sections titled "Putting," "Chipping and Pitching," and "Sand." Further segments on practicing and the selection of equipment are also useful but, in many ways, the most interesting is a final chapter called "Putting Theory into Play." Here Watson takes us through his final nine holes at the 1982 U.S. Open, wherein four greens were missed but the short game (and a solid dose of course management) saved the day.

A very popular work.

Under $25

Golf • *Henry Longhurst*
J.M. Dent, London • 335pp • 1937
1st US edition: Davis McKay 1937
Reprinted by the Sportsman's Book Club (1949)

Bernard Darwin once wrote of this book that, "Longhurst has achieved that which is extremely rare by combining instruction with amusement," and Henry Cotton called it, "A veritable encyclopaedia." So the early reviews, one might conclude, were decidedly favorable.

This is, in fact, an instruction book composed not by a great champion but rather by a golf writer, though we must recall that Longhurst did captain the squad at Cambridge and thus was somewhat accomplished as a player. More importantly, he understood the game, its quirks, and its absurdities as well as anyone—though whether that translates into helping the average player actually improve by reading this book is anybody's guess.

Original: $40 • Sportsman's: $40

Golf from Two Sides •
Roger and Joyce Wethered
Longmans, Green London • 197pp • 1922 (w/revised 1925 edition)

Offering few of the career reminiscences inherent to *Golfing Memories and Methods*, this unique 1922 volume is primarily instructive, with an obvious accent on gender differences. Indeed, eight of 12 chapters deal with issues of style and technique, though Roger chips in three more diverse sections (including his thoughts on golf in America) toward the close.

It might be argued that this book is really more a novelty than a necessity, but to do so, I think, is to vastly underestimate the stature and importance of these terribly talented siblings in prewar British golf.

$115

Golf Fundamentals: Orthodoxy of Style • *Seymour Dunn*
Privately printed, Lake Placid, NY • 283pp • 1922
Reprinted (as "Golf Fundamentals") by Golf Digest (1977 & 1988)

Aside from being both a teacher and player of great repute, Seymour Dunn came from the purest of golfing bloodlines: Willie Dunn Sr. was his grandfather while his mother came from the famous Gourlays of Musselburgh. Having come to America to make his fortune, Dunn penned this early classic in 1922, dividing it into four sections. The first is called "Mechanical Laws of the Golf Swing," the second "Dynamic Laws of the Golf Stroke." "Golf Psychology" comes next, followed by an untitled final segment dedicated to situational shotmaking.

Considered a standard in its time, inexpensive reprints of *Golf Fundamentals* are readily available today.

Original: $225 • Golf Digest: Under $25

The Golfing Machine • *Homer Kelley*
Star System, Seattle • 241pp • 1969

This is, by acclamation, the most complicated book of golf instruction ever written—but might it also be the best? Addressing the swing in terms of angles, force vectors, and the like, it requires a college-level physics background just to digest such things as "dual horizontal hinge action," the "Catalogue of Basic Component Variations," and assembly of the elusive "Power Package."

Those few who have mastered it, however, generally call it the gospel, and its most famous proponent, the young Bobby Clampett, really was a remarkable advertisement. Still, beyond the technical jargon, I shall more remember a long-hitting pro for whom I once worked belting drives over the horizon, then mumbling that "the power package was fully assembled" as he strode confidently from the tee.

$65

Golfing Memories and Methods • *Joyce Wethered*
Hutchinson, London • 255pp • 1933
Reprinted by Sportsman's Book Club (1951) and Classics of Golf (2000)

Bobby Jones once called Joyce Wethered the finest golfer—male or female—that he had ever played with, automatically making this combination autobiography/instruction book well worth our attention. The opening six chapters recount Ms. Wethered's life story, no dull read given both the family she grew up in and the four British Women's Championships she won during the 1920s. From then on, the book becomes tutorial, save for several late chapters on prominent events and Scottish courses.

In the preface Wethered writes that with regard to technique, "I am not speaking about 'ladies' golf,' because, strictly speaking, there is no such thing as ladies' golf at all—only good or bad golf as played by members of either sex."

So there.

Original: $120 • Sportsman's: $35 • COG: New ($29)

Golf My Way • *Jack Nicklaus (with Ken Bowden)*
Simon & Schuster, New York • 264pp • 1974 (w/PBKs)
1st UK edition: Wm. Heinemann 1974 (w/PBKs)

It is difficult to keep track of all the instructional books sporting Jack Nicklaus's name, but I think that most would consider *Golf My Way* to be the closest to definitive. Written during one of Jack's several golfing primes, it is broken into three sections: "Beliefs and Attitudes," "Down the Fairway," and "Around and on the Green." Within these, a total of 22 chapters lay out Jack's overall approach, and while there's little here that's truly groundbreaking, how can one possibly have a golf library without the Golden Bear's thoughts on the swing?

Under $25

The Golf Swing • *David Leadbetter (with John Huggan)*
Stephen Greene, Lexington, MA • 143pp • 1990
1st UK edition: William Collins Sons (1990)
Reprinted by Dutton (2001)

This was the first of Leadbetter's instructional books and even now represents the most undiluted collection of his thoughts on the ideal swing. Most interesting, I think, is that few (if any) "new" ideas appear here—proving, perhaps, that the best golf teachers possess more in the way of great diagnostic and communicative skills than innovative swing thoughts.

With Nick Faldo and Nick Price at the top of Leadbetter's resumé, it is interesting to note that the player pictured in the book's drawings appears to be David Frost.

Under $25

The Golf Swing • *Cary Middlecoff*
Prentice-Hall, Englewood Cliffs, NJ • 230pp • 1974
1st UK edition: Robert Hale 1974
Reprinted by Burford Books (1999 PBK)

One of the more overlooked volumes in the instruction library, *The Golf Swing* first gets our attention for its detailed breakdowns of the swings of Vardon, Jones, Hogan, Snead, Nelson, Armour, Nicklaus, Player, Palmer, and Littler. But even more interesting, I think, are Dr. Middlecoff's dissections of what these same men have themselves written about the swing, his comparisons of their differences, and his debunking of a few of their apparent contradictions.

A neat and decidedly unsung book.

Under $25

Harvey Penick's Little Red Book •
Harvey Penick
Simon & Schuster, New York • 175pp •
1992 (w/PBKs)

As a jumping-off point for one of the most popular series of instructional volumes ever published, the *Little Red Book* is a collection of ideas recorded over the years (in *his* little red book) by renowned Texas teaching pro Harvey Penick. Nearly 90 entries are presented here, some as short as a paragraph, others running several pages. Beyond simple instruction, two of the longer "chapters" offer Penick's comments on the great players, male and female, that he has known, which serves as an interesting diversion from the instruction.

Multiple volumes (in a variety of colors) have followed, proving that Penick's simple, down-to-earth style makes for highly agreeable reading.

Under $25

How I Play Golf • *Tiger Woods*
Warner, New York • 320pp • 2001

As early as it is in an already stunning career, there very well may come a better instructional book authored by Eldrick "Tiger" Woods—but for the time being, *How I Play Golf* isn't too bad a start. Profusely illustrated and laudably thorough, it covers every aspect of the game including the mental side, the one area where every golfer enjoys at least the *potential* to keep up with Tiger. Few are physically capable of matching the rest of Woods's arsenal, of course, but at least there's a lot here to build on.

New ($19)

How to Build a Classic Golf Swing • *Ernie Els*
(with Steve Newell)
HarperCollins, New York • 144pp • 1996 (w/PBK)

Beyond simply showcasing the prettiest swing in contemporary golf, this detailed yet easy-to-digest volume is an excellent primer on golf's long game. Though the final three chapters ("Developing Your Own Best Rhythm," "How to Hit the Ball Further," and "Shaping the Ball") are of particular interest, the centerpiece is an initial 20-page swing sequence which beautifully lays out, in vivid words and pictures, the keys to a reliable modern swing. As a famous New York sportscaster used to say, "You could turn your sets off right there . . ."
New ($28)

How to Keep Your Temper on the Golf Course •
Tommy Bolt
David McKay, New York • 145pp • 1969

No golfing library would seem truly complete without this superbly named volume. Fittingly, Bolt begins by observing that "the title certainly sounds weird coming from me and could easily arouse the same lifted eyebrows that would accompany one called *How to Get Along with Your Neighbors* by Fidel Castro."
   Half instructive, half anecdotal.
   "Throw it, Tommy, throw it!"
Under $25

How to Perfect Your Golf Swing • *Jimmy Ballard*
Golf Digest, Norwalk, CT • 160pp • 1981 (w/PBKs)

Preaching his theory of "connection," Jimmy Ballard was among golf's most sought-after instructors during the late 1970s and early 1980s, working with as many top Tour pros as the Leadbetters and McLeans do today. This book, which was the holy grail to many, lays out all sorts of information regarding proper technique and misconceptions.
   Hardcover copies in particular are surprisingly difficult to find.
$85+

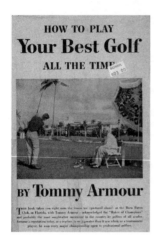

How to Play Your Best Golf All the Time • *Tommy Armour*

Simon & Schuster, New York • 151pp •
1953 (w/revised 2nd edition 1961)
1st UK edition: Hodder & Stoughton
1954
Reprinted by Classics of Golf (1984)

The original dust jacket of this volume must have one of the most appropriate cover photos ever: Armour, seated beneath his umbrella, dispensing advice to a young pupil with the palm-lined Boca Raton Club in the background.

But ambience aside, the Silver Scot was even more highly thought of as a teacher than as a player (despite winning three Major championships!) and this, the first of his three books on the subject, is widely considered his best. Armour offered little theory that was truly new or different, save one important thing: He was among the first to advocate aggressive, all-out use of the right hand in generating power.

This book reportedly sold 400,000 copies in its first year, an impressive number in any era.

Original: Under $25 • COG: New ($29)

Lessons from the Golf Greats •
David Leadbetter (with Richard Simmons)
HarperCollins, New York • 160pp • 1995

The concept of a book analyzing famous swings is hardly a new one, but I doubt if it has been done better than *Lessons from the Golf Greats*. In this full-color volume, the ubiquitous Leadbetter dissects the actions of 25 contemporary stars with eight-image side and rear sequences that are precisely in synch. Beyond these excellent pictures, he also adds a bit of biographical and swing history for each player, plus specific tips and drills that the reader can glean from each sequence. The book's only flaw, perhaps, is its limitation to modern players, for it would be most interesting to hear Leadbetter's thoughts on Vardon, Jones, Hagen, Nelson, Snead, etc.

Under $25

The Master of Putting • *George Low (with Al Barkow)*
Atheneum, New York • 84pp • 1983 (w/later PBK)

Though a bit of a cult figure compared to famous stars like Bobby Locke or Ben Crenshaw, George Low has long been acknowledged as one of the game's truly great putters. His brief but highly functional book is divided into seven chapters: "The Grip," "The Stance," "The Stroke," "Reading the Greens," "Picking a Putter," "Practice," and "The Styles of the Best." Though each section is plainly useful, the last is especially interesting for its studies of Watson, Nicklaus, Palmer, Jones, Hagen, Locke, Mangrum, Casper, Archer, and Crenshaw—an all-time A list of the greens.
Under $25

The Methods of Golf's Masters •
Dick Aultman and Ken Bowden
Coward, McCann & Geoghegan, New York • 191pp • 1975 (w/PBK)
1st UK edition (as "Masters of Golf, learning from their methods"): Stanley Paul 1976
Reprinted by Classics of Golf (1987)

Like David Leadbetter's *Lessons from the Golf Greats,* this 1975 volume provides an analysis of a number of famous golf swings, ranging chronologically from Vardon to Nicklaus. There is a fair amount of biographical information in addition to the instruction, which itself is technical but easy to digest. About the only negative is the quality of many of the older images, though for me this is at least partially offset by the detailed breakdown of the differences between Ben Hogan's early and later swings, a genuine treat which any student of technique should find especially interesting.
Original: Under $25 • COG: New ($33)

Natural Golf • *Sam Snead*
A.S. Barnes, New York • 208pp • 1953

Over his storied and seemingly endless career, Sam Snead's name appeared on not less than 15 books on golf instruction. I have chosen *Natural Golf* to represent this body of work because of its thoroughness, its timing (his career having peaked in the years just preceding its publication), and because an old professional friend who used to winter at the Boca Raton Club once told me that this was in fact Snead's personal favorite of the bunch.

The book features 11 chapters covering all aspects of the game and is illustrated with photos and diagrams. There is, of course, much to be gleaned here, though given Snead's legendary woes on the greens, chapter VII ("Putting the Natural Way") might well be avoided by beginners or the faint of heart. [Aside: Hogan, another balky putter, ignores the subject completely in *The Modern Fundamentals of Golf*, so this suggestion is not entirely tongue-in-cheek.]

$45

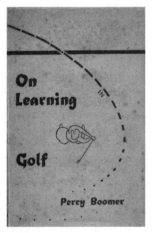

On Learning Golf • *Percy Boomer*
John Lane, London • 215pp • 1942
1st US edition: Knopf 1946
Reprinted by Classics of Golf (1988)

This old classic stands among the most detailed instruction books ever, written by one of the best-named teachers imaginable. In a novel turn, it concentrates not on the swing mechanics themselves, but rather on how to learn those mechanics, a process that Boomer ultimately breaks down to the development of feel.

Rather like *The Golfing Machine*, I'm not certain how many golfers will actually want to *read* this book, but it surely belongs in any instruction-oriented collection.

Original: $50 • COG: New ($33)

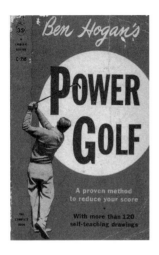

Power Golf • *Ben Hogan*

A.S. Barnes, New York • 166pp • 1948 (w/numerous reprints & editions, incl PBK)
1st UK edition: Kaye & Ward 1949

Fully nine years before he wrote *The Modern Fundamentals of Golf,* Hogan wrote the frequently overlooked *Power Golf.* The book represents a complete golfer's guide with 11 chapters ranging from "Evolution of the Hogan Grip" and "Clubs . . . Selection and Use" to "Uphill and Downhill Shots" and the closing "Now, It's Up to You." Perhaps a bit less technical than its best-selling successor, *Power Golf* features a younger, pre-accident Hogan, with body more supple and backswing well beyond parallel. Also, unlike *The Modern Fundamentals,* it utilizes photographs (which illustrate, among other things, the unbelievable flexibility of Hogan's wrists) and also includes an unabashedly sentimental dedication to golfer Henry Picard.

The *Modern Fundamentals* is the Bible for many, but for the less technically inclined, *Power Golf* might be the more enjoyable choice.

$50

Present Day Golf • *George Duncan and Bernard Darwin*

Hodder & Stoughton, London • 309pp • 1921 (w/revised 1922 2nd edition)
1st US edition: George H. Doran 1921

Duncan, the 1920 Open champion, was among the first successors to the Great Triumvirate and was generally considered among the world's elite in the years following World War I. What makes this book notable is the appearance of Darwin, whose only other instructive turns were the relatively minor *Golf: Some Hints and Suggestions*

(1920, 32pp) and *Hints on Golf* (1912, 55pp)—both small and decidedly rare today. Curiously, his association with this volume was itself rather short-lived as his chapters and name were both dropped from the revised 1922 edition. The original 1921 model, however, still remains relatively easy to find.

Original: $110 • 1922 (Darwin-less): $50

Pure Golf • *Johnny Miller (with Dale Shankland)*
Doubleday, New York • 191pp • 1976
1st UK edition: Hodder & Stoughton 1976

Like some others, this book offers little revolutionary material, and it can be reasonably argued that the average golfer is physically incapable of matching Miller's long, lanky early-1970s swing anyway. But when this volume was written, Johnny Miller was playing some of the finest golf in the game's history, making his thoughts of the period at least of historical interest if nothing else.

$35

A Round of Golf with Tommy Armour • *Tommy Armour*
Simon & Schuster, New York • 143pp • 1959
1st UK edition: Hodder& Stoughton 1960

Written several years after the immensely successful *How to Play Your Best Golf All the Time*, Armour's second instructional book takes rather a novel approach. Though several chapters on technique are interspersed, it essentially recounts a semifictional nine holes played with a semifictional average golfer, with Armour's advice on strategy, course management, and the like liberally dispensed throughout.

Astute readers will recognize the holes as a thinly-veiled version of the front nine of the West course at Winged Foot, the Silver Scot's longtime summer home.

$30

Shape Your Swing the Modern Way • *Byron Nelson*
Golf Digest, Norwalk, CT • 127pp • 1976 (w/PBK)
Reprinted by Classics of Golf (1985)

I don't suppose that many great players write instruction books fully 30 years after retiring, yet this 1976 effort by Byron Nelson is generally ranked among the best of the modern era. It actually offers very little that is new (Lord Byron having shaped *his* modern swing about four decades previous) but it does include a variety of very interesting chapters among its three primary sections: "The Modern Swing—How It All Began," "New Techniques to Correct Old Habits," and "Using Your Head to Lower Your Score."

In addition to the usual Wind foreword, Tom Watson contributes an afterword to the Classics of Golf edition, perhaps making it preferable to the original.

Original: $35 • COG: New ($29)

Shark Attack: Greg Norman's Guide to Aggressive Golf •
Greg Norman
Macmillan, Melbourne • 191pp • 1987 (w/PBKs)
Expanded American edition: Simon & Schuster 1988 (w/PBKs)

Some may argue that there's little inventive material here which, strictly speaking, might be correct. But as one of the greatest drivers of the ball ever to tee it up, Norman's long-game thoughts are of obvious relevance. The "Aggressor's Edge" and "I Dare You" sections that close each chapter might, at a glance, appear gimmicky. Then again, considering how few golfers can play an aggressive game without shooting themselves into oblivion, they might turn out to be just the thing.

Under $25

Swing Easy, Hit Hard • *Julius Boros*
Harper & Row, New York • 158pp • 1965 (w/multiple PBK editions)

This might not be the most prominent book in one's instructional section, but anyone who ever witnessed the results of Boros's syrupy, is-he-actually-awake swing knows exactly why it's here.
Under $25

Swing the Clubhead • *Ernest Jones*
Dodd, Mead, New York • 126pp • 1952

Despite losing a leg in World War I, Ernest Jones was a fine player and famous teacher whose philosophy was nicely summed up by Dr. Alister MacKenzie when he wrote: "Ernest Jones' teaching consists in three words and three words only: 'Swing club head.' He believes that if one gets a correct mental picture of swinging the club head like a weight at the end of a string the necessary body movements will automatically adjust themselves."

Enough people must have agreed; this relatively modern volume is surprisingly difficult to find.
$110+

This Game of Golf • *Henry Cotton*
Country Life, London • 248pp • 1948
1st US edition: Scribner's 1948

As professional golfers go, three-time Open champion Henry Cotton was a most prolific writer, authoring some 13 books on the game over a period of nearly 50 years. Whether or not *This Game of Golf* represents the best of the bunch, of course, is an entirely subjective thing. It is, however, almost certainly the most well-rounded, following in the Harry Vardon/J.H. Taylor tradition of omnibus works.

Of the book's five sections, Part One is autobiographical while Parts Two and Three fulfill the instructive role. Where things really get interesting, however, are Parts Four and Five. In the former, Cotton travels the world of golf, recounting favorite stories, events, and venues. In the latter, he profiles three generations of great players from Vardon to Hogan, ultimately joining Bobby Jones in calling Joyce Wethered the finest player (relative to the competition) he had ever seen.

$45

Trouble-Shooting • *Seve Ballesteros (with Robert Green)*
Broadway, New York • 174pp • 1996

Though Broadway Book's "Masters of Golf" series seems to have gone quickly by the wayside, it did leave us with two worthwhile volumes, Gary Player's *Bunker Play* and this. In the well-illustrated *Trouble-Shooting,* Ballesteros demonstrates many of the off-balance, one-handed, blindfolded sort of shots that made him famous, plus a healthy dose of basic (and helpful) uphill and downhill stuff. I'm not sure how successful this volume was but whatever the take, Seve truly earned his cut just by posing in so many hunched-over, contorted positions. Then again, he was certainly well-practiced . . .

Under $25

The Venturi Analysis • *Ken Venturi (with Al Barkow)*
Atheneum, New York • 160pp • 1981
Reprinted by Classics of Golf (1985)

Like David Leadbetter's *Lessons from the Golf Greats* (and several others), this volume is composed primarily of Venturi's breaking down the swings of 28 top stars. Its images are entirely black and white, and vary in their numbers, angles, and overall quality. However, while Leadbetter's volume may be both deeper and more visually appealing, *The Venturi Analysis* includes sequences of Hogan, Nelson, and Snead, giving it an historical component that many modern entries lack.

Original: Under $25 • COG: New ($33)

Winning Golf • *Byron Nelson*
A.S. Barnes, New York • 192pp • 1946
1st UK edition: MacDonald 1947
Reprinted by Taylor Publishing, Dallas, TX (1973)

Most observers will agree that this, Lord Byron's initial book of instruction, is somewhat less substantial than 1976's *Shape Your Swing the Modern Way* (see above). Still, I find it distinctly enjoyable as a time capsule, for the 85+ full-page photos are documenting the swing which, just months previous, had won a record 19 tournaments during a magical 1945 season.

Perhaps not indispensable, but a pleasant addition nonetheless.

Original: $45 • Taylor: Under $25

The Winning Shot • *Jerome D. Travers and Grantland Rice*
Doubleday, Garden City, NY • 258pp • 1915
1st UK edition: Werner Laurie 1915

In the preface to *The Winning Shot* the authors state that ". . . there is a great deal more to golf than any mere mechanism of form. There is also a wonderful psychology, an elastic humor, the thrill of many mighty matches and miraculous shots that add greatly to its lure." Consequently, though unquestionably a book of instruction, this volume works the edges of the field, concentrating little on mechanics but passing along numerous tips and instructive stories involving some of the game's all-time greatest players.

Though perhaps not essential, this enjoyable work remains, for its vintage, a relatively strong presence in the marketplace.

$250+

You Can Hit the Golf Ball Farther •
Evan "Big Cat" Williams (with Larry Sheehan)
Golf Digest, Norwalk, CT • 127pp • 1979 (w/PBK)

I'm not certain how many books have been produced strictly about hitting a golf ball for distance, but who better than Evan "Big Cat" Williams—the original long-driving King—to write one? This small volume covers virtually every aspect of driving for power . . . except, perhaps, how to stand 6'6".

Under $25

SECTION VIII
BIOGRAPHIES

O ur criteria here are likely the simplest of any of our genres. For much like the previous section on instruction, it is my goal to provide biographies for as many of golf's great players as have been written, dating from the first known volume (John Low's *F.G. Tait: A Record*) to those of today's top stars. In many cases these books have been authored by some of golf's finest writers, while some others have been included simply because their subject was too important a part of the game's history to omit.

One major difference from the instruction category is the infrequent reprinting of most earlier biographies, making books on many pre–World War II players a potentially expensive proposition. Newer volumes, however, tend to be easily found in all manner of places.

Allan Robertson, Golfer: His Life and Times •
Alistair Adamson
Grant, Droitwich • 90pp • 1985

As St. Andrews' Keeper of the Green, the unquestioned "Best Golfer in the World" (for a time) and the creator of the Road Hole as we know it, Allan Robertson's place on golf's mantle of legends is carved in granite. Less concrete, however, is the contemporary writer's ability to research the everyday events of a life which began roughly two centuries ago, thus explaining the relative brevity of this book.

Nicely covered is Robertson's playing record (challenge matches only, there not yet being an Open Championship) as well as his career as a topflight club and feathery ball maker. Of additional interest to the reader will be "Allan Robertson's album," a large collection of period news clippings which occupy the second half of the book.

Printed in limited edition (1,055 copies), this fine record may be a bit narrow for the general readers but it certainly fills an important hole on the shelf of the historically minded.

$50

The Autobiography of an Average Golfer • *O.B. Keeler*
Greenberg, New York • 247pp • 1925
Reprinted by Flagstick Books (1999)

With a talent far better suited to writing than teeing it up, Keeler dedicates this volume "To Bobby Jones: born to the purple of golf, as far ahead of the average golfer as ever the author was behind him, this humble memoir of stress and struggle is affectionately inscribed."

Largely overlooked, this Golden Age book represents an amusing account of Keeler's own life, with a heavy emphasis on the role that golf has played in it. It is an interesting and enjoyable read, though material directly related to Jones is at a relative minimum.

"I was not intended to be a great golfer. I was not intended to be a good golfer..."

Original: $300+ • Flagstick: New ($29)

Ben Hogan: The Man Behind the Mystique • *Martin Davis*
American Golfer, Greenwich, CT • 216pp • 2002

This attractive, oversized biopic was the third of the American Golfer series profiling legendary players of the past. It follows a pattern similar to its sister volumes on Bobby Jones and Byron Nelson (see below), beginning with essays penned by Martin Davis, Valerie Hogan (with Dave Anderson), and Dan Jenkins, plus swing analysis by Jim McLean and eyewitness tournament accounts from radio broadcaster John Derr. The "Photography and Commentary" which occupies the book's latter half includes virtually every event of importance during Hogan's playing career, as well as all manner of ephemera, news clippings, and sidebars. A complete playing record rounds out a package that, for any Hogan fan, is truly essential.

Be forewarned: Most will find it difficult to purchase one of these relatively unique American Golfer books and not be tempted to surround it with its equally stylish siblings.

New ($50)

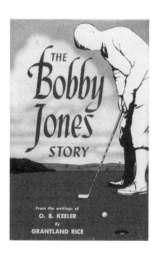

The Bobby Jones Story •
Grantland Rice
Tupper & Love, Atlanta • 303pp • 1953
1st UK edition: W. Foulsham 1953
Reprinted by Old Golf Shop (1980) and Triumph (2003)

I'm not sure how many biographies of Bobby Jones a golfer's library requires, and on the whole this might well be considered the least essential of one's choices, but . . .

The Bobby Jones Story represents the effort of the great Grantland Rice, collecting and editing the contemporary writings of Jones's talented sidekick O.B. Keeler. The source is remarkably primary, the literary hands considerably gifted. Thus while you may not absolutely *need* this volume, what golfer isn't going to want it?

The 1953 editions remain easy to find but at widely varying prices—a question rendered moot by Triumph's mass-market 2003 reprint.

Original: $200 • Old Golf (300 copies): $175 • Triumph: New ($20)

The Boy's Life of Bobby Jones • *O.B. Keeler*
Harper's, New York • 308pp • 1931
Reprinted by Sleeping Bear (2002) and Ann Arbor Media Group
(2004)

Down the Fairway, the collaborative effort of Bobby Jones and O.B.
Keeler, is generally held up as *the* Bobby Jones biography, and from a
purely literary perspective, this may be rightly so. But *Down the Fairway*
was published in 1927, three years before Jones won the Grand Slam,
leaving it fundamentally lacking as a complete career retrospective.

Enter *The Boy's Life,* written entirely by Keeler in the aftermath of
the "Impregnable Quadrilateral," following the Immortal Bobby's retirement. The epic story, of course, we are all familiar with. But of the
author's perspective Keeler wrote: "I saw much of his game. I attended
twenty-seven major, or national, championships with him and numerous lesser events. I traveled with him 120,000 miles. And I am the only
person in the world who saw him win all thirteen of his major titles."

Definitely a primary source.

Original: $300 • Sleeping Bear: New ($35) • AAMG: New ($18)

Byron Nelson: The Story of Golf's Finest Gentleman and the Greatest Winning Streak in History • *Martin Davis*
American Golfer, Greenwich, CT • 160pp • 1997

The second of Martin Davis's American Golfer series, *Byron Nelson*
opens with a foreword by fellow Texan Ben Crenshaw, then moves into
essays by Tom Watson, Dan Jenkins, Dave Anderson, and Nick Seitz,
plus an analysis of Lord Byron's swing by his friend and protégé Ken
Venturi. For its "Photography and Commentary" segment it focuses upon
Nelson's five Major championship victories and, of course, his legendary 11-event winning streak of 1945, which is profiled in great depth,
event-by-event.

Like its sisters, a highly attractive volume.

New: ($60)

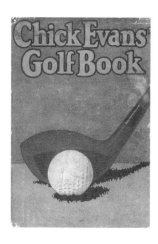

Chick Evans' Golf Book •
Charles "Chick" Evans Jr.
Thos. E. Wilson, Chicago • 343pp • 1921
(w/1969 PBK)
Reprinted by Old Golf Shop (1978) and
the Memorial Tournament (1985)

This book's subtitle, "The Story of the Sporting Battles of the Greatest of all Amateur Golfers," was not simple marketing fodder, for we must remember that Bobby Jones was still a year or two away from making his splash at the time of its publication. As a recounting of one's "sporting battles," this thorough and well-written work is worthy of the plaudits it has long received, with 24 biographical chapters and a final two reserved for instruction. There is a good deal of historical context within these pages, but one senses that Evans had an eye for this sort of thing as all 65 of the book's photos (most not only of himself) were drawn from his private collection.

  With both reprints in very limited editions, one is frequently best off shelling out for the relatively available original.

Original: $175+ • Old Golf (30 copies): $175 • Memorial (425 copies): $175

Comeback: The Ken Venturi Story • *Ken Venturi*
(with Oscar Fraley)
Duell, Sloan and Pearce, New York • 184pp • 1966

Though a series of health problems (including a rare circulatory disorder) conspired to prevent 1964 U.S. Open champion Ken Venturi from securing a place among golf's all-time greats, his story was remarkable enough to be featured in the well-known book *Gifford on Courage*. Here is the roller-coaster tale as seen directly through Venturi's eyes, an honest recounting of a career that twice plummeted to the depths, only to be resuscitated through hard work, talent, and guts.

  A book which proves the tired cliché that the truth really is stranger than fiction.

$30

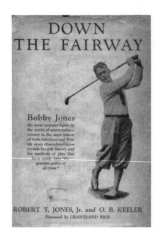

Down the Fairway • *Bobby Jones and O.B. Keeler*
Minton, Balch, New York • 239pp • 1927
1st UK edition: George Allen & Unwin 1927
Reprinted by Blue Ribbon (1927), Classics of Golf (1983), and Longstreet (2001)

In his foreword to the 1983 Classics of Golf reprint, Herbert Warren Wind wrote that "There are quite a few people, myself included, who consider *Down the Fairway* the best book about golf ever written"—and how many volumes get to bask in that sort of praise?

In hindsight, the decision by Jones to write an autobiography at age 25, three years prior to winning the Grand Slam, may seem a strange one. But at the time, he had just become the first man ever to capture both the Open Championship and the U.S. Open in the same season, a feat he evidently considered unlikely to be usurped. It is also worth noting that Jones himself was actually responsible for writing the majority of this book (initially for serial presentation in the magazine *Liberty*), a rarity among famous athletes of any era.

Similar to his later works *Golf Is My Game* and *Bobby Jones on Golf, Down the Fairway* mixes autobiographical material with instructional hints, this time in a ratio of the 11 opening chapters to the six closers. The book is fairly well illustrated with nearly 40 black and white photos, and a career chronology is included at the close. It is, then, a standard against which many golfing biographies are judged, leaving one only to wonder if Jones ever considered revising it after his 1930 retirement.

Original: $275+ • COG: New ($33) • Longstreet: New ($25)

The Education of a Golfer •
Sam Snead (with Al Stump)
Simon & Schuster, New York • 248pp •
1962 (w/PBK)
1st UK edition: Cassell 1962
Reprinted by Sportsman's Book Club
(1964) and the Memorial Tournament
(1984)

It is entirely debatable whether *The Education of a Golfer* should be categorized under Instruction or Biography, for it is loaded equally with playing tips and stories from Snead's background and golfing life. But why get wrapped up in semantics? It is, by nearly universal acclaim, one of the finest golf books ever written—a bellwether entry in either category.

The book contains 10 chapters, each focused on a particular instructional theme but filled mostly with amusing and informative stories. The instruction is slipped in here and there before a recap at each chapter's end serves as more of a standard lesson. Snead produced numerous tutorial books and several autobiographies but on balance, this represents the best of each.

Original: $50 • Sportsman's: $30 • Memorial (410 copies): $60+

The Education of a Woman Golfer • *Nancy Lopez*
(with Peter Schwed)
Simon & Schuster, New York • 191pp • 1979 (w/PBK)
1st UK edition: Pelham 1980

It cannot, of course, be coincidence that this volume's title runs so close to Sam Snead's famous work but no matter, for Lopez has truly enjoyed a career of comparably grand stature. Like Snead's, this is a book that mixes biography with instruction, though given their more clear-cut divisions within the text, this work can safely be classified under the former.

Lopez's story—which begins well outside of golf's traditional milieu—is, on its own, more than a little compelling. But some particularly interesting material is also included here on men's golf vs. women's golf

and the mental side of the game, making this a good all-around read from a player who, just like Snead, failed only to win a U.S. Open.
Under $25

A Feel for the Game • *Ben Crenshaw (with Melanie Hauser)*
Doubleday, New York • 221pp • 2001

Written shortly after his captaincy of an emotional (and controversial) American Ryder Cup victory, Crenshaw's *A Feel for the Game* tells the life story of golf's strongest modern-day traditionalist. Save for recounting his two Masters wins, it spends little time cataloging a great PGA Tour career, focusing instead upon his youth and amateur days, a famous putter ("Little Ben"), an even more famous temper, his beautifully stated love for Augusta National, and golf course architecture.

In hindsight, perhaps a disproportionate amount of attention is paid to the 2000 Ryder Cup and its aftermath, though given the book's timing, such was probably a commercially dictated inevitability. One hates to think, however, that such coverage came at the expense of further observations on the game from one of its greatest-ever supporters.
New ($25)

The Fifth Estate: Thirty Years of Golf • *Jerome D. Travers and James R. Crowell*
Knopf, New York • 259pp • 1926

This relatively forgotten effort by five-time Major champion Jerry Travers is a combination autobiography/history book, recounting Travers's exceptional career within the context of golf's early twentieth-century growth in America. The book is divided into seven sections: "The Dude Era of Golf," "The Reign of the Old Man," "Nerves: Spectre on the Links," "Your True Self Revealed," "Golf Scales Its Summit," "English Versus American Golf," and "An Informal Ranking of the Stars."

Though all are of real historical value, the last might be of greatest interest to many. For while it does discuss and dissect Travers's talented contemporaries, it also offers a brief recounting of the genesis of Pine Valley, as related by George Crump himself. The story of legendary British architect H.S. Colt pitching a tent in the middle of the woods, then emerging days later with a routing plan, is especially enjoyable.

The best of Travers's three books, *The Fifth Estate* is easier to find than one might think—but at a price.

$175+

Fifty Years of Golf: My Memories • *Andrew Kirkaldy*
(as told to Clyde Foster)
T. Fisher Unwin, London • 224pp • 1921
1st US edition: Dutton 1921
Reprinted by the USGA (1993)

As Harry Vardon writes of "Andra" Kirkaldy at the front of *Fifty Years of Golf,* "Andra looked at everything and everybody with his own eyes, and he never called a spade anything but a spade." Indeed, Kirkaldy, a St. Andrews man, was far more famous for his pointed opinions than his golf, though as a constant contender in the Open Championship, he was in fact a topflight player.

Within these pages Kirkaldy's text lives up to both his reputation and the book's title, recounting the many people and occurrences of a patently eventful golfing life. Of greatest interest, I believe, are Andra's candid profiles of British golf's early stars. We anticipate his thoughts on Vardon, Taylor, Braid, and Herd, of course, but a few words on Young Tom Morris—whom Kirkaldy frequently saw play as a youth—are a great bonus.

Original editions are more accessible than one might guess, and are perhaps easier to locate than copies of the USGA reprint.

Note: A second 1921 edition, rather inexplicably titled *My Fifty Years of Golf: Memories,* was produced as well.

Original: $150 • USGA (1,500 copies): $100

A Game of Golf • *Francis Ouimet*
Houghton Mifflin, Boston • 273pp • 1932
1st UK edition: Hutchinson 1933
Reprinted by Ouimet Caddie Scholarship Fund (1963) and Old Golf Shop (1978)

Ouimet's autobiography—written within a year of his second U.S. Amateur title, and apparently without help from a ghostwriter—is another historically important book that seems to cry out for a modern reprinting. Though not quite a classic of the biography genre, it does recount firsthand the young Massachusetts amateur's defeat of British superstars Harry Vardon and Ted Ray in a play-off for the 1913 U.S. Open, as well as his various other triumphs.

Not terribly hard to find, but usually fairly expensive.

Original: $250+ • Old Golf (250 copies): $150

Gary Player: World Golfer • *Gary Player*
(with Floyd Thatcher)
Word, Waco, TX • 193pp • 1974
1st UK edition: Pelham 1975

Though written when Player was only 38, *World Golfer* stands up just fine as an effective autobiography—perhaps because Player won only one of his nine Major championships (the 1978 Masters) subsequent to its publication. What makes this volume especially interesting, of course, is that Player's story differs so greatly from those of most American and British stars, and his world travel (estimated at over four million miles in 1974) is the stuff of legends.

As an original inductee into golf's Hall of Fame, his biography is important to any golfer's library.

Under $25

Golf at the Gallop • *George Duncan*
Sporting Handbooks, London • 192pp • 1951

Open champion in 1920, George Duncan was among the first of Britain's post-Triumvirate stars, an underrated group due to their failure to head off the Golden Age dominance of Americans Hagen, Jones, and Sarazen. *Golf at the Gallop* is Duncan's autobiography and, despite being half-filled with instruction, makes for a lively and relatively timeless read.

The book's first half recounts an active playing career and, beyond Duncan's own competitive stories, is filled with profiles of nearly every great player, professional or amateur, from J.H. Taylor right on through to Babe Zaharias. Given Duncan's timing—essentially as a bridge between the greats of the Victorian age and the stars of the mid-twentieth-century—this colorful work probably deserves a larger place than it has ever occupied on the game's historical shelf.

$75

Golf Is My Game • *Robert Tyre (Bobby) Jones*
Doubleday, Garden City, NY • 255pp • 1960
1st UK edition: Chatto & Windus 1961
Reprinted by A&C Black (1990 PBK) and Flagstick Books (1997)

While Jones's 1927 collaboration with O.B. Keeler, *Down the Fairway*, may well be considered better literature, *Golf Is My Game* covers the Immortal Bobby's entire career—a not unimportant difference considering, for example, that the Grand Slam was won in 1930.

This volume reverses the formula used by *Down the Fairway* (and many other such books) in that it opens with instruction, specifically eight chapters under the section titled "Improving Your Golf." It then moves into "Competition and the Grand Slam," a six-chapter stretch, the final four entries of which cover each of the great 1930 triumphs. The final segment, titled "And After," is especially interesting, offering Jones's thoughts on the evolution of the game, the founding of Augusta National (including a hole-by-hole tour), and finally his being uniquely honored with the Freedom of the City award at St. Andrews.

It is difficult to imagine cramming a life as rich as Jones's into 255 pages, but *Golf Is My Game* touches all the key bases. An important entry.

Original: $100 • A&C Black: $30 • Flagstick: New ($33)

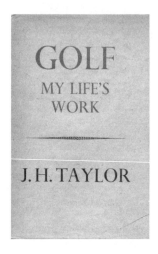

Golf: My Life's Work • *J.H. Taylor*
Jonathan Cape, London • 236pp • 1943

Though less wide-ranging than 1902's *Taylor on Golf*, this difficult-to-find autobiography recounts the life of the immensely popular five-time Open champion from his "Early Days" (chapter one) through to his activities of later life. Completed without the aid of a ghostwriter, it tells one of golf's all-time greatest stories, beginning life as a caddie and domestic servant for Horace Hutchinson's father, rising to the top of the golf world, being instrumental in the founding of the PGA and the building of public golf courses, and generally leaving a legacy matched by very, very few.

Beyond taking us back to that splendid Victorian era when Vardon, Taylor, and Braid ruled golf, this volume also provides a stark reminder of the darker years later to follow. For across from the title page is stamped an ominous "Book Production War Economy Standard" logo, and Joseph Murdoch has noted copies whose jackets were actually printed on the reverse sides of already-used dust covers!

$225

Good Bounces & Bad Lies • *Ben Wright*
Sleeping Bear, Chelsea, MI • 304pp • 1999

Few voices were more familiar to international golf fans during the 1980s and '90s than that of Ben Wright, *Financial Times* writer turned BBC and CBS television broadcaster. In this long and entertaining volume, Wright recounts his life from a youth in war-torn England to his late-'90s battles with American political correctness, all the way recounting one amusing story after another. Naturally the book is heavy on broadcasting tales, providing candid glimpses of everyone from Pat Summerall and Gary McCord to Wright's early mentor, the legendary Henry Longhurst.

Though some off-color material may seem nonessential, I consider any man who uses the phrase "he's hooked this comprehensively" to be well worth reading.

Under $25

The Greatest Game of All: My Life in Golf •
Jack Nicklaus (with Herbert Warren Wind)
Simon & Schuster, New York • 416pp • 1969
1st UK edition: Hodder & Stoughton 1969
Reprinted by Flagstick Books (1998)

Though obviously written too early to be a definitive profile of the Golden Bear's career, the thorough coverage of Jack's formative years and Wind's standard literary excellence make *The Greatest Game of All* perhaps the finest of volumes by or about Jack Nicklaus. It is divided into five sections: The first details Jack's experiences and relationships with Bobby Jones, Ben Hogan, and Arnold Palmer, the second his youth and amateur career, the third his pre-1969 professional career. The fourth shifts into an extensive segment of instruction, while the fifth concludes with, among other things, a chapter on golf course architecture.

More recent Nicklaus bios tell a longer story, but I sincerely doubt that any cover their subject with quite so much depth and style.

Original: $35 • Flagstick: New ($33)

The Greatest of Them All: The Legend of Bobby Jones •
Martin Davis
American Golfer, Greenwich, CT • 200pp • 1996

This attractive volume was the first of the American Golfer series profiling legendary players of the past. It follows (or rather sets) a pattern similar to its sister books on Ben Hogan and Byron Nelson, beginning with essays penned by Alistair Cooke, Dave Anderson, Ben Crenshaw, and Peter Dobereiner (among others) and reprints of period coverage by Bernard Darwin, O.B. Keeler, and Grantland Rice. The "Photography and Commentary" section includes Jones's Major championship wins, a study of his swing, and his lifelong relationship with the city of St. Andrews. The building of Augusta National, however, is essentially omitted.

Like its sisters, this genuinely oversized book eats up a lot of shelf space, but most will find it well worth it.

New ($60)

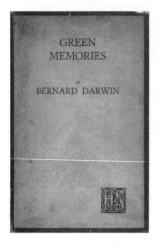

Green Memories • *Bernard Darwin*
Hodder & Stoughton, London • 332pp • 1928
Reprinted by Flagstick Books (1998)

Green Memories is the first of four autobiographical volumes produced by Darwin (see *Life Is Sweet Brother, Pack Clouds Away,* and *The World That Fred Made*), though this one is easily the most "golfing" of the bunch, reading almost like a prewar history of the game. It is remarkably thorough, with detailed sections on Darwin's own successful playing career, great Open Championships, trips to the United States, the historic 1913 U.S. Open and 1922 Walker Cup (in which he participated), portraits of favorite courses and players, and so on.

Suffice to say that in his foreword to the Flagstick Books reprint, John Hopkins, a Darwin successor at the *Times,* writes that *Green Memories* "is the best of Darwin's books, which, in turn, makes it the best book on golf."

Very possibly.

Original: $225+ • Flagstick: New ($33)

Harold Hilton—His Golfing Life and Times •
John L.B. Garcia
Grant, Droitwich • 121pp • 1992

This limited edition (750 copies) chronicles the remarkable career of seven-time Major champion Harold H. Hilton, a legend of late nineteenth-century British golf. The book is arranged chronologically over nine chapters, with particular attention paid to Hilton's unique championship feats: being the lone amateur to win two Open Championships and the lone Briton to capture the U.S. Amateur. A 31-page appendix is another valuable component, highlighting Hilton's record, contemporary views of his game (including those of Francis Ouimet and Bernard Darwin), his thoughts on technique, and a highly detailed bibliography.

$35

Harry Vardon: The Revealing Story of a Champion Golfer • *Audrey Howell*
Stanley Paul, London • 184pp • 1991 (w/revised PBK 2001)

One of the genuine mysteries in the annals of golf literature is how, save for his own self-written effort, not a single biography of Harry Vardon was ever produced prior to 1991. Further, Vardon's book (see *My Golfing Life*) was strictly limited to his playing career, leaving readers still to wonder about so many other aspects of this modest legend's up-and-down life.

Enter Audrey Howell, the Greyhound's daughter-in-law, with this fine volume which delves as much into Vardon the man as King Harry the player. To be sure, its chief revelation is the existence of Vardon's out-of-wedlock son, an unconventional element hitherto unknown (or, perhaps, deliberately overlooked). But far more importantly, it provides our first detailed look behind the quiet confidence and the "Vardonic" smile, profiling this decidedly unassuming figure whose presence, some 70 years hence, still looms large upon the golfing landscape.

Nearly a century past his prime, we finally get to meet Harry Vardon.
Original: $40 • PBK: Under $25

Hogan • *Curt Sampson*
Rutledge Hill, Nashville • 262pp • 1996 (w/PBK)

This 1996 volume is generally considered the best Hogan biography to date, though the field remains a surprisingly lean one. Of course, prospective writers weren't about to get much help from the reclusive Hawk in researching such projects, so perhaps the scarcity is just as Mr. Hogan wanted it.

In any event, Sampson's book is well-detailed, yet a fast and pleasant read. Its eight chapters cover nearly the entirety of Hogan's life which, without any sort of contrived amplification, reads like a Hollywood script. Full chapters are dedicated to both the epic 1953 season (when Hogan won three Major titles) and the legendary question of "The Secret." But in the end, this book succeeds mostly because it does a fine job of capturing the persona of a man who, in the author's words, "became an idea quite apart from golf."

New ($25)

Hogan: The Man Who Played for Glory • *Gene Gregston*
Prentice-Hall, Englewood Cliffs, NJ • 192pp • 1978

This, the first full Hogan biography, preceded Curt Sampson's work by nearly two decades. Gregston reportedly gathered material for many years in preparing this manuscript, and it does cover Hogan's competitive successes in fine detail. For my money, however, Sampson's volume goes deeper into Hogan the man which, considering how well documented his playing career has become, is really the more valuable ticket. Still, this earlier book will hold great appeal for those who simply cannot get enough regarding the legend—and there are a lot of us.

$50

The Hogan Mystique • *The American Golfer*
American Golfer, Greenwich, CT • 132pp • 1994

The forerunner of the American Golfer's oversized biopics of Jones, Nelson, and Hogan, this similarly large volume features over 70 black-and-white images of Hogan shot by photographer Jules Alexander between 1959 and 1971. Like the AG's later books, *The Hogan Mystique* also features some high-profile essays, this time from Dave Anderson ("Standards of the Man"), Ben Crenshaw ("The Hawk"), and Dan Jenkins ("Hogan His Ownself"). But perhaps of greatest interest are the swing comments of Ken Venturi, a Hogan friend and disciple who surely knows more about the Hawk's technique (and, perhaps, his "Secret?") than he will ever divulge.

Though not quite as full as the books to follow, *The Hogan Mystique* is most attractive and interesting in its own right, and essential to the great man's legions of fans.

New ($50)

How I Played the Game •
Byron Nelson
Taylor, Dallas • 271pp • 1993

In a charming throwback to a less preten-
tious era, Byron Nelson actually wrote this
manuscript himself, making it about as primary a source as the modern golf reader is
likely to encounter. Over 11 chapters it covers Nelson's life, from the early years in Ft.
Worth right on into the 1990s. All of the landmark moments are detailed, of course, with
a full chapter set aside for the pinnacle season of 1945. Of special interest, I think, is a
chapter providing Nelson's thoughts on 45 prominent golfers with whom
he has played, many of them Hall-of-Famers. Finally, historians will
value a remarkably detailed appendix listing, year-by-year, every Tour
event in which Lord Byron participated, including his score and position, the purse, the winner, and other salient facts.

In short, *How I Played the Game* is a uniquely personal look at a
legendary golfing life by one of the game's all-time great gentlemen.
$30

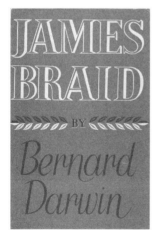

James Braid • *Bernard Darwin*
Hodder & Stoughton, London • 196pp •
1952 (w/PBK)
Reprinted by Old Golf Shop (1981) and
Flagstick Books (2003)

I must confess that *James Braid* is my least
favorite of Darwin's golf books which, I suppose, is roughly akin to saying that Pebble
Beach just doesn't measure up to Pine Valley
or Cypress Point—the distinction seems almost
pointless, but there it is. The book is a biography of the legendary Braid, and is certainly
not without real merit, yet I've always found

it to lack that certain *je ne sais quoi* that generally distinguishes Darwin's uniquely special prose. Some—if not most—may perhaps disagree.

The 1981 reprint, by the way, was limited to 200 copies, making the sometimes-expensive 1952 edition generally the easier find.

Original: $150 • Old Golf (200 copies): $50 • Flagstick: New ($29)

James Braid: Champion Golfer • *Bob MacAlindin*
Grant, Droitwich • 110pp • 2003

Perhaps mindful that Bernard Darwin had already left his imprint on the Braid legacy, Bob MacAlindin's modern volume is intended not so much as a biography but rather as the definitive record of Braid's playing career. In this light the book succeeds nicely, recording much of Braid's competitive travels around the UK as well the occasional sea-sickness-plagued visit to the Continent. Much attention is of course paid to his five Open championships, but also to countless lesser events, a ledger of which appears at the close.

Though several chapters do address both biographical and golf architecture aspects, such information might better be pursued through Darwin, or John Moreton's *The Golf Courses of James Braid.*

New ($45)

John Ball of Hoylake • *John Behrend*
Grant, Droitwich • 108pp • 1989

In the pre-Triumvirate era, when so many of Britain's top golfers eschewed turning professional, John Ball Jr. won an incomparable *eight* British Amateur titles—and then added the 1890 Open Championship for good measure. This brief but detailed work, written by a leading British historian and longtime member of Royal Liverpool (Hoylake), chronicles Ball's career over 15 chapters, with an appropriate emphasis on his competitive record.

Some American readers may be less interested in this story, but Bobby Jones notwithstanding, John Ball may well have been the greatest amateur of all time.

New ($30)

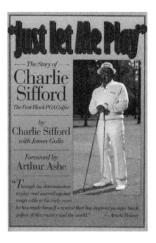

Just Let Me Play • *Charles Sifford*
(with James Gullo)
British American, Latham, NY • 237pp •
1992

Long before there was a Tiger, there was
Charles Sifford, a genuine pioneer whose road
to victory on the PGA Tour made even Jackie
Robinson's path seem relatively smooth. This
typically overlooked volume chronicles
Sifford's story, a harsh and decidedly sad epic
but one also dotted with great moments of
triumph. Hardly pleasant bedtime reading,
this important book serves to remind that
while golf's traditions of challenge and character aren't for everyone,
the game's boundaries of inclusiveness should never, ever have been drawn
along racial lines.
$55+

Life & Times of Bobby Jones • *Sidney L. Matthew*
Sleeping Bear, Chelsea, MI • 296pp • 1995

Considering the large amount of autobiographical material written by
Jones himself (or his ardent chronicler O.B. Keeler), a detailed biography per se likely wouldn't add much to our Jones file. Thus Sid Matthew
played it smart, making this really more of a pictorial bio, a grand scrapbook of Jones images detailing the Immortal Bobby's amazing life.

As many of the pictures came from private collections, there is much
new material here, and I doubt that any reader can come away without
gaining a stronger appreciation of the sheer magnitude of the Jones story.
Architectural buffs will also find several new early images of Augusta
National, though nothing that will dramatically rewrite the course's
occasionally murky design history.
$75

Life Is Sweet Brother •
Bernard Darwin
Collins, London • 285pp • 1940

The second of Darwin's four autobiographical works, *Life Is Sweet Brother* is probably the closest thing to a "normal" autobiography in the bunch. It recounts the great scribe's youth, his school days at Eton and Cambridge, his brief time as a solicitor, and, ultimately, his shift to a life of writing. All told, there are only two purely golfing chapters ("Changing Golf" and "Some Golfers of My Time"), making this an ideal volume for Darwin lovers, but perhaps less so for those interested strictly in the game.
$40

Links of Life • *Joe Kirkwood*
Privately published • 141pp • 1973

This highly rewarding little work has been largely overlooked for three decades now, perhaps because it was privately published long before the Internet made such ventures truly viable. Essentially it is a travelogue, recapping the worldwide wanderings of Kirkwood, the fine Australian player who is best remembered as golf's first great trick-shot artist. The travel angle (which includes visits to all six inhabited continents) works nicely, but what makes the book special is that the majority of this touring was done with the great Walter Hagen, whose legendary personality springs vibrantly to life within these pages.

Indeed, *Links of Life*'s only problem is that it leaves one wondering about the many additional stories that were doubtless omitted.
$55

A Love Affair with the Game • *Frank "Sandy" Tatum Jr.*
The American Golfer, Greenwich, CT • 221pp • 2002

Former USGA President Sandy Tatum's autobiography is less a narrative than a series of vignettes touching upon the many people, places, and events that he has seen during his 60+ years in golf. As it ever was, Tatum's perspective is that of the great traditionalist, a man who loves the game for its character and challenge while resenting its modern commercialization and the breaking down of its core values. There are many fascinating stories and profiles, all experienced by the author firsthand, but in the end, *A Love Affair with the Game* stands out mostly for its refreshing honesty. For here is a uniquely knowledgeable man rejecting the notions of greed, corporatization, and equipment manufacturers ruling the modern game.

I wonder if any of his disciples in Far Hills are listening.

New ($25)

My Golfing Life • *Sandy Herd*
Chapman & Hall, London • 246pp • 1923
1st US edition: Dutton 1923

As the so-called fourth member of the Triumvirate, Sandy Herd may be less well-known (at least to American readers) than Vardon, Taylor, or Braid, but he was the 1902 Open Champion and a legitimately great player in his own right. In this 14-chapter autobiography, the St. Andrews native recounts his career, his experiences with his famous contemporaries, plus stories of additional legends like Old Tom Morris, the Kirkaldy brothers, John Ball, and Walter Hagen. Toward the close it offers the seemingly obligatory "Golf among the Americans" section, as well as two chapters of instruction.

Perhaps not having five or six Open Championship victories to retell provided Herd the latitude for a wider-ranging narrative, giving this relatively hard-to-find volume a certain charm of its own.

$135

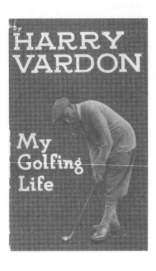

My Golfing Life • *Harry Vardon*
Hutchinson, London • 281pp • 1933
Reprinted by the Memorial Tournament (1981) and Ellesborough (1985)

Vardon essentially wrote this volume himself, having the dual effect of making it less professionally polished than some but more genuine than most. It traces his legendary career from its beginnings on the Isle of Jersey right on through to his retirement days at Totteridge, covering every major event and all three American trips en route. The upside to such a work is obvious, as it has bequeathed us the firsthand views of perhaps the most talented golfer who ever lived. The downside too is clear, for given the values of the time, we are left without many details of King Harry's somewhat sad personal life (see *Harry Vardon: The Revealing Story of a Champion Golfer*, page 177). Similarly, so gentlemanly a man as Vardon is seldom critical of others and offers no sense whatsoever as to just how good he considered himself.

With reprint editions even more scarce than originals, *My Golfing Life* represents an expensive acquisition no matter how one chooses to pursue it.

Original: $650 • Memorial (300 copies): $350 • Ellesborough (200 copies): $350

My Life and Soft Times • *Henry Longhurst*
Cassell, London • 366pp • 1971

Few will argue that *My Life and Soft Times* is much of a golf book; in fact as the great Longhurst recounts his life we are rather surprised (at least on the Western side of the Atlantic) at how relatively minor a role the Royal & Ancient game plays in it. Yet a fascinating and exciting life it was, traveling to nearly every corner of the globe and engaging in a surprisingly high degree of adventure. A romantic throwback to the last years of the British Empire, this remains one of golf's most unique and interesting stories.

Under $25

My Partner, Ben Hogan •
Jimmy Demaret
McGraw-Hill, New York • 214pp • 1954
1st UK edition: Davies 1954 (w/PBK)
Reprinted by the Memorial Tournament
(1990)

This somewhat rare title stands out as perhaps the only time one of golf's brightest stars ever wrote an entire book about another. Demaret, of course, was closer than most to Hogan, and thus was able to profile him in a more intimate (and humorous) manner than might any professional writer. An eminently pleasant biographical read, *My Partner, Ben Hogan* probably seemed more groundbreaking in 1954, when the Hogan myth had not yet been so thoroughly analyzed and the Hawk was still silently steamrolling the competition.

Original: $125 • Memorial: $125

Not Only Golf • *Pat Ward-Thomas*
Hodder & Stoughton, London • 206pp • 1981

Unless the scribe happens to be Henry Cotton or Peter Thomson, or perhaps the globetrotting Mr. Longhurst, skeptics may well question the value of a golf *writer's* autobiography—but I doubt that they should continue to do so upon reading *Not Only Golf*. For aside from the book's pleasant-yet-direct style, Ward-Thomas enjoyed, by any standard, a most fascinating life. In what other golf biography, for example, will one encounter the exploits of a World War II RAF pilot and the building of a makeshift prison-camp golf course to idle away four years spent as a POW?

Equally interesting, however, are the author's recountings of his many travels, which included regular visits to the United States and further treks to Australia, South Africa, and elsewhere. And despite the title, this book is absolutely rife with golfing material. Indeed, it is Ward-Thomas's candid and up-close portrayals of the great players of the 1950s and '60s that most make *Not Only Golf* a desirable addition for any wide-ranging collection.

Under $25

The Old Man: The Biography of Walter J. Travis •
Bob Labbance
Sleeping Bear, Chelsea, MI • 259pp • 2000

Though the Apple Tree Gang and C.B. Macdonald may have done more to get the ball rolling, no man was more important to the growth of American golf than Walter Travis, champion player, golf course architect, and editor of the *American Golfer* magazine—all after taking up the game at the then-not-so-young age of 35.

Amazingly *The Old Man* stands as the first genuine Travis biography and though written a full century after his initial U.S. Amateur triumph, it offers a very high measure of detail. Divided into three sections ("The Golfer," "The Editor," and "The Architect"), *The Old Man* concisely and effectively profiles an American golfing icon.

New ($30)

Pack Clouds Away • *Bernard Darwin*
Collins, London • 288pp • 1941

For me, *Pack Clouds Away* has long been the toughest Darwin book to get a handle on, perhaps because it really isn't about anything in particular. Written in the Cotswolds during a blitz-inspired war relocation, it is considered by many to be autobiographical, though really it tends to offer more about Darwin's opinions (on fashion, dogs, St. Moritz, etc.) than specific recountings of his life. Like *Every Idle Dream,* the focus is not on golf, though unlike that distinguished book of essays, the game does worm its way consistently into things here, particularly in the chapter "On Tour" and two others chronicling visits to America. Though more for the hard-core Darwin fan, I suppose, *Pack Clouds Away* still strikes me as a fascinating and beautifully written document indicative of a besieged Britain looking back on better days.

Note: First editions of this and *Life Is Sweet Brother*—both published by Collins—are bound and lettered identically, giving a distinct (though not necessarily accurate) feel of being sister volumes.

$60

The Parks of Musselburgh: Golfers, Architects, Clubmakers • *John Adams*
Grant Books, Droitwich • 154pp • 1991

This limited edition (750 copies) hasn't taken long in becoming relatively scarce. It represents a detailed look at one of the game's legendary families, two generations of golfers who accounted for seven Open Championships, numerous advances in clubmaking, a pioneering golf book, and the design of over 125 courses worldwide.

Though Willie Sr. and Mungo are covered as thoroughly as modern research will allow, the centerpiece of the book is Willie Jr., the most versatile and entrepreneurial of all nineteenth-century golf professionals. Young Willie's was a most fascinating of golfing lives, from his two Open Championships and numerous club design patents to his international architectural practice and status as the lone professional to regularly stake his own money in the high-profile challenge matches of the day.

One wishes that more could be written about these fascinating people, but *The Parks of Musselburgh* probably includes all that recorded history will allow.

$125

Peter Alliss: An Autobiography • *Peter Alliss*
Collins, London • 192pp • 1981 (w/PBK)

Coming some 18 years after 1963's *Alliss Through the Looking Glass*, this is in fact the fine British player-turned-commentator's second autobiography. As TV viewers well know, Alliss has a great facility with words, making this jaunt through his early years, competitive career, television work, and entry into the field of golf course architecture a very pleasant read.

I will be the first to admit that two autobiographies for a man who never won a Major championship seems like a lot—but who, over the last half-century, has experienced so many aspects of the game more fully?

Under $25

Shark: The Biography of Greg Norman • *Lauren St. John*
Rutledge Hill, Nashville • 288pp • 1998

Shark is a fairly candid volume, profiling one of the modern game's most compelling figures through a star-crossed career that Hollywood itself could not have invented. Most valuable, I think, is that St. John seems to have approached the project with great objectivity, neither fawning over her subject nor setting out to deliberately ridicule or embarrass him. The result is a deep and authentic account owing, perhaps, to some very well-placed sources. Notably, the author's first acknowledgment is to Greg and Laura Norman, "who not only gave generously of their time but were much kinder and nicer than they actually needed to be while doing so."

Readers who like this will also enjoy the autobiographical *Greg Norman: My Story,* a less-objective but highly engaging text whose only real fault was being written way too early (1983).

Under $25

Sir Walter and Mr. Jones •
Stephen Lowe
Sleeping Bear, Chelsea, MI • 387pp • 2000

Written by a college history professor, *Sir Walter and Mr. Jones* possesses a degree of scholarly research not often found in modern golf literature. Essentially a dual biography, it closely follows the lives of those polar opposites, Walter Hagen and Bobby Jones, who, despite their antithetical backgrounds and personalities, became closely intertwined during the 1920s peaks of their respective golfing careers.

Though both men have been chronicled on other occasions, it is doubtful that any volume captures the day-to-day paths of either's life as well as this one—especially with regard to Hagen who has not enjoyed quite as much posthumous adoration as the Immortal Bobby. Though Joe Kirkwood's *Links of Life* may show something more of his wild side, *Sir Walter and Mr. Jones* probably allows us greater access to the "real" Walter Hagen than any book yet written.

New ($35)

They Call Me Super Mex • *Lee Trevino (with Sam Blair)*
Random House, New York • 202pp • 1982
1st UK edition ("Super Mex"): Stanley Paul 1983

With two U.S. Opens, two Open Championships, and two PGAs in his pocket, Lee Trevino's place in golf history is more than secure. But despite so stellar a record, Trevino will likely be better remembered for his wisecracks and pleasant on-course demeanor, a carefree style that is also apparent throughout this autobiography. From growing up fatherless in Dallas to winning six Majors, Trevino's story is genuinely an American classic—but one told here in a decidedly lighthearted style.

Under $25

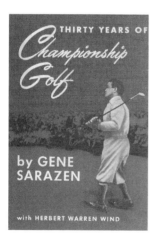

Thirty Years of Championship Golf • *Gene Sarazen (with Herbert Warren Wind)*
Prentice-Hall, New York • 276pp • 1950 (w/PBK)
Reprinted by Classics of Golf (1987)

Long cited among the elite of the game's biographies, *Thirty Years of Championship Golf* likely held as much literary potential as any volume undertaken in its genre. For a subject there was Sarazen, a tough, entertaining, and occasionally controversial superstar who lived the American dream, going, quite literally, from rags to riches. For a writer there was Wind, a celebrated talent and one particularly adept at this sort of work. The result, not surprisingly, fully lives up to the billing, recounting not only the Squire's great championship triumphs but also his impoverished roots, his seemingly endless travels, and his days cavorting with Roaring Twenties society.

In the early 1950s Henry Longhurst wrote that *Thirty Years* "has given me more pleasure than any golfing book I have read for many years." Even today, a half-century later, the life of a man who competed against everyone from Vardon to Nicklaus still makes for a fresh and truly fascinating read.

Original: $275 • COG: New ($33)

This Life I've Led • *Babe Didrikson Zaharias*
(as told to Harry Paxton)
A.S. Barnes, New York • 242pp • 1955 (w/later PBK)
1st UK edition: Robert Hale 1956
Reprinted by the Memorial Tournament (1991)

While many believe that Babe Didrikson Zaharias was the greatest female athlete that ever lived, it can also be reasonably argued that she was the best female golfer as well. For while other players may match her tournament records (most having played the game for many more years), the Babe remains the only woman to qualify for a men's PGA Tour event—the 1945 Los Angeles Open—under equal playing conditions.

Though *This Life I've Led* won't be confused with the writings of Darwin or Wind, its autobiographical account of a truly extraordinary life is a fine addition to any sports-oriented library.

By the way, in 1945, playing at Riviera, the Babe made the cut.

Original: $40 • Memorial (200 copies): $150

The Unsinkable Titanic Thompson • *Carlton Stowers*
Eakin, Burnet, TX • 234pp • 1982 (w/PBK)

Given that wagering between players is so integral a part of golf (accepted, as it is, even by the staid old USGA), it hardly seems surprising that among the more famous names of the sport stands A.C. (Titanic) Thompson, legendary gambler and hustler extraordinaire. This volume covers his life and schemes perhaps as well as is posthumously possible, attempting to separate myth from reality so many years after the fact. I doubt that anyone with a sporting interest will be bored by this colorful work, though it is the rare golf-oriented book indeed that devotes substantial space to such upstanding citizens as Al Capone, Arnold Rothstein, and Nick the Greek.

Both hardcover and paperback copies are a tough find.

Original: $250+ • PB: $100

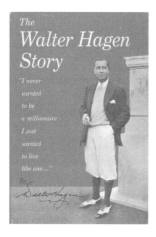

The Walter Hagen Story •

Walter Hagen

Simon & Schuster, New York • 341pp • 1956

1st UK edition: Heinemann 1957

Reprinted by the Memorial Tournament (1977), Vintage (2001 PBK), and Classics of Golf (2003)

Golf has had its great players and its colorful characters, but I sincerely doubt that it— or any other sport—has ever enjoyed a competitor who pushed harder for the blue ribbon in both categories than the legendary Walter Hagen.

The problem, at least from the perspective of dictating an autobiography, is that the "character" category is less easily expounded upon in the first person, particularly with publishers and editors clamoring for the safety of simply recounting famous championship victories. Consequently *The Walter Hagen Story,* while genuinely excellent in many ways, does not truly do justice to the Haig's various and highly entertaining off-the-course adventures. Oh, a great deal of splendid material does appear, but we would be remiss not to note that Joe Kirkwood's little-known *Links of Life* (see page 182) manages to recount not just individual stories but entire intercontinental tours that are completely omitted here.

Still, *The Walter Hagen Story* has much to offer, and it's difficult to imagine a golfer's library being truly complete without it. Given a huge 1956 printing, original copies are still very much in circulation today.

Original: $80 • Memorial (250 copies): $150 • Vintage (PBK): New ($10) • COG: New ($33)

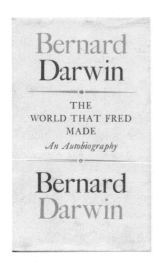

The World That Fred Made •
Bernard Darwin
Chatto & Windus, London • 256pp •
1955

The last of Darwin's four autobiographical volumes, *The World That Fred Made* was also his final book of any sort, being published not very far from his 80th birthday in 1955. It recounts with remarkable clarity his formative years, family memories, and educational experiences, with golf inevitably "breaking in sooner or later since it has played so large a part in a possibly mis-spent life."

Like the Dean's other autobiographical works (save for *Green Memories*), the narrowly focused golf fan may at times feel lost within this text. Yet to read eight decades' worth of recollections from so remarkable a man is itself fascinating, as is the sense of youthful nostalgia that must pervade all of our advancing years. For as Darwin wrote in closing out this final opus: "We now live in such a dreadfully grown-up world."

$55

SECTION IX
REFERENCE/MISCELLANEOUS

A mongrelized section if ever there was one.

Our reference choices are fairly self-explanatory. I have tried to select as varied a group as might be found in covering a single game, recognizing that not all encyclopedias are arranged from A–Z and that there genuinely is *a lot* of information to be digested about several hundred years' worth of golf. Numerous volumes may duplicate the information provided by those selected, but I doubt that very many can improve upon it.

As for the handful of miscellaneous books, suffice it to say that while all are too good or too important to pass over, they simply don't fit among any of our other categories.

The American Annual Golf Guide
Angus, New York • 1916 (w/13 subsequent annual editions)

It can be fairly argued that Richardson and Werden's *Golfer's Year Book*
(see below) provides a wider range of information, but based simply
upon its relative longevity, *The American Annual Golf Guide* remains
best known among prewar American guidebooks. Published 14 times
between 1916 and 1931 (1919 and 1930 being dark years), it provided
the most thorough state-by-state listings of courses on the market, offering detailed information on yardage, par, club officers, playing policies,
and fees. Historians lament an occasional fuzziness of establishment
dates (the *club's* initial year is generally listed, not the course's) and the
usual lack of architectural credits. But any way one looks at it, this was
the most prominent record going.

Despite so many editions, good copies are definitely at a premium
today.

$300+

Aspects of Collecting Golf Books • *Various*
Grant, Droitwich • 195pp • 1996

A perfectly titled volume for our purposes, this modern anthology includes 10 sections created by a variety of experts, each featuring a specific area of golfing literature. Among the highlights are Fred Hawtree's
section on architectural books, the great modern collector Alastair
Johnston's profiling of early British works, essays on Bernard Darwin
and Horace Hutchinson, and a section on women's golf books. Some
listed volumes carry descriptive notations, though these are generally
not expansive.

Nowhere near as comprehensive as Murdoch and Donovan's *The
Game of Golf and the Printed Word 1566–1985*, this is still an important collection as its focus on certain chosen areas provides a high yield
of valuable information. With only 425 copies printed, however, it is a
particularly difficult find.

$450

Australian Golf • *Jack Pollard*
Angus & Robertson, Sydney • 398pp • 1990

Though the word doesn't appear in the title, this is in fact an encyclopedic volume, covering more than 180 years of Australian golf, arranged from A–Z. What makes it particularly worthwhile is the depth of the author's knowledge, for the book's 600+ entries are thorough and well-written, providing a good deal more information than most books of this type.

Under $25

Cobble Valley Yarns •
A.W. Tillinghast
Philadelphia Printing, Philadelphia •
295pp • 1915
Reprinted by the USGA (1994)

A glance at this book's date of publication suggests that Tillinghast fancied himself an author several years before truly establishing himself as a world-class architect. I use the word "fancied" because few consider either this or a later volume, *The Mutt and Other Golf Yarns* (1925) to represent high golfing literature. After all, Tillinghast's own daughter referred to them as "immense, gushing sentimentalism" and the former executive director of the USGA, Frank Hannigan, has written: "Let's not fool ourselves. These are not works of high art."

They are, however, a curious footnote of some real historical interest. Enough so, in fact, that copies are extremely difficult to find, even of the USGA's 1994 reprint that paired both volumes in a single slipcase.

Originals (either book): $400 • USGA (1,500 copies): $175+

Collecting Golf Books, 1743–1938 • *Cecil Hopkinson*
Constable, London • 56pp • 1938 (w/PBK)
Reprinted (with addenda by Joseph Murdoch) by Grant (1980)

In deciding to write *The Golfer's Library*, I must admit to having been heartened considerably upon discovering how relatively limited Hopkinson's little volume actually is. For despite an obvious historical importance, it cannot remotely be compared to Joseph Murdoch's eventual attempts at cataloging *everything*. In truth, it really only discusses a handful of important volumes.

For the record, *Collecting Golf Books* is divided into sections entitled "Bibliographies," "Poetry," "Rules," "Instruction," "Histories," "Annuals," "Fiction," "Humour," "Essays," "Collections and Symposiums," "Americana," and a miscellaneous group simply called "Various." Equally for the record, the hands-down winner for the most pages goes to Poetry, an interesting commentary on the game's literary roots.

Original: $1,000 • Grant: $350+

The Complete Encyclopedia of Golf • *Derek Lawrenson*
Carlton, London • 648pp • 1999

This large encyclopedia is not a traditional A–Z affair, instead breaking down the game's vast body of information into seven sections: "The Early History of Golf," "The Major Tournaments," "The Other Tournaments," "The Top 200 Players (Men)," "The Top 50 Players (Women)," "The Top 100 Courses," and "Records." At 648 pages the book is obviously thorough and Lawrenson, as a popular international golf writer, enjoys strong credentials.

Still available new, frequently remaindered.

New ($45)

The Complete Golf Gamesmanship • *Stephen Potter*
Heinemann, London • 177pp • 1968
1st US edition ("Golfmanship"): McGraw-Hill 1968

I must admit to being generally averse to this sort of "how-to-win-without-really-cheating" stuff, but Potter's masterpiece is simply too amusing to be discarded. How, for example, can we possibly omit a work which acknowledges Henry Longhurst for "a few of the more sophisticated ploys" included therein?

But the author calls forth a great deal of his own creativity as well. For example, he suggests that one should always saddle a big hitter with "a caddie who never says 'good shot' but often points to a place, 30 yards ahead, which was reached by Byron Nelson when he played the course in 1946, or, better still, by J.H. Taylor, when he played there with the gutty in '98."

One might genuinely gain an edge from this stuff—if able to apply it with anything resembling a straight face.

Under $25

Dead Solid Perfect • *Dan Jenkins*
Atheneum, New York • 234pp • 1974 (w/PBKs)

As off-color golf books go, this stands unchallenged as the heavyweight champion. The story of journeyman tour player Kenny Puckett's run at winning a U.S. Open, *Dead Solid Perfect* offers up more sex, violence, and foul language than an R-rated movie. At the same time, however, it is—like most of Jenkins's work—both funny and, in its own way, rather traditional with regard to the game and its values.

Personally, I prefer the author's 1991 entry *You Gotta Play Hurt*, a tremendously entertaining sports book, though only tangentially about golf.

Under $25

The Duffer's Handbook of Golf •
Grantland Rice
Macmillan, New York • 163pp • 1926
Reproduced by Classics of Golf (1988)

The Duffer's Handbook might well be the standard-bearer of the Miscellaneous category, for there is no other section into which it truly fits. It is, in great measure, a book of humor, with Rice's miniessays often instructing us "How to Lose Distance," "How to Make a Hole in 9," and so on, and period cartoonist Clare Briggs lampooning the game (and its players) at every turn. Yet interspersed throughout are legitimate tips, both from Rice and luminaries like Hagen and Jones, making this a book which gives one every chance to improve without taking the game too seriously.

Few golf volumes bear a more appropriate title.

Original: $100 • COG: New ($29)

The Encyclopedia of Golf • *Malcolm Campbell*
Dorling Kindersley, London • 336pp • 1991 (w/1994 & 2001 revised editions)
1st US edition (as "Random House International Encyclopedia of Golf"): Random House 1991

Though perhaps not on par with the remarkable thoroughness of 1975's classic *Shell Encyclopedia*, Malcolm Campbell's frequently printed effort is certainly more visually impressive, being in full color and including numerous photos and annotated course diagrams. It is divided into five sections—"The Early Game," "The Modern Game," "Championship Courses of the World," "The Hall of Fame," and "Records and Reference"—and, in point of fact, tends to read more like a book than as a reference collection.

Buyer's note: The most recent reissue is titled *The New Encyclopedia of Golf* and is readily available as of this writing.

New ($40)

The Game of Golf and the Printed Word 1566–1985 •
Richard E. Donovan and Joseph S.F. Murdoch
Castalio, Endicott, NY • 658pp • 1987

Though one of the least "readable" books one will ever encounter, this is, without question, as valuable a golf volume as has ever been published. Quite simply, it is a bibliography of every book on the game for which the authors could find record—no small number given their exhaustive research and the late Mr. Murdoch's status as perhaps the game's most voracious literary collector. There is indeed little to be read here, for the entries are brief, to the point, and lacking any form of annotation. But for a record of who wrote what and when (complete with publishers, page counts, later editions, etc.), this remains the universal gold standard.

Its price has really taken off since the millennium.

$90

Goldfinger • *Ian Fleming*
Jonathan Cape, London • 318pp • 1959 (w/further editions/ reprints too numerous to count)
Reprinted by Flagstick Books (2000)

Though few works of fiction have been included in *The Golfer's Library, Goldfinger,* as one of the more famous novels of its time, is highly significant in its detailed portrayal of James Bond's high-stakes golf match with the eponymous villain. The match is played at "Royal St. Marks" (a thin cover for the author's beloved Royal St. Georges) and is described with great realism, right down to a rules violation that ultimately determines the winner. Curiously, Fleming does appear to have erred in his interpretation of the rule in question—an oddity for an author who took such great pride in the details.

Under $25+ • Flagstick: New ($29)

Golf Clubs of the Empire: The Golfing Annual •
T.R. Clougher
Clougher, London • 1926 (w/six subsequent annual editions)

Though not markedly different in style from most prewar guidebooks, *Golf Clubs of the Empire* remains a striking testimonial to both the sheer size of the "Greater Britain" and the vast distances over which her agents transported the game of golf. Throughout its seven years of publication it provided comprehensive listings of established clubs and courses both at home and in numerous colonial territories worldwide. And while its relative scarcity may render it economically unessential to many readers, I personally find the glimpses of golf in such far-flung locales as Hong Kong, Nyasaland, and Ceylon to be endlessly fascinating.

$175

Golf: The Passion and the Challenge • *Mark Mulvoy and Art Spander*
Prentice-Hall, Englewood Cliffs, NJ • 256pp • 1977

This colorful edition provides a fine picture of the game as it was in the late 1970s, featuring chapters on equipment, life on the PGA Tour, swing techniques, and putting. Very well. But what stands out about this volume, at least to my mind, are its first and last chapters. The former is a detailed study of course architecture through the words of a young Pete Dye, followed by a blow-by-blow recounting of his design process at Florida's John's Island Club. The latter is a fantasy match-play tournament featuring 16 of golf's greatest-ever players. Both represent enjoyable and unique reading.

Under $25

Golfer's Handbook

Given over a century of evolution, it is impossible to provide bibliographic specs for the game's longest-running (by a mile!) annual publication. Currently titled *The Royal & Ancient Golfer's Handbook*, this venerated backbone of golfing reference has been in existence since 1899, shepherded by numerous well-known editors (presently Renton Laidlaw) and omitting only the war years, 1942–1946. As such, its lengths and contents have varied greatly, though certain components manage to remain constant a full century on.

Earlier editions often exceeded 800 pages and resembled similar period yearbooks, featuring championship records (from *everywhere*), rules, international directories of clubs, a who's who of golf, and a famous section detailing oddities and accomplishments of the game, far and wide. Modern editions (which can push 1,000 pages) have added historical features and the like, though club directories have been scaled back in detail, and now include only the UK and Europe.

Old or new, the massive amount of information included herein makes the *Golfer's Handbook* a valuable edition to any collection.

Early: $175+ • PostWar: $50+ • Modern: New ($43)

Golfer's Year Book • *William D. Richardson and Lincoln A. Werden (Editors)*
Golfer's Year Book, New York • 1930 (w/several subsequent annual editions)

Rather the ambitious volume, *The Golfer's Year Book* was an even grander version of the *American Annual Golf Guide,* including numerous interesting features along with its voluminous listings of American, Canadian, and Caribbean/Mexican courses. Prominent player biographies, regional historical pieces, and championship records are everywhere, boasting writers such as Darwin, Keeler, Darsie L. Darsie, and the architect Charles Banks.

Interestingly, this was one of the very few annuals to actually expand during the Depression, growing from 1930 to '31, then becoming oversized in '32. It apparently disappeared by 1934 but returned for several more WWII-era editions.

$75

Golfing in Southern Africa • *Robert Fall*
South African Golf, Cape Town • 324pp • 1958

Obviously intended as an annual publication, this catalog of South African golf saw only a 1958 edition, perhaps explaining why it stands as a relatively rare title today. Modeled, it seems, after the *Golfer's Handbook*, it presents a similar plethora of information on the history, records, players, and venues of this fertile golfing country. In addition to its comprehensive guide to courses, it features a *Handbook*-like section of "Extraordinary Happenings," a detailed who's who of regional golfers, and articles on greenkeeping and golf course architecture.

Extraneous to some, but well worth the effort to anyone interested in the game's long and storied South African past.

$100

How to Become a Scratch Golfer • *Patrick Campbell*
Anthony Blond, London • 144pp • 1963
Reprinted by Classics of Golf (1998)

Among pretenders to P.G. Wodehouse's undisputed crown as golf's fun-
niest writer, *Sunday Times* humorist Patrick Campbell states his case
with this brief but decidedly amusing volume. Purporting to guide the
beginner through the intricacies of learning the game, it starts with the
basics ("Select a professional who really knows what he's talking about.
There are several of them around."), touches upon the need to acquire
the proper equipment ("professionals only have to take a brief look at
their client to decide which combination is best for him. They always
have it in stock."), then moves on to cover all manner of missed shots,
etiquette breaches, and, most memorably, the "style" of the faux scratch
player.

Lest one take this all in jest, however, the book concludes with a
recounting of the author's own deep run at the 1949 British Amateur
when, at Portmarnock's famous 15th, the gallery awaited his "high, loop-
ing hook which would not be seen again or, alternatively, a furtive, de-
fensive socket onto the beach."

Good stuff.

$30 • COG: New ($29)

The Library of Golf 1743–1966 • *Joseph S.F. Murdoch*
Gale Research, Detroit • 314pp • 1968

As the first known attempt to codify the game's *entire* body of writing,
this, Murdoch's first book, represents a landmark in the golf literature
field. The content is arranged alphabetically, by author, but indexed alphabetically, chronologically, and by subject matter. Some volumes are
accompanied by extensive annotation (highlighted by Murdoch's irreverent wit), others, unfortunately, by none at all.

Never having been reprinted, *The Library of Golf* is a genuine collectors' item, with clean copies costing a pretty penny. The book's massive importance notwithstanding, however, I would suggest the following
economically appealing alternative: First, acquire the relatively common *The Game of Golf and the Printed Word*. Then order a copy of *The
Murdoch Golf Library* (Grant Books, 1991) that lists, with many comments, the late Mr. Murdoch's entire collection. So armed, the reader

will possess about 90 percent of this volume's precious information for roughly one-fifth the price.

$500+

My Greatest Day in Golf • *Darsie L. Darsie*
A.S. Barnes, New York • 210pp • 1950
1st UK edition: Alvin Redman 1952

With appropriate apologies to Pembroke Vaile, Waxo Green, and Otis Dypwick, Darsie L. Darsie, long ago of Los Angeles, must surely have enjoyed the greatest name in the history of golf writing. Yet beyond enjoying such obvious marquee value, *My Greatest Day in Golf* is an enjoyably original book, chronicling the greatest golfing day of 51 top mid-twentieth century players, both professional and amateur. Some of the selections are predictable, others decidedly offbeat. But all are couched in a sense of context and history, as well as the smooth, knowledgeable writing style of one of the last of the old-fashioned scribes.

Blandly illustrated in black and white, but all of the era's top stars, plus an engaging array of amateurs, are here.

$35

The Principles Behind the Rules of Golf • *Richard S. Tufts*
Privately published, Pinehurst • 102pp • 1960 (w/1961 2nd edition)
Reprinted by the USGA (1989)

Our collection would not be complete without at least a nod toward that complicated backbone of the game, the Rules of Golf. In this relatively rare volume, Pinehurst scion and USGA veteran Richard Tufts takes on this task not simply by recounting the rules themselves but rather by examining the fundamental concepts that have given rise to them. As the author puts it: "Running through the rules are underlying principles, that, like the steel rods which lie below the surface of reinforced concrete, serve to bind together the brittle material and to give it strength."

For those less inclined to spend big dollars on their least-favorite aspect of the game, there is always Tom Watson and Frank Hannigan's 1980 collaboration *The Rules of Golf: Illustrated and Explained.* A more recent option—though perhaps the most hypocritical golf book of all time—is Arnold Palmer's *Playing by the Rules,* a remarkably ironic entry in that it was published shortly after Palmer's high-profile endorsement of an illegal club.

Original: $110 • USGA (1,500 copies): $150

The Shell International Encyclopedia of Golf •
Donald Steel and Peter Ryde
Ebury, London • 480pp • 1975
1st US edition (as "The Encyclopedia of Golf"): Viking 1975

Herbert Warren Wind has referred to this as being "one of the few indispensable golf books," and with only the briefest of looks, any knowledgeable reader will find themselves readily in agreement.

To begin with, it was put together by an all-star cast. For while Steel and Ryde's names appear on the title page (along with Wind, as "American Advisory Editor"), nearly 25 additional contributors (from 10 countries and five continents) provided all manner of materials. Consequently this volume likely contains more information on players, events, equipment, rules, courses, and just about any other aspect of golf than has otherwise been assembled within a single cover. It is also, we should note, profusely illustrated with photos, diagrams, and basic course maps, and it just happens to be an extremely pleasant read as well.

I'm not certain that anyone knows exactly how many entries are included, but I can state unequivocally that in the course of my own research, I have rarely turned to its pages and come up wanting.

$40

Twentieth Century Golf Chronicle • *Various*
Publications International, Lincolnwood, IL • 608pp • 1998

This large volume is precisely as advertised: a year-by-year account of the game throughout the last century, focusing on the people, places, and events that came to dominate each golfing season. The method, perhaps, is nothing unique but the depth of coverage just might be, with smaller tournaments, rule changes, and the openings of famous courses representing just some of the miscellaneous information that regularly appears. A great deal of energy clearly went into the assembling of this book, and a great deal of research time can often be saved by consulting it.

Under $25

SECTION X
COURSE AND CLUB HISTORIES

There are, of course, hundreds upon hundreds of club history books out there, and so narrowly defined a genre should not be allowed to consume too many of our precious 400 spaces. Consequently, I have selected 25 that meet the dual conditions of (a) representing a legitimately world-class facility, and (b) illustrating the golf course's history and design to a genuinely high degree.

Because these are nearly always privately published (and in limited edition), locating many can be both difficult and expensive. Is it worth it? I suppose that depends upon one's budget, shelf space, and degree of affection for a particular golf course. But for most of the 25 selected, one can at least rest assured that a more detailed and accurate picture of a given facility can only be achieved by a first-hand visit.

Notes: These volumes are arranged in the alphabetical order of the club's name, *not* the title of the book itself. Also, several of the more contemporary editions are stocked by the clubs themselves, and may well be sold to nonmembers following a polite inquiry.

The Story of the Augusta National Golf Club •
Clifford Roberts
Doubleday, Garden City, NY • 255pp • 1976

Though obviously a bit dated, this remains the closest thing available to a true club history of Augusta National. Perhaps the ultimate in primary sources, Roberts recounts stories of the club's creation and profiles a number of early members and staff. He also provides a detailed list of course changes up to that time—though with the current regime apparently determined to obliterate all that came before it, the relevance of this list is declining by the minute.

$95

Baltusrol 100 Years • *Robert S. Trebus and*
Richard C. Wolffe Jr.
Baltusrol GC • 166pp • 1995

Among the most attractive and detailed of club histories, this colorful volume richly details Baltusrol's early layouts (upon which several Major championships were played), its Tillinghast-designed Upper and Lower courses, and the many important events (including seven U.S. Opens) that have taken place here since 1895.

More thorough—and easily found—than James J. Mahon's earlier *Baltusrol: 90 Years in the Mainstream of American Golf.*

$65

Cherry Hills Country Club 1922–1997 •
George E. Brown III
Cherry Hills CC • 168pp • 1998

Though this volume fails to detail the club's present-day golf course to the usual standard, it draws alternative kudos for reprinting William Flynn's original Golden Age hole drawings, a rare treat indeed. Hardcore collectors will note that these same drawings also appeared in the club's smaller 50th-anniversary book, *Fifty Years of Mostly Fun,* in 1972.

$50

Chicago Golf Club 1892–1992 • *Ross Goodner*
Chicago GC • 157pp • 1991

As one might expect from such a golfing shrine, this volume provides much detail regarding C.B. Macdonald and the club's illustrious early years. Also especially noteworthy is the hole-by-hole tour of the golf course guided by Ben Crenshaw.
"Far & Sure."

$125+

The Legacy Continues: A 50-Year History of Colonial Country Club • *Russ Pate*
Colonial CC • 156pp • 1986

A large and nicely illustrated book, *The Legacy Continues* profiles what is comfortably the youngest of our featured clubs—though with a U.S. Open, Ben Hogan, and so many PGA Tour visits under its belt, Colonial's pedigree stands well above reproach. Architecture fans will find the replacement of three original holes with today's "horrible horseshoe" particularly interesting.

$70

Alister MacKenzie's Cypress Point Club •
Geoff Shackelford
Sleeping Bear, Chelsea, MI • 189pp • 2000

It is the rare club history that is not published directly by the club, but then Cypress Point is one very rare club. The highlights of this volume, by far, are hole-by-hole photos of course architect Dr. Alister MacKenzie playing the legendary layout shortly after its opening—an utterly remarkable documentation of the artist and his creation. Comprehensive biographies of MacKenzie and his right hand, Robert Hunter, are a fine bonus.

New ($35)

Sixty-Seven Years of the Fishers Island Golf Club Links •
Charles B. Ferguson
Fishers Island GC • 69pp • 1993

This hard-to-find volume is refreshingly simple, presenting Seth Raynor's wonderfully unaltered golf course in great detail. The endpapers, an Olmsted Brothers map which includes the routing of a never-built second 18, are especially fascinating.

$200+

The Maidstone Links • *David Goddard*
Maidstone Club • 144pp • 1997

A beautifully researched work, this volume covers in great detail the evolution of Maidstone's famous and highly exclusive links. Primarily black and white photos (with a brief color insert) are a small disappointment but a gallery of aerial surveys, dating from 1930 to 1994, more than makes up for it.

$45

Golf at Merion • *Desmond Tolhurst*
Merion GC • 176pp • 1989

Among the very finest of club history books, this nicely illustrated work highlights the club's development, the layouts of both the East and West courses, and a uniquely rich tournament history. Of particular note are the maps and old photos detailing the East course's modernization in the mid-1920s.

    With the USGA hesitant to bring the U.S. Open back for face-saving and profit-margin reasons, no revised edition figures to be necessary.

$100+

Muirfield: Home of the Honourable Company •
Norman Mair
Mainstream, Edinburgh • 168pp • 1994

The Honourable Company is, by most reasonable accounts, the oldest golfing club in the world, so a first-class history book would certainly seem in order. This attractive (and relatively findable) volume fits the bill in terms of both content and style. The obvious question: How did Mair make it all fit?

$30

The Evolution of a Legacy/The Crowned Jewels of Oak Hill • *Donald M. Kladstrup*
Oak Hill CC • 42pp/46pp • 1995/1989 • PBK

This pair of paperback booklets does a fine job of profiling the club's famous East course, particularly *The Evolution of a Legacy,* which superimposes Donald Ross's original designs over drawings of the present holes. Proof that a massive budget isn't necessary to produce a club record of quality.

$25

Oakmont Country Club: The First Seventy-Seven Years •
Edward B. Foote
Oakmont CC • 80pp • 1980

The publication of this detailed book predates most in this section, thus two memorable U.S. Opens (1983 and 1994) are not covered. But the creation and evolution of this legendary golf course is nicely documented—and that's the stuff we can't easily find elsewhere.

$140

The Pasatiempo Story • *Margaret Koch*
Pasatiempo Inc. • 126pp • 1990 (w/PBK + 1997 reprinting)

Though this book is not entirely about golf, it attractively presents the fascinating history of the MacKenzie-designed course that would also serve as the good doctor's final residence and resting place. Though hole illustrations are infrequent, the reproduction of the 1929 Olmsted Bros. property survey makes for fine compensation.

Hardcover: $50

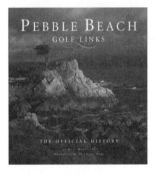

Pebble Beach Golf Links •
Neil Hotelling
Sleeping Bear, Chelsea, MI • 224pp • 1999

Prepared in advance of the 2000 U.S. Open, this colorful volume features numerous photos (old and new) of Pebble Beach and the surrounding development. A detailed history of the celebrated course's evolution (particularly Chandler Egan's 1928 renovation) is provided, though there is no hole-by-hole profile.

Under $25

Pine Valley Golf Club: A Chronicle • *Warner Shelly*
Pine Valley GC • 107pp • 1982

From a golf course perspective, this is easily the best of Pine Valley's three history volumes as it profiles all 18 holes individually, each with historic and modern photographs. There is plenty of background on George Crump and the course's illustrious design process as well.

$75

Pinehurst Stories: A Celebration of Great Golf and Good Times • *Lee Pace*
Resorts of Pinehurst • 224pp • 1991 (w/expanded 2nd edition 1999)

Obviously operating on the promotional budget of a large resort, this attractively produced volume succeeds nicely in capturing a piece of Pinehurst's special golfing atmosphere. A heavy nod is made to the resort's history, to Donald Ross, and to years of tournament action, but the detailed profiling of the legendary No. 2 course isn't bad either.
Original: $70 • 1999: New ($50)

Prestwick Golf Club: Birthplace of The Open •
David Cameron Smail (Editor)
Prestwick GC • 238pp • 1989

Prestwick was initially the sole home of the Open Championship and on its hallowed grounds names like Willie Park Sr. and Jr., Old and Young Tom Morris, John Ball, Harry Vardon, and James Braid combined to win an incredible 18 championship belts and claret jugs. Talk about your historical treasure troves . . .
$85

The Riviera Country Club: A Definitive History •
Geoff Shackelford
Riviera CC • 196pp • 1995

Along with *Baltusrol 100 Years* and *Golf at Merion,* this stands among the elite of American club history volumes. Aside from its scores of historic, tournament, and golf course photos, the book stands out both for its thoroughness and for the presence of the many stars and celebrities that have, over the years, helped to define this Los Angeles golfing mecca.
$60

A History of the Royal Dornoch Golf Club 1877–1999 •
John Macleod
Moravian, Elgin • 120pp • 2000

Though visual coverage of the course is limited to only a few color photos and three period routing maps, this informative volume captures much of what is special about Dornoch and, for that matter, the whole of Scottish golf. The obligatory section on Donald Ross is very much in evidence.

New ($32)

The Royal Melbourne Golf Club: A Centenary History •
Joseph Johnson
Royal Melbourne GC • 256pp • 1991

Strictly speaking, this book pays less attention to the golf course(s) than is our standard—rather a surprise given the utterly superlative nature of the club's 36 holes. But the aerial surveys that are included (complete with overdrawn highlights) are revealing, as is an early Alex Russell map of Dr. MacKenzie's West course.

$90

Golf at St. Andrews • *Keith Mackie*
Pelican, Gretna, LA • 192pp • 1995
1st UK edition: Aurum 1995

There is, of course, no shortage of books chronicling the history of St. Andrews, and the reality is that the majority are highly similar in overall content. This particular volume, penned by a former editor of Britain's *Golf World* magazine, is my personal choice, largely on the strength of its graphics. For in addition to the usual array of historical and contemporary photos, it includes highly detailed maps of each hole on the Old Course—just the type that come in handy when sitting down to watch the Open Championship.

$40

St. Andrews • *Louis T. Stanley*
Salem House, Topsfield, MA • 216pp • 1986
1st UK edition: W.H. Allen 1986

If professional writing is considered an important quality among club histories, then Louis Stanley's rendition of the St. Andrews narrative is likely worth acquiring. This volume is not as well-illustrated as Mackie or David Joy's (see below), but when the story is one we've largely heard before, having a strong storyteller on board becomes valuable. Hole-by-hole diagrams included.

$30

St. Andrews & The Open Championship • *David Joy*
Sleeping Bear, Chelsea, MI • 240pp • 1999

What course but St. Andrews would qualify for three separate selections here? This version recounts the first 25 Open Championships played over the Old Course while offering a particularly wide range of photos, both old and contemporary.

$35

Waialae Country Club: The First Half Century •
Thomas Hitch and Mary Kuramoto
Waialae CC • 220pp • 1981

Though worthwhile for presenting early aerial photos and a map of Seth Raynor's much-altered original design, this coffee-table-sized tome scores bonus points for a detailed 34-page section on the history of golf (and courses) throughout Hawaii.

$45

Winged Foot Story • *Douglass L. Smith*
Winged Foot GC • 192pp • 1984 (w/revised 1994 edition & PBK)

This volume's subtitle ("The Golf, the People, the Friendly Trees") will certainly ring true to players and arborists alike. But between detailed tours of the property's abundant flora, it finds time to recount Winged Foot's remarkable history and profile all 36 of its famously challenging Tillinghast holes.

Original: $40

Appendix

Part I—The Complete Book Titles of Golf's Landmark Writers (arranged chronologically within each writer, from date of first book)

Notes: – Only books with golf-oriented subject matter are included.
   – Only bold-faced titles appear in *The Golfer's Library*.
   – Any material under 20 pages not included.
   – Subsequent revised or abridged editions and reprints are not listed, nor are overseas titles (see main text).

Bernard Darwin

The Golf Courses of the British Isles • Duckworth • 253pp • 1910
Tee Shots and Others • Kegan Paul • 271pp • 1911
Golf from the Times • The Times • 141pp • 1912
Hints on Golf • Burberry's • 55pp • 1912
Golf: Some Hints and Suggestions • Country Life • 32pp • 1920
Present Day Golf • Hodder & Stoughton • 309pp • 1921
A Friendly Round • Mills & Boon • 142pp • 1922
A Round of Golf on the L&NER • London & Northeastern Railway • 127pp • c1925
The Golf Courses of Great Britain • Jonathan Cape • 287pp • 1925
Six Golfing Shots by Six Famous Players • Dormeuil Freres • 46pp • 1927
Green Memories • Hodder & Stoughton • 332pp • c1928

Golf in Great Britain and Ireland • Travel Assoc. of Great Britain • 39pp • c1930
Second Shots • George Newnes • 178pp • 1930
Out of the Rough • Chapman & Hall • 336pp • c1932
Playing the Like • Chapman & Hall • 246pp • 1934
Rubs of the Green • Chapman & Hall • 260pp • 1936
Life Is Sweet Brother • Collins • 285pp • 1940
Pack Clouds Away • Collins • 288pp • 1941
Golf Between Two Wars • Chatto & Windus • 227pp • 1944
British Golf • Collins • 47pp • 1946
Golfing By-Paths • Country Life • 203pp • 1946
Every Idle Dream • Collins • 254pp • 1948
James Braid • Hodder & Stoughton • 196pp • 1952
A History of Golf in Britain • Cassell • 312pp • 1952
    (with Longhurst, Cotton, etc.)
Golf: The Pleasures of Life Series • Burke • 222pp • 1954
The World That Fred Made • Chatto & Windus • 256pp • 1955
Mostly Golf • A&C Black • 198pp • 1976
A Round with Darwin • Souvenir • 223pp • 1984
Darwin on the Green • Souvenir • 240pp • 1986
The Darwin Sketchbook • Classics of Golf • 384pp • 1991
The Happy Golfer • Flagstick • 264pp • 1997
Bernard Darwin on Golf • Lyons • 414pp • 2003

Peter Dobereiner

The Game with a Hole in It • Faber & Faber • 142pp • 1970
The Glorious World of Golf • McGraw-Hill • 250pp • 1973
Stroke, Hole or Match? • David & Charles • 192pp • 1976
For the Love of Golf • Stanley Paul • 256pp • 1981
Down the Nineteenth Fairway • Andre Deutch • 205pp • 1982
The Golfers—The Inside Story • Collins • 190pp • 1982
The Book of Golf Disasters • Stanley Paul • 179pp • 1983
Jacklin's Golf Secrets • Stanley Paul • 109pp • 1983
Golf à la Carte • Stanley Paul • 219pp • 1991

Horace G. Hutchinson

Hints on the Game of Golf • William Blackwood • 69pp • 1886
Golf: The Badminton Library • Longmans, Green • 495pp • 1890

Famous Golf Links • Longmans, Green • 199pp • 1891
Golfing: The Oval Series of Games • George Routledge • 120pp •
  1893
After Dinner Golf • Hudson • 124pp • 1896
British Golf Links • J.S. Virtue • 331pp • 1897
A Golfing Pilgrim on Many Links • Methuen • 287pp • 1898
The Book of Golf and Golfers • Longmans, Green • 316pp • 1899
Aspects of Golf • J.W. Arrowsmith • 150pp • 1900
Bert Edward, the Golf Caddie • John Murray • 257pp • 1903
Golf Greens and Green-Keeping • Country Life • 219pp • 1906
The New Book of Golf • Longmans, Green • 361pp • 1912
Fifty Years of Golf • Country Life • 229pp • 1919
The Lost Golfer • John Murray • 335pp • 1930

Dan Jenkins

Sports Illustrated's the Best 18 Golf Holes in America • Delacorte
  • 160pp • 1966
The Dogged Victims of Inexorable Fate • Little Brown • 298pp •
  1970
Dead Solid Perfect • Atheneum • 234pp • 1974
You Gotta Play Hurt • Simon & Schuster • 353pp • 1991
Fairways and Greens • Doubleday • 247pp • 1994

O.B. Keeler

The Autobiography of an Average Golfer • Greenberg • 247pp •
  1925
Down the Fairway • Minton, Balch • 239pp • 1927 (with Bobby
  Jones)
The Boy's Life of Bobby Jones • Harpers' • 308pp • 1931
Golf in North Carolina • NC Dept of Conservation & Develop-
  ment • 52pp • c1938

Henry Leach

Great Golfers in the Making • Methuen • 299pp • 1907
The Spirit of the Links • Methuen • 314pp • 1907
Letters of a Modern Golfer to His Grandfather • Mills & Boon •
  309pp • 1910
The Happy Golfer • Macmillan • 414pp • 1914

Henry Longhurst

Candid Caddies • Duckworth • 120pp • 1935
Golf • J.M. Dent • 303pp • 1937
Go Golfing • Duckworth • 105pp • 1937 (with Archie Compston)
It Was Good While It Lasted • J.M. Dent • 342pp • 1941
Golf Mixture • Werner Laurie • 203pp • 1952
A History of Golf in Britain • Cassell • 312pp • 1952 (with
    Darwin, Cotton, etc.)
Round in Sixty-Eight • Werner Laurie 173pp 1953
The Old Course at St. Andrews • A.G. Spalding • 39pp • 1961
Only on Sundays • Cassell • 259pp • 1964
Ryder Cup, 1965 • Stanley Paul • 64pp • 1965 (with Geoffrey
    Cousins)
Talking about Golf • Macdonald • 150pp • 1966
How to Get Started in Golf • Hodder & Stoughton • 92pp • 1967
Never on Weekdays • Cassell • 182pp • 1968
Southport: Golf Centre of Europe • County Borough • 32pp •
    c1969
My Life and Soft Times • Cassell • 366pp • 1971
The Best of Henry Longhurst • Collins • 206pp • 1979
The Essential Henry Longhurst • Willow • 320pp • 1988

H.B. Martin

Golf Yarns: The Best Things about the Game of Golf • Dodd
    Mead • 85pp • 1913
Sketches Made at the Winter Golf League . . . • Publishers
    Typesetting • 102pp • 1915
Pictorial Golf • Dodd Mead • 243pp • 1928
The Making of a Champion • Harry C. Lee • 32pp • 1928
What's Wrong with Your Golf Game • Dodd Mead • 240pp •
    1930
Golf for Beginners • Modern Sports • 98pp • 1930
Great Golfers in the Making • Dodd Mead • 268pp • 1932
Fifty Years of American Golf • Dodd Mead • 423pp • 1936
How to Play Golf • Modern Sports • 98pp • 1936
St. Andrews Golf Club 1888–1938 • Privately printed • 146pp •
    1938 (with A.B. Halliday)
The Garden City Golf Club 1899–1949 • Privately printed • 67pp
    • 1949

Charles Price

Golf Magazine's Pro Pointers and Stroke Savers • Harpers • 253pp
• 1960
The World of Golf • Random House • 307pp • 1962
Shell's Wonderful World of Golf 1963 • Shell Oil • 24pp • 1963
The American Golfer • Random House • 241pp • 1964
Sports Illustrated Book of Golf • Lippincott • 73pp • 1970
Esquire's Golfer's Guide • Esquire • 28pp • 1972
The World Atlas of Golf • Mitchell Beazley • 280pp • 1976
   (with Ward-Thomas, Wind, etc.)
Black's Picture Sports: Golf • A&C Black • 95pp • 1976
The Carolina Lowcountry, Birthplace of American Golf • Sea Pines
   • 76pp • 1980 (with G. Rogers)
Golfer-at-Large • Atheneum • 241pp • 1982
A Golf Story • Atheneum • 161pp • 1987

Grantland Rice

The Winning Shot • Doubleday, Page • 258pp • 1915 (with Jerome
   Travers)
The Duffer's Handbook of Golf • Macmillan • 163pp • 1926
Fore—With a Glance Aft • Conde Nast • 47pp • c1929
The Bobby Jones Story • Tupper & Love • 303pp • 1953

Garden G. Smith

Golf • Lawrence & Bullen • 104pp • 1897
The World of Golf • A.D. Innis • 330pp • 1898
Side Lights on Golf • Sisley's • 153pp • 1907
The Royal and Ancient Game of Golf • Golf Illustrated • 275pp •
   1912 (with Harold Hilton)

Louis T. Stanley

Green Fairways • Methuen • 204pp • 1947
Fresh Fairways • Methuen • 220pp • 1949
Master Golfers in Action • Macdonald • 143pp • 1950
Style Analysis • Naldrett • 103pp • 1951
The Woman Golfer • Macdonald • 128pp • 1952
The Faulkner Method • Hutchinson • 62pp • 1952 (with Max
   Faulkner)

This Is Golf • W.H. Allen • 192pp • 1954
The Golfer's Bedside Book • Methuen • 197pp • 1955
Fontana Golf Book • Collins • 127pp • 1957
Swing to Better Golf • Collins • 256pp • 1957
This Is Putting • W.H. Allen • 191pp • c1957
The Book of Golf • Max Parrish • 147pp • 1960
Golf with Your Hands • Collins • 256pp • 1966
Pelham Golf Year • Pelham • 443pp • 1981 (w/2 subsequent editions)
St. Andrews • W.H. Allen • 216pp • 1986
A History of Golf • Weidenfeld & Nicolson • 218pp • 1991

Pat Ward-Thomas

Masters of Golf • Heinemann • 257pp • 1961
The Long Green Fairway • Hodder & Stoughton • 192pp • 1966
Shell Golfer's Atlas of England, Scotland and Wales • George Rainbird • 76pp • 1968
The World Atlas of Golf • Mitchell Beazley • 280pp • 1976 (with Wind, Price, etc.)
The Royal and Ancient • R&A Golf Club • 124pp • 1980
Not Only Golf • Hodder & Stoughton • 206pp • 1981

Herbert Warren Wind

The Story of American Golf • Farrar, Strauss • 502pp • 1948
Thirty Years of Championship Golf • Prentice-Hall • 276pp • 1950 (with Gene Sarazen)
The Complete Golfer • Simon & Schuster • 315pp • 1954
Tips from the Top • Prentice-Hall • 105pp • 1955
Tips from the Top: Book 2 • Prentice-Hall • 105pp • 1956
Five Lessons: The Modern Fundamentals of Golf • A.S. Barnes • 127pp • 1957 (with Ben Hogan)

On Tour with Harry Sprague • Simon & Schuster • 94pp • 1960
Shell's Wonderful World of Golf 1962 • Shell Oil • 24pp • 1962
The Greatest Game of All • Simon & Schuster • 416pp • 1969
(with Jack Nicklaus)
Herbert Warren Wind's Golf Book • Simon & Schuster • 317pp •
1971
The World Atlas of Golf • Mitchell Beazley • 280pp • 1976
(with Ward-Thomas, Price, etc.)
Golf Quiz • Golf Digest • 248pp • 1980
Following Through • Ticknor & Fields • 414pp • 1985

P.G. Wodehouse

The Clicking of Cuthbert • Herbert Jenkins • 256pp • 1922
The Heart of a Goof • Herbert Jenkins • 314pp • 1926
Wodehouse on Golf • Doubleday, Doran • 844pp • 1940
The Golf Omnibus • Barrie & Jenkins • 467pp • 1973
Fore: The Best of Wodehouse on Golf • Ticknor & Fields • 259pp
• 1983

Part II—The Complete Book Titles of Golf's Greatest Players (arranged chronologically within each writer, from date of first book)

Notes: – Only bold-faced titles appear in *The Golfer's Library.*
– Any material under 20 pages not included.
– Subsequent revised or abridged editions and reprints are
not listed, nor are overseas titles (see main text).

Tommy Armour

How to Play Your Best Golf All the Time • Simon & Schuster •
151pp • 1953
A Round of Golf with Tommy Armour • Simon & Schuster •
143pp • 1959
Tommy Armour Speaks • Macgregor • 20pp • c1960
Play Better Golf: The Irons • The News • 22pp • 1963
Play Better Golf: The Drive • The News • 23pp • 1964
Tommy Armour's ABC's of Golf • Simon & Schuster • 187pp •
1967

Severiano Ballesteros

Seve Tours: Golf Tours of Spain • Iberia Air Lines • 64pp • 1981
Seve: The Young Champion • Hodder & Stoughton • 156pp •
1982
Natural Golf • Athenuem • 219pp • 1988
Trouble-Shooting • Broadway • 174pp • 1996

James Braid

Golf Guide and How to Play Golf • British Sports • 144pp • 1906
How to Play Golf • American Sports • 123pp • 1907 (with Harry
Vardon)
Advanced Golf • Methuen • 322pp • 1908
Ladies' Field Golf Book • George Newnes • 85pp • 1908

Henry Cotton

Golf • Eyre & Spottiswoode • 147pp • 1931
Hints on Play with Steel Shafts • British Steel Golf Shafts • 40pp •
c1933
Some Golfing Ifs • British Steel Golf Shafts • 40pp • c1938
This Game of Golf • Country Life • 248pp • 1948
A History of Golf in Britain • Cassell • 312pp • 1952
(with Longhurst, Darwin, etc.)
My Swing • Country Life • 144pp • 1952
My Golfing Album • Country Life • 248pp • 1959
Henry Cotton Says . . . • Country Life • 80pp • 1962
Study the Golf Game with Henry Cotton • Country Life • 236pp •
1964
The Picture Story of the Golf Game • World Distributors • 157pp
• c1965
Henry Cotton's Guide to Golf in the British Isles • Cliveden •
124pp • 1969
Golf: A Pictorial History • Collins • 240pp • 1975
Thanks for the Game: The Best of Golf with Henry Cotton •
Sidgwick & Jackson • 176pp • 1980

Nick Faldo

The Rough with the Smooth • Stanley Paul • 172pp • 1980
Enjoying Golf with Nick Faldo • St. Michael • 128pp • 1985

On Course for the Open: A Pictorial Biography • Stanley Paul •
 128pp • 1987
Golf—The Winning Formula • Stanley Paul • 239pp • 1990
Faldo: In Search of Perfection • Weidenfeld & Nicolson • 159pp •
 1994
Faldo: A Swing for Life • Viking Penguin • 224pp • 1995

Walter Hagen

Golf Clubs and How to Use Them • W.J. Brueckman • 22pp • 1929
The How and Why of Golf • L.A. Young • 31pp • c1932
The Walter Hagen Story • Simon & Schuster • 341pp • 1956

Harold Hilton

My Golfing Reminiscences • James Nisbet • 247pp • 1907
The Royal and Ancient Game of Golf • Golf Illustrated • 275pp •
 1912 (with Garden Smith)
Modern Golf • Outing • 140pp • 1913

Ben Hogan

Here's Your Free Golf Lesson • Bromo-Seltzer • 56pp • c1940
Power Golf • A.S. Barnes • 166pp • 1948
The Complete Guide to Golf • Bobbs-Merrill • 144pp • 1955
 (with others)
Five Lessons: The Modern Fundamentals of Golf • A.S. Barnes •
 127pp • 1957 (with H.W. Wind)

Bobby Jones

Down the Fairway • Minton, Balch • 239pp • 1927 (with O.B.
 Keeler)
How to Play Golf • Bell Syndicate • 32pp • 1929
My Twelve Most Difficult Shots • B&B • 63pp • c1929
Bobby Jones on Golf • New Metropolitan • 112pp • 1930
Golf Bobby Jones—Out of the Rough and Putt • Flicker • 100pp •
 1930
Golf Shots by Bobby Jones—Driver and Mashie Shots • Flicker •
 100pp • c1930
Short Cuts to Par Golf • Fawcett • 65pp • 1931 (with Sarazen,
 Hagen, Armour, etc.)

Rights and Wrongs of Golf • A.G. Spalding • 45pp • 1935
Some Tips from Bobby Jones • A.G. Spalding • 22pp • c1935
How To Run a Golf Tournament • American Golf Inst. • 32pp •
  c1936
Group Instructions in Golf • American Sports • 63pp • 1939
  (with Harold Lowe)
The Masters Tournament • Privately printed • 32pp • c1952
  (with Clifford Roberts)
Golf Is My Game • Doubleday • 255pp • 1960
Bobby Jones on Golf • Doubleday • 246pp • 1966
Bobby Jones on the Basic Golf Swing • Doubleday • 63pp • 1969

Bobby Locke

Bobby Locke on Golf • Country Life • 196pp • 1953
Golf Hints • Lotus • 36pp • c1955

Byron Nelson

Winning Golf • A.S. Barnes • 190pp • 1946
How to Score Better than You Swing • Golf Digest • 32pp • c1955
Shape Your Swing the Modern Way • Golf Digest • 127pp • 1976
The Byron Nelson Story • Old Golf Shop • 130pp • 1980 (com-
  piled by Mort Olman)
How I Played the Game • Taylor • 271pp • 1993
The Little Black Book • Summit • 175pp • 1995

Jack Nicklaus

My 55 Ways to Lower Your Golf Score •
  Simon & Schuster • 125pp • 1964
The Best Way to Better Golf • Fawcett •
  128pp • 1966
The Best Way to Better Golf, Number 2 •
  Fawcett • 127pp • 1968
Jack Nicklaus: Profile of a Champion •
  Ohio Promotion • 50pp • 1968
Take a Tip from Me • Simon & Schuster
  • 125pp • 1968
The Greatest Game of All • Simon &
  Schuster • 416pp • 1969 (with H.W.
  Wind)

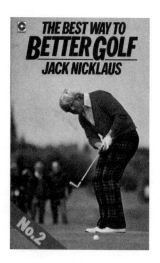

The Best Way to Better Golf, Number 3 • Fawcett • 128pp • 1969
Jack Nicklaus Plays the NCR South • Ohio Promotion • 46pp • 1969
Winning Golf • Grow Ahead • 32pp • 1969
18 Holes • Grow Ahead • 32pp • 1970
Jack Nicklaus Golf Handbook • Benjamin • 60pp • 1973
Golf My Way • Simon & Schuster • 264pp • 1974
Jack Nicklaus' Lesson Tee • Golf Digest • 157pp • 1977
On & Off the Fairway: A Pictorial Autobiography • Simon &
 Schuster • 255pp • 1978
Play Better Golf, the Swing from A–Z • Pocket Books • 200pp • 1980
Play Better Golf, Volume II • Pocket Books • 207pp • 1981
Jack Nicklaus' Playing Lessons • Golf Digest • 142pp • 1981
Play Better Golf, Volume III • Pocket Books • 207pp • 1983
The Full Swing • Golf Digest • 205pp • 1984
My Fifty Most Memorable Shots in the Majors • Golf Digest •
 126pp • 1988
The Best of Nicklaus' Golf • Chancellor • 205pp • 1992
My Story: An Autobiography • Simon & Schuster • 505pp • 1997
My Golden Lessons • Simon & Schuster • 176pp • 2002
Nicklaus by Design • Harry N. Abrams • 288pp • 2002

Greg Norman

Greg Norman: My Story • Harrap • 160pp • 1983
Shark Attack: Greg Norman's Guide to Aggressive Golf •
 Macmillan • 191pp • 1987
Greg Norman's Instant Lessons • Simon
 & Schuster • 221pp • 1993
Advanced Golf • George E. Tuttle •
 208pp • 1995

Arnold Palmer

Arnold Palmer's Golf Book • Ronald •
 142pp • 1961
Graph-Check System for Golf • Graph-
 Check • 72pp • c1963
Portrait of a Professional Golfer • Golf
 Digest • 110pp • 1964
My Game and Yours • Simon & Schuster
 • 158pp • 1965

The Arnold Palmer Method • Dell •
   235pp • 1968
Situation Golf • McCall • 83pp • 1970
Arnold Palmer Plays Merion • Arnold
   Palmer Enterprises • 44pp • 1971
Go for Broke: My Philosophy of Win-
   ning Golf • Simon & Schuster •
   252pp • 1973
495 Golf Lessons • Follett • 128pp •
   1973
Arnold Palmer's Best 54 Golf Holes •
   Doubleday • 206pp • 1977
Arnold Palmer's Complete Book of
   Putting • Atheneum • 163pp • 1986

Play Great Golf • Doubleday • 181pp • 1987
Honor & Glory: Arnold Palmer's Guide to the 1995 Ryder Cup •
   Crow International • 168pp • 1995
Golf Academy Golf Journal • Triumph • 138pp • 1997
A Golfer's Life • Ballentine • 420pp • 1999
Playing by the Rules • Pocket Star • 336pp • 2002

Willie Park Jr.

The Game of Golf • Longmans, Green • 277pp • 1896
The Art of Putting • J&J Gray • 47pp • 1920

Gary Player

Gary Player's Golf Secrets • Prentice-Hall • 146pp • 1962
Play Golf with Player • Collins • 190pp • 1962
Improve Your Golf • Vacuum Oil • 20pp • c1962
Grand Slam Golf • Cassell • 133pp • 1966
Positive Golf • McGraw-Hill • 119pp • 1967
Gary Player's Golf Class [Book I] 100 Lessons • Beaverbrook •
   84pp • 1967
124 Golf Lessons • Golfer's Digest Assoc. • 50pp • 1968
Gary Player's Golf Class • The Star • 48pp • 1968
More Tips from Gary Player • The Star • 64pp • 1968
Gary Player's Golf Class [Book II] 100 Lessons • Beaverbrook •
   83pp • 1969

Play Better Golf with Gary Player Edutext • Outmart • 128pp • 1970

Good Test for the 1970 U.S. Open, Hazletine National Golf Club • Outmart • 44pp • 1970

The Medium Iron to the Green • Visual Instruction Booklets • 144pp • c1971

The Tee Shot • Visual Instruction Booklets • 144pp • c1971

395 Golf Lessons • Follett • 112pp • 1972

Gary Player: World Golfer • Word Books • 193pp • 1974

Gary Player's Golf Guide • The Star • 24pp • c1974

Gary Player's Golf Class [Book III] 162 Lessons • Sunday Express • 100pp • 1975

Gary Player on Fitness and Success • Worlds Work • 102pp • 1979

Gary Player's Golf Book for Young People • Golf Digest • 110pp • 1980

Gary Player's Golf Class [Book IV] 170 Lessons • Sunday Express • 100pp • 1980

Gary Player's Golf Clinic • DBI Books • 160pp • 1981

Golf Begins at Fifty • Simon & Schuster • 254pp • 1988

Fit for Golf • Weidenfeld & Nicolson • 175pp • 1994

Bunker Play • Broadway • 160pp • 1996

The Complete Golfer's Handbook • New Holland • 160pp • 1999

Gary Player's Top Golf Courses of the World • Lyons • 160pp • 2001

Golfer's Guide to the Meaning of Life • Rodale • 144pp • 2001

Gene Sarazen

Gene Sarazen's Common Sense Golf Tips • Wilson Sporting Goods • 104pp • 1924

From Tee to Cup • Wilson Sporting Goods • 64pp • 1937 (with others)

Want to Be a Golf Champion? • General Mills • 29pp • 1945

The Golf Clinic • Ziff-Davis • 157pp • 1949 (with Snead and others)

Thirty Years of Championship Golf • Prentice-Hall • 276pp • 1950

Golf: New Horizons • Thomas Y. Crowell • 276pp • 1966
Better Golf after Fifty • Harper & Row • 120pp • 1967
Gene Sarazen's World Golf Directory • World Sports • 208pp •
  1977

Sam Snead

Sam Snead's Quick Way to Better Golf • Sun Dial • 76pp • 1938
How to Play Golf, and Professional Tips on Improving Your Score
  • Garden City • 173pp • 1946
How to Hit a Golf Ball from Any Sort of Lie • Doubleday • 74pp
  • 1950
Natural Golf • A.S. Barnes • 208pp • 1953
Sam Snead's Celebrity Golf Tips • Golf Digest • 31pp • 1960
Sam Snead's Secrets of Golf • Consolidated • 96pp • c1960
Stop-Action Golf Book, 2–4 Iron • Coca-Cola • 46pp • c1960
Sam Snead on Golf • Prentice-Hall • 146pp • 1961
The Education of a Golfer • Simon & Schuster • 248pp • 1962
The Driver Book • Golf Digest • 126pp • 1963
Short Cuts to Long Drives • Golf Digest • 23pp • c1965
Sam Snead Teaches You His Simple Key Approach to Golf •
  Atheneum • 178pp • 1975
Golf Begins at Forty • Dial Press • 175pp • 1978
Slammin' Sam • Donald Fine • 238pp • 1986
Pigeons, Marks, Hustlers and Other Golf Bettors You Can Beat •
  Stanley Paul • 112pp • 1987
The Lessons I've Learned • Macmillan • 173pp • 1989
The Game I've Loved • Ballentine • 223pp • 1997

J.H. Taylor

Taylor on Golf: Impressions, Comments and Hints • Hutchinson •
  328pp • 1902
Golf Faults Illustrated • George Newnes • 140pp • 1905
  (with George Beldam)
Golf: My Life's Work • Jonathan Cape • 236pp • 1943

Peter Thomson

This Wonderful World of Golf • Pelham • 222pp • 1969
  (with Desmond Zwar)

The World Atlas of Golf • Mitchell Beazley • 280pp • 1976
(with Ward-Thomas, Price, etc.)

Walter Travis

Practical Golf • Harper's • 225pp • 1901
The Art of Putting • Macmillan • 31pp • 1904

Lee Trevino

Lee's Secret: The Fascinating Success Story of Lee Trevino •
    Confidence • 21pp • 1969
I Can Help Your Game • Fawcett • 112pp • 1971
Groove Your Golf Swing My Way • Atheneum • 184pp • 1976
They Call Me Super Mex • Random House • 202pp • 1982
The Snake in the Sandtrap • Holt, Rinehart & Winston • 166pp •
    1985

Harry Vardon

How to Play Golf • American Sports • 123pp • 1907
    (with James Braid)
The Complete Golfer • Methuen • 283pp • 1905
How to Play Golf • Methuen • 298pp • 1912
Success at Golf • Fry's Magazine • 143pp • 1914 (with others)
Golf Club Selection • Burke Golf Co. • 48pp • 1916
Progressive Golf • Hutchinson • 160pp • 1920
My Golfing Life • Hutchinson • 281pp • 1933

Tom Watson

The Rules of Golf: Illustrated and Explained • Random House •
    200pp • 1980
Getting Up and Down • Random House • 192pp • 1983
The New Rules of Golf • Random House • 181pp • 1984
Tom Watson's Getting Back to Basics • Pocket Star • 127pp • 1992
Tom Watson's Strategic Golf • Pocket Books • 120pp • 1993
The 25 Greatest Achievements in Golf • Triumph • 132pp • 1997

Tiger Woods

How I Play Golf • Warner • 320pp • 2001

ACKNOWLEDGMENTS

In addition to the three major acknowledgments mentioned in the introduction, I must offer my sincere thanks to several additional people.

Most prominent among these must surely be my mother Roberta, who performed a splendid edit of this text despite having virtually no interest in the subject at hand. Further editorial thanks go to my father Hannan, my sister Joanna, and to my friend Geoff Shackelford, an invaluable resource both in selecting the chosen 400 and assembling some coherent remarks about them.

I would also wish to extend my sincere appreciation to the staffs of two very special Southern California institutions, the Amateur Athletic Foundation and the Riviera Country Club. Without the support I have received in both of these wonderful places, this and several other projects could never have come to fruition.

And finally my thanks to my agent, Marilyn Allen, as well as to everyone at Ann Arbor Media Group who helped to make *The Golfer's Library* a reality.

—DW

INDEX

Great Britain, 15, 26, 46, 124–25. *See
    also* England, Scotland
*Great Donald Ross Golf Courses You
    Can Play* 129
Great Golf Courses of Canada 129–30
Great Golf Courses of Ireland 130
Great Golf Courses of the World 130
Great Golfers in the Making xiv, 18
*Great Golfers: Their Methods at a
    Glance* xiv, 19
*Greatest Game of All: My Life in Golf,
    The* xviii, 175
*Greatest of Them All: The Legend of
    Bobby Jones, The* 175
Green Fairways 73
Green Memories xv, 176
Green, Robert 43, 159
Greg Norman: My Story 188
Gregston, Gene 178
Grounds for Golf xix, 108
*Guide to Southern African Golf
    Courses,* 131
Gullo, James 181

Haddock, Raymund M. 109
Hagen, Walter xiv, xv, xviii, 34, 49,
    182
  autobiography of 191
  biography of 188–89
  ghostwriter for. *See* Martin, H.B.
  list of golf book titles by 223
Hamilton, David xx
Hamilton, Don 48–49
handbooks xii, xiv, xvi, 15–16, 21,
    197–98, 200
Hannigan, Frank, 195, 203
Hanse, Gil 94, 103, 108
Happy Golfer, The 19, 73–74
Hargreaves, Ernest 34
Harmsworth, Vyvyan 26
*Harold Hilton—His Golfing Life and
    Times* 176
Harper's Official Game Guide 1901
    20
Harris, Robert 55
*Harry Vardon: The Revealing Story of
    a Champion* 177

Harvey Penick's Little Red Book 150
Haultain, Arnold 25, 29
Hauser, Melanie 170
Hawaii, 213
Hawtree, Fred 22, 96, 98–99, 108, 194
Hazards 108
Heart of a Goof, The xv, 70
Hebron, Michael 141–42
Hecker, Genevieve xiv, 12–13, 23
Henderson, Ian T. 45, 47–48
Herbert Warren Wind's Golf Book xix,
    74
Herd, Sandy xv, 19, 78, 183
Hezlet, May xiv, 23
Hill, Dave 91
Hilton, Harold xiv
  biography of 24, 176
  contributing author 6, 13, 19, 26,
    28, 68
  list of golf book titles by 223
Hints on Golf 156
Hints on the Game of Golf xiii, 20
Historic Golf Courses of America 131
*Historic Golf Courses of the British
    Isles* 127
*Historical Gossip about Golf and
    Golfers* xii, 21
History of Golf, A (Browning) xvii,
    49–50
History of Golf, A (Stanley) 50
History of Golf Illustrated, A 43
History of Golf in Britain, A 51
History of the PGA Tour, The 88
*History of the Royal and Ancient Golf
    Club, St. Andrews, A* xiv, 21
*History of the Royal Dornoch Golf
    Club 1877–1999, A* 212
Hitch, Thomas 213
Hogan 177
Hogan, Ben xvii, 64, 69, 74
  biography of 165, 177, 178, 185
  golf swing of 145, 153
  instructional book by 144, 155
  list of golf book titles written by 223
Hogan Mystique, The 178
*Hogan: The Man Who Played for
    Glory* 178